# Tableau 10 Complete Reference

Transform your business with rich data visualizations and interactive dashboards with Tableau 10

**Joshua N. Milligan**
**Tristan Guillevin**

**BIRMINGHAM - MUMBAI**

# Tableau 10 Complete Reference

First Published: December 2018

Production Reference: 1211218

Published by Packt Publishing Ltd.
Livery Place, 35 Livery Street
Birmingham, B3 2PB, U.K.

ISBN 978-1-78995-708-2

www.packtpub.com

`mapt.io`

Mapt is an online digital library that gives you full access to over 5,000 books and videos, as well as industry-leading tools to help you plan your personal development and advance your career. For more information, please visit our website.

## Why Subscribe?

- Spend less time learning and more time coding with practical eBooks and Videos from over 4,000 industry professionals

- Improve your learning with Skill Plans built especially for you

- Get a free eBook or video every month

- Mapt is fully searchable

- Copy and paste, print, and bookmark content

## Packt.com

Did you know that Packt offers eBook versions of every book published, with PDF and ePub files available? You can upgrade to the eBook version at `www.packt.com` and as a print book customer, you are entitled to a discount on the eBook copy. Get in touch with us at `customercare@packtpub.com` for more details.

At `www.packt.com`, you can also read a collection of free technical articles, sign up for a range of free newsletters, and receive exclusive discounts and offers on Packt books and eBooks.

# Contributors

## About the Authors

**Joshua N. Milligan** has been with Teknion Data Solutions since 2004 and currently serves as a Principal Consultant. With a strong background in software development and custom .NET solutions, he brings a blend of analytical and creative thinking to BI solutions, data visualization, and data storytelling. His years of consulting have given Joshua hands-on experience with all aspects of the BI development cycle from data modeling, ETL, enterprise deployment, data visualization, and dashboard design. He has worked with clients in numerous industries including financial, energy, healthcare, marketing, government, and services. Joshua has been named by Tableau as a Tableau Zen Master every year since 2014. This places Joshua in a group of individuals recognized by Tableau as not only masters of the tool but also who have a deep desire to teach and help others. As a Tableau Ambassador, trainer, mentor, and leader in the online Tableau community, Joshua is passionate about helping others gain insights from their data. He frequently broadcasts webinars to educate and inform the Tableau community and the world at large about the wonders of Tableau and is a much sought after featured speaker at Tableau conferences, user groups, and various technology and industry functions. He thrives on helping others. Joshua is the author of the first edition of Learning Tableau, which quickly became one of the highest acclaimed Tableau books for users at all levels. He was a technical reviewer of the *Tableau Data Visualization Cookbook, Creating Data Stories with Tableau Public*, and his work has been featured multiple times on Tableau Public's Viz of the Day and Tableau's website. He also shares frequent Tableau tips, tricks, and advice along with a variety of dashboards on his fun and creative blog site. You can follow Joshua on Twitter at @VizPainter.

**Tristan Guillevin** is a true data lover who likes to share his passion. He graduated from engineering school in 2015. During these years, he went to Burkina Faso to teach computer science in schools around the country. The will to share and help people never left him since then. He started his professional life as a consultant at Actinvision, where he discovered Tableau. Soon, data visualization became a passion that has taken him around the world. In 2017, he won the Iron Viz (the ultimate data visualization battle organized by Tableau every year) in Las Vegas. Since his winning, he helps people with Tableau by making webinars, conferences, blog articles, and finally, this book! He's currently working at Ogury as a business analyst.

# Packt Is Searching for Authors Like You

If you're interested in becoming an author for Packt, please visit `authors.packtpub.com` and apply today. We have worked with thousands of developers and tech professionals, just like you, to help them share their insight with the global tech community. You can make a general application, apply for a specific hot topic that we are recruiting an author for, or submit your own idea.

# Table of Contents

# Preface

Graphical presentation of data enables us to easily understand complex data sets. Tableau 10 Complete Reference provides easy-to-follow recipes with several use cases and real-world business scenarios to get you up and running with Tableau 10.

This Learning Path begins with the history of data visualization and its importance in today's businesses. You'll also be introduced to Tableau - how to connect, clean, and analyze data in this visual analytics software. Then, you'll learn how to apply what you've learned by creating some simple calculations in Tableau and using Table Calculations to help drive greater analysis from your data. Next, you'll explore different advanced chart types in Tableau. These chart types require you to have some understanding of the Tableau interface and understand basic calculations. You'll study in detail all dashboard techniques and best practices. A number of recipes specifically for geospatial visualization, analytics, and data preparation are also covered. Last but not least, you'll learn about the power of storytelling through the creation of interactive dashboards in Tableau.

Through this Learning Path, you will gain confidence and competence to analyze and communicate data and insights more efficiently and effectively by creating compelling interactive charts, dashboards, and stories in Tableau.

## Who This Book Is For

Tableau 10 Complete Reference is designed for anyone who wants to understand their data better and represent it in an effective manner. It is also used for BI professionals and data analysts who want to do better at their jobs.

## What This Book Covers

*Chapter 1*, *Creating Your First Visualizations and Dashboard*, introduces the basic concepts of data visualization and shows multiple examples of individual visualizations that are ultimately put together in an interactive dashboard.

*Chapter 2*, *Working with Data in Tableau*, explains that Tableau has a very distinctive paradigm for working with data. This chapter explores that paradigm and gives examples of connecting to and working with various data sources.

*Chapter 3*, *Moving from Foundational to More Advanced Visualizations*, expands upon the basic concepts of data visualization to show how to extend standard visualization types.

*Chapter 4*, *Using Row-Level, Aggregate, and Level of Detail Calculations*, introduces the concepts of calculated fields and the practical use of calculations. The chapter walks through the foundational concepts for creating Row Level, Aggregate, and Level of Detail calculations.

*Chapter 5*, *Table Calculations*, is about table calculations, one of the most complex and most powerful features of Tableau. This chapter breaks down the basics of scope, direction, partitioning, and addressing to help you understand and use them to solve practical problems.

*Chapter 6*, *Formatting a Visualization to Look Great and Work Well*, is about formatting, which can make a standard visualization look great, have appeal, and communicate well. This chapter introduces and explains the concepts around formatting in Tableau.

*Chapter 7*, *Telling a Data Story with Dashboards*, dives into the details of building dashboards and telling stories with data. It covers the types of dashboards, objectives of dashboards, and concepts such as actions and filters. All of this is done in the context of practical examples.

*Chapter 8*, *Deeper Analysis – Trends, Clustering, Distributions and Forecasting*, explores the analytical capabilities of Tableau and demonstrates how to use trend lines, clustering, distributions, and forecasting to dive deeper into the analysis of your data.

*Chapter 9*, *Making Data Work for You*, shows that data in the real world isn't always structured well. This chapter examines the structures that work best and the techniques that can be used to address data that can't be fixed.

*Chapter 10*, *Advanced Visualizations, Techniques, Tips, and Tricks*, builds upon the concepts in previous chapters and expands your horizons by introducing non-standard visualization types along with numerous advanced techniques while giving practical advice and tips.

*Chapter 11*, *Sharing Your Data Story*, once you've built your visualizations and dashboards, you'll want to share them. This chapter explores numerous ways of sharing your stories with others.

*Chapter 12*, *Catching Up with Tableau 2018*, details of every new feature of the different Tableau 2018 versions. You'll learn how to use them with clear explanations, examples, and tutorials. This chapter is the best way to catch up with the new releases if you already have some Tableau knowledge.

*Chapter 13*, *Deal with Security*, is the last technical chapter of this book and focuses on three ways to secure your data: permissions on Tableau Server, user filters on Tableau Desktop, and row-level data security in your data.

*Chapter 14*, *How to Keep Growing Your Skills*, is a non-technical but essential chapter. You'll discover many ways of learning new things and growing your Tableau skills thanks to community projects. The chapter is also a tribute to the Tableau community, presenting many ways to be part of that big family, which shares a passion for data visualization with Tableau.

# To Get the Most out of This Book

You will need a licensed or trial version of Tableau Desktop to follow the examples contained in this book. You may download Tableau Desktop from Tableau Software at http://www.tableau.com/. The examples in this book use the interface and features of Tableau 10.0. Many of the concepts will apply to previous versions, though some interface steps and terminology may vary. The provided workbooks may be opened in Tableau 10.0 or later, though you may use any version to connect to the provided data files to work through the examples. Tableau Public is also available as a free download (http://www. tableau.com/) and may be used with many of the examples.

You may use a PC or a Mac to work through the examples in this book. Mac users may notice slight changes in user interface and will need to make note of the following changes in keys and clicks:

- Right-click can be accomplished by holding the Command key while clicking
- Right-click and drag and drop can be accomplished by holding the option *(Alt)* key while dragging and dropping

# Download the Example Code Files

You can download the example code files for this book from your account at www.packt.com. If you purchased this book elsewhere, you can visit www.packt.com/support and register to have the files emailed directly to you.

You can download the code files by following these steps:

1. Log in or register at www.packt.com.
2. Select the **SUPPORT** tab.
3. Click on **Code Downloads & Errata**.
4. Enter the name of the book in the **Search** box and follow the onscreen instructions.

Once the file is downloaded, please make sure that you unzip or extract the folder using the latest version of:

- WinRAR/7-Zip for Windows
- Zipeg/iZip/UnRarX for Mac
- 7-Zip/PeaZip for Linux

The code bundle for the book is also hosted on GitHub at https://github.com/PacktPublishing/Tableau-10-Complete-Reference. In case there's an update to the code, it will be updated on the existing GitHub repository.

We also have other code bundles from our rich catalog of books and videos available at https://github.com/PacktPublishing/. Check them out!

# Conventions Used

In this book, you will find a number of text styles that distinguish between different kinds of information. Here are some examples of these styles and an explanation of their meaning.

Code words in text, database table names, folder names, filenames, file extensions, pathnames, dummy URLs, and user input are shown as follows: "We'll create a calculated field named Floor to determine if an apartment is upstairs or downstairs."

A block of code is set as follows:

```
IF [Apartment] >= 1 AND [Apartment] <= 3
 THEN "Downstairs"
ELSEIF [Apartment] > 3 AND [Apartment] <= 6
 THEN "Upstairs"
ELSE "Unknown"
END
```

**Bold**: Indicates a new term, an important word, or words that you see onscreen. For example, words in menus or dialog boxes appear in the text like this. Here is an example: "When you open Tableau, on the left, in the **Connect** area, click on **Microsoft Excel**."

 Warnings or important notes appear like this.

 Tips and tricks appear like this.

# Get in Touch

Feedback from our readers is always welcome.

**General feedback**: If you have questions about any aspect of this book, mention the book title in the subject of your message and email us at customercare@packtpub.com.

**Errata**: Although we have taken every care to ensure the accuracy of our content, mistakes do happen. If you have found a mistake in this book, we would be grateful if you would report this to us. Please visit www.packt.com/submit-errata, selecting your book, clicking on the Errata Submission Form link, and entering the details.

**Piracy**: If you come across any illegal copies of our works in any form on the Internet, we would be grateful if you would provide us with the location address or website name. Please contact us at copyright@packt.com with a link to the material.

**If you are interested in becoming an author**: If there is a topic that you have expertise in and you are interested in either writing or contributing to a book, please visit authors.packtpub.com.

# Reviews

Please leave a review. Once you have read and used this book, why not leave a review on the site that you purchased it from? Potential readers can then see and use your unbiased opinion to make purchase decisions, we at Packt can understand what you think about our products, and our authors can see your feedback on their book. Thank you!

For more information about Packt, please visit packt.com.

# 1
# Creating Your First Visualizations and Dashboard

Tableau is an amazing platform for seeing, understanding, and making key decisions based on your data. With it, you can achieve incredible data discovery, analysis, and storytelling. You'll accomplish these tasks and goals visually using an interface that is designed for a natural and seamless flow of thought and work. Tableau accomplishes this using VizQL, a visual query language. You won't have to learn VizQL. It's all done behind the scenes and you won't be forced to write tedious SQL scripts, MDX code, or painstakingly work through numerous wizards to select a chart type and then link everything to data.

Instead, you will be interacting with your data in a visual environment where everything that you drag and drop will be translated into the necessary queries and then displayed visually. You'll be working in real-time, so you will see results immediately, get answers as fast as you can ask questions, and be able to iterate through dozens of ways to visualize the data to find a key insight or tell a piece of the story.

Tableau allows you to accomplish numerous tasks, including:

- **Data connection, integration, and preparation**: Tableau allows you to connect to data from sources and, if necessary, create a structure that is ready to use. Most of the time this is as easy as pointing Tableau to a database or opening a file, but Tableau gives you the tools to bring together even complex and messy data from multiple sources.
- **Data exploration**: You can visually explore a dataset using Tableau in order to understand what data you have.
- **Data visualization**: This is the heart of Tableau. You can iterate through the countless ways of visualizing the data to ask and answer questions, raise new questions, and gain new insights.
- **Data analysis**: Tableau has an ever growing set of analytical functions that allow you to dive deep into understanding complex relationships, patterns, and correlations in the data.

- **Data storytelling**: Tableau allows you to build fully interactive dashboards and stories with your visualizations and insights so that you can share the data story with others.

We'll take a look at each of these tasks in the subsequent chapters. This chapter introduces the foundational principals of Tableau and focuses on data visualization. We'll accomplish this through a series of examples that will introduce the basics of connecting to data, exploring and analyzing the data visually, and finally putting it all together in a fully interactive dashboard. These concepts will be developed far more extensively in the subsequent chapters. But don't skip this chapter, as it introduces key terminology and foundational concepts, including:

- Connecting to data
- Foundations for building visualization
- Visualizing the data
- Creating bar charts
- Creating line charts
- Creating geographic visualizations
- Using Show Me
- Bringing everything together in a dashboard

# Connecting to data

Tableau connects to data stored in a wide variety of files and databases. This includes flat files, such as Excel and text files; relational databases, such as SQL Server and Oracle; cloud-based data sources, such as Google Analytics and Amazon Redshift; and OLAP data sources, such as Microsoft Analysis Services. With very few exceptions, the process of building visualizations and performing analysis will be the same no matter what data source you use. We'll cover the details of connecting to different data sources in Chapter 2, *Working with Data in Tableau.*

For now, we'll connect to a text file, specifically, a comma-separated values file (.csv). The data itself is a variation of the sample data provided with Tableau for Superstore, a fictional retail chain that sells various products to customers across the United States. It's preferable to use the supplied data file instead of the Tableau sample data as the variations will lead to differences in visualizations.

The Chapter 1 workbook, included with the code files bundle, already have connections to the file; however, for this example, we'll walk through the steps of creating a connection in a new workbook:

1. Open Tableau; you should be able to see the home screen with a list of connection options on the left, thumbnail previews of recently edited workbooks in the center, links to various resources on the right, and sample workbooks on the bottom.

2. Under **Connect** and **To a file**, click **Text File**.

3. In the **Open** dialogue box, navigate to the `\Learning Tableau\Chapter 01\` directory and select the `Superstore.csv` file.

4. You will now see the data connection screen, which allows you to visually create connections to data sources. We'll examine the features of this screen in detail in the *Connecting to data* section of `Chapter 2`, *Working with Data in Tableau*. For now, notice that Tableau has already added and given a preview of the file for the connection:

5. For this connection, no other configuration is required, so simply click on the **Sheet 1** tab at the bottom to start visualizing the data! You should now see the main work area within Tableau, which looks similar to the following screenshot:

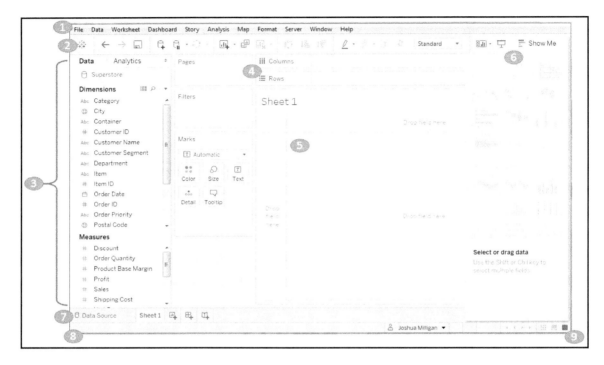

We'll refer to elements of the interface throughout the book using specific terminology, so take a moment to get familiar with the terms used for various components numbered in the preceding image:

1. The menu contains various menu items for performing a wide range of functions.
2. The toolbar allows for common functions, such as undo, redo, save, adding a data source, and so on.
3. The sidebar contains tabs for **Data** and **Analytics**. When the **Data** tab is active, we'll refer to the sidebar as the data pane. When the **Analytics** tab is active, we'll refer to the sidebar as the analytics pane. We'll go into detail later in this chapter, but for now, note that the data pane shows the data source at the top and contains a list of fields from the data source and is divided into dimensions and measures.

4. Various shelves, such as **Columns**, **Rows**, **Pages**, and **Filters,** serve as areas to drag and drop fields from the data pane. The **Marks** card contains additional shelves, such as **Color**, **Size**, **Text**, **Detail**, and **Tooltip**. Tableau will visualize data based on the fields you drop on the shelves.

Data fields in the data pane are available to be added to the view. Fields that have been dropped on a shelf are called in the view or active fields, because they play an active role in the way Tableau draws the visualization.

5. The canvas or view is where Tableau will draw the data visualization. You may also drop fields directly onto the view. In Tableau 10, you'll observe the seamless title at the top of the canvas. By default, it will display the name of the sheet, but it can be either edited or hidden.

6. **Show Me** is a feature that allows you to quickly iterate through various types of visualizations based on data fields of interest. We'll look at **Show Me** towards the end of the chapter.

7. The tabs at the bottom of the window gives you the option of editing the data source, as well as navigating between and adding any number of sheets, dashboards, or stories. Many times a tab (whether it is a sheet, dashboard, or story) is referred to, generally, as a sheet. We'll also often use these specific terms for a tab:

   - **A sheet**: A sheet is a single data visualization (such as a bar chart or line graph). Since sheet is also a generic term for any tab, we'll often refer to a sheet as a **view** because it is a single view of the data.
   - **A dashboard**: A dashboard is a presentation of any number of related views and other elements (such as text or images) arranged together as a cohesive whole to communicate a message to an audience. Dashboards are often interactive.
   - **A story**: A story is a collection of dashboards or single views arranged to communicate a narrative from the data. Stories can also be interactive.

A Tableau workbook is the collection of data sources, sheets, dashboards, and stories. All of this is saved as a single Tableau workbook file (.twb or .twbx). We'll look at the difference in file types and explore details of what else is saved as a part of a workbook in later chapters.

8. As you work, the status bar will display important information and details about the view and selections.

9. Various controls allow you to navigate between sheets, dashboards, and stories, as well as view the tabs as a filmstrip or switch to a **Sheet Sorter** showing an interactive thumbnail of all sheets in the workbook.

Now that you have worked through connecting to the data, we'll explore some examples that lay the foundation for data visualization and then move into building some foundational visualization types. To prepare for this, do the following:

1. From the menu, navigate to **File | Exit.**

2. When prompted to save changes, select **No.**

3. From the \Learning Tableau\Chapter 01 directory, open the file Chapter 01 Starter.twbx. This file contains a connection to the **Superstore** data file and is designed to help you walk through the examples in this chapter.

 The files for each chapter include a Starter workbook that allows you to work through the examples given in this book. If at any time, you'd like to see the completed examples, open the Complete workbook for the chapter.

With a connection to the data, you are now ready to visualize and analyze the data. As you start doing so, you will take on the role of an analyst at the retail chain. You'll ask questions of the data, build visualizations to answer those questions, and ultimately design a dashboard to share the results. Let's start by laying down some foundations to understand how Tableau visualizes data.

# Foundations for building visualizations

When you first connect to a data source, such as the Superstore file, Tableau will display the data connection and the fields in the data pane on the left sidebar. Fields can be dragged from the data pane onto the canvas area or onto various shelves, such as **Rows**, **Columns**, **Color**, or **Size**. We'll see that placement of the fields will result in different encodings of the data, based on the type of field.

# Measures and dimensions

The fields from the data source are visible in the data pane and are divided into measures and dimensions. The difference between measures and dimensions is a fundamental concept to understand when using Tableau:

- **Measures**: Measures are values that are aggregated. That is, they can be summed, averaged, and counted, or have a minimum or maximum.
- **Dimensions**: Dimensions are values that determine the level of detail at which measures are aggregated. You can think of them as slicing the measures or creating groups into which the measures fit. The combination of dimensions used in the view defines the view's basic level of detail.

As an example (which you can view in the `Chapter 01 Starter` workbook on the **Measures and Dimensions** sheet), consider a view created using the fields **Region** and **Sales** from the Superstore connection, as shown here:

The **Sales** field is used as a measure in this view. Specifically, it is being aggregated as a sum. When you use a field as a measure in the view, the type aggregation (such as **SUM**, **MIN**, **MAX**, **AVG**) will be shown on the active field. In the preceding example, the active field on **Rows** clearly indicates the sum aggregation of Sales: **SUM(Sales)**.

The Region field is a dimension with one of four values for each record of data: **Central**, **East**, **South**, or **West**. When the field is used as a dimension in the view, it slices the measure. So instead of an overall sum of sales, the preceding view shows the sum of sales for each region.

# Discrete and continuous

Another important distinction to make with fields is whether a field is being used as discrete or continuous. Whether a field is discrete or continuous, determines how Tableau visualizes it based on where it is used in the view. Tableau will give you a visual indication of the default for a field (the color of the icon in the data pane) and how it is being used in the view (the color of the active field on a shelf). Discrete fields, such as **Region** in the previous example, are blue, and continuous fields, such as **Sales**, are green.

In the screenshots, in the print version of this book, you should be able to distinguish a slight difference in shading between discrete (green) and continuous (blue) fields, but pay special attention to the interface as you follow along using Tableau.

## Discrete fields

Discrete (blue) fields have values that are shown as distinct and separate from each other. Discrete values can be reordered and still make sense.

When a discrete field is used on the **Rows** or **Columns** shelves, the field defines headers. Here the discrete field Region defines column headers:

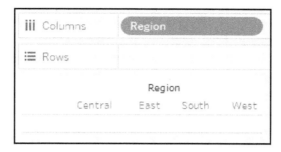

Here, it defines row headers:

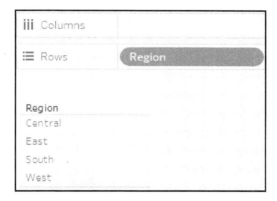

When used for color, a discrete field defines a discrete color palette in which each color aligns with a distinct value of the field:

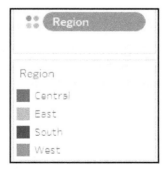

# Continuous fields

Continuous (green) fields have values that flow from first to last. Numeric and date fields are often used as continuous fields in the view. The values of these fields have an order, which would make little sense to change.

When used on **Rows** or **Columns**, a continuous field defines an axis:

When used for color, a continuous field defines a gradient:

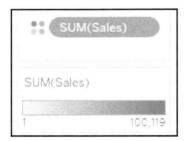

It is very important to note that continuous and discrete are different concepts from measure and dimension. While most dimensions are discrete by default and most measures are continuous by default, it is possible to use any measure as a discrete field and some dimensions as continuous fields.

To change the default of a field, right-click on the field in the data pane and select **Convert to Discrete** or **Convert to Continuous**. To change how a field is used in the view, right-click on the field in the view and select it to be either discrete or continuous.

In general, you can think of whether a field is continuous or discrete, as telling Tableau, how to display the data (header or axis, single colors or gradient) and measure or dimension, and how to organize the data (aggregate it or slice/group it).

As you work through the examples in this chapter, pay attention to the fields you are using to create the visualizations, whether they are dimensions or measures, and whether they are discrete or continuous. Experiment with changing fields in the view from continuous to discrete and vice versa to gain an understanding of the difference in the visualization.

# Visualizing data

A new connection to a data source is an invitation to explore. At times you may come to the data with very well defined questions and a strong sense of what you expect to find. Other times, you will come to the data with general questions and very little idea of what you will find. The data visualization capabilities of Tableau empower you to rapidly and iteratively explore the data, ask new questions, and make new discoveries.

The following visualization examples cover a few of the foundational visualization types. As you work through the examples, keep in mind that the goal is not simply to learn how to create a specific chart. Rather, the examples are designed to help you think through the process of asking questions of the data and getting answers through iterations of visualization. Tableau is designed to make that process intuitive, rapid, and transparent. Far more important than memorizing steps to create a bar chart is understanding how and why to use a Tableau to create a bar chart and then adjust your visualization to gain new insights as you ask new questions.

# Creating bar charts

Bar charts visually represent data in a way that makes comparisons of value across different categories easy. Length of the bar is the primary means by which you will visually understand the data. You may also incorporate color, size, stacking, and order to communicate additional attributes and values.

Creating bar charts in Tableau is quite easy. Simply drag and drop the measure you want to see on either the **Rows** or **Columns** shelf and the dimension that defines the categories onto the opposing **Rows** or **Columns** shelf.

As an analyst for the Superstore, you are ready to begin a discovery process focused on sales (especially the dollar value of sales). As you follow the examples, work your way through the sheets in the `Chapter 01 Starter.twbx` workbook. The `Chapter 01 Complete.twbx` workbook will contain the complete example, so you can compare your results at any time:

1. Navigate to the **Sales by Department** sheet (view).
2. Drag and drop the **Sales** field from **Measures** in the data pane to the **Columns** shelf. You now have a bar chart with a single bar representing the sum of sales for all the data in the data source.
3. Drag and drop the **Department** field from **Dimensions** in the data pane to the **Rows** shelf. This slices the data to give you three bars, representing the sum of sales for each department:

You now have a horizontal bar chart. This makes the comparison of sales between the departments easy. Notice how the mark type in the drop-down menu on the **Marks** card is set to **Automatic** and shows an indication that Tableau has determined that bars are the best visualization given the fields you have placed in the view. As a discrete dimension, the **Department** field defines row headers for each department in the data. As a continuous measure, the **Sales** field is defining an axis with the length of the bar extending from 0 to the value of the sum of sales for each department.

Typically, Tableau draws a mark (bar, shape, circle, square, and so on.) for every intersection of dimensional values in the view. In this simple case, Tableau is drawing a single bar mark for each dimensional value (**Furniture, Office Supplies**, and **Technology**) of **Department**. The type of mark is indicated and can be changed in the drop-down-menu on the **Marks** card. The number of marks drawn in the view can be observed on the lower-left status bar. Tableau draws different marks in different ways. For example, bars are drawn from 0 (or the end of the previous bar, if stacked) along the axis. Circles and other shapes are drawn at locations defined by the value(s) of the field defining the axis. Take a moment to experiment with selecting different mark types from the dropdown on the **Marks** card. Having an understanding of how Tableau draws different mark types will help you master the tool.

# Iterations of bar charts for deeper analysis

Using the preceding bar chart, you can easily see that the **Technology** department has more total sales than either **Furniture** or **Office Supplies**, which has fewer total sales compared to any other department. What if you want to further understand sales amounts for departments across various regions?

1. Navigate to the **Bar Chart (two levels)** sheet where you will find an initial view identical to the one you created previously.

2. Drag the **Region** field from **Dimensions** in the data pane to the **Rows** shelf and drop it to the left of the **Department** field already in the view, as shown:

You still have a horizontal bar chart. But now you've introduced **Region** as another dimension that changes the level of detail in the view and further slices the aggregate of the sum of **Sales**. By placing **Region** before **Department**, you will be able to easily compare sales for each department within a given region.

Now you are starting to make some discoveries. For example, the **Technology** department has the most sales in every region, except in the **East** where **Furniture** has higher sales. **Office Supplies** never has the highest sales in any region.

Let's take a look at a different view, using the same fields arranged differently:

1. Navigate to the **Bar Chart (stacked)** sheet where you will find an initial view identical to the one you created previously.
2. Drag the **Region** field from the **Rows** shelf and drop it on the **Color** shelf:

Instead of a side-by-side bar chart, you now have a stacked bar chart. Notice how each segment of the bar is color-coded by the **Region** field. Additionally, a color legend has been added to the workspace. You haven't changed the level of detail in the view, so sales is still summed for every combination of region and department.

The **Level of Detail** or **View Level of Detail** is a key concept when working with Tableau. In the most basic visualizations, the combination of values of all the dimensions in the view defines the lowest level of detail for that view. All measures will be aggregated or sliced by the lowest level of detail. In the case of most basic views, the number of marks (indicated in the lower-left corner of the status bar) corresponds to the number of intersections of dimensional values. If **Department** is the only field used as a dimension, you will have a view at the department level of detail and all measures in the view will be aggregated as per the department. If **Region** is the only field used as a dimension, you will have a view at the region level of detail and all measures in the view will be aggregated as per the region. If you use both **Department** and **Region** as dimensions in the view, you will have a view at the level of department and region. All measures will be aggregated per the unique combination of department and region.

Stacked bars are useful when you want to understand part-to-whole relationships. It is now fairly easy to see what portion of the total sales of each department is made in each region. However, it is very difficult to compare sales for most of the regions across departments. For example, can you easily tell which department had the highest sales in the **East** region? It is difficult because, with the exception of **West**, every segment of the bar has a different starting place.

Now, take some time to experiment with the bar chart to see what variations you can create:

1. Navigate to the **Bar Chart (experimentation)** sheet.
2. Try dragging the **Region** field from **Color** to the other shelves on the **Marks** card, such as **Size**, **Label**, and **Detail**. Observe that in each case, the bars remain stacked but are redrawn based on the visual encoding defined by the **Region** field.
3. Use the **Swap** button on the toolbar to swap fields on **Rows** and **Columns**. This allows you to very easily change from a horizontal bar chart to a vertical bar chart (and vice versa):

4. Drag and drop **Sales** from the **Measures** section of the data pane on top of the **Region** field on the **Marks** card to replace it. Drag the **Sales** field to **Color** if necessary and notice how the color legend is a gradient for the continuous field.

5. Further experiment by dragging and dropping other fields onto various shelves. Note the behavior of Tableau for each action you take.

6. From the **File** menu, select **Save**.

At the time of writing of this book, Tableau does not have an autosave feature. You will want to get in the habit of saving the workbook early and then pressing *Ctrl + S* or selecting **Save** from the **File** menu often to avoid losing your work.

# Creating line charts

Line charts connect the related marks in visualization to show movement or relationship between connected marks. The position of the marks and the lines that connect them are the primary means of communicating the data. Additionally, you can use size and color to visually communicate additional information.

The most common kind of line chart is a time series chart. Time series show the movement of values over time. They are very easy to create in Tableau and require only a date and a measure.

Continue your analysis of Superstore sales using the Chapter 01 Starter workbook that you saved earlier. The following are the steps to get the output of the **Sales over time** graph:

1. Navigate to the **Sales over time** sheet.
2. Drag the **Sales** field from **Measures** to **Rows**. This will give you a single, vertical bar representing the sum of all the sales in the data source.

3. To turn this into a time series, you must introduce a date. Drag the **Order Date** field from **Dimensions** in the data pane on the left and drop it on **Columns**. Tableau has a built-in date hierarchy and the default level of the year has given you a line chart connecting four years. Notice that you can clearly see an increase in sales year after year:

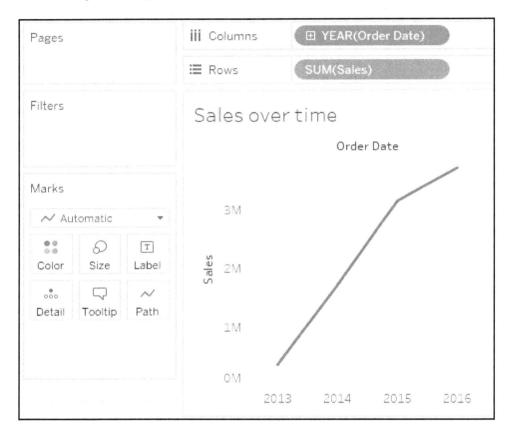

4. Use the drop-down menu of the **YEAR(Order Date)** field on **Columns** (or right-click the field) and switch the date field to use the **Quarter**. You may observe that **Quarter** is listed twice in the drop-down menu. We'll explore the various options for date parts, values, and hierarchies in the *Visualizing dates and times* section of Chapter 3, *Moving from Foundational to More Advanced Visualizations*. For now, select the second option:

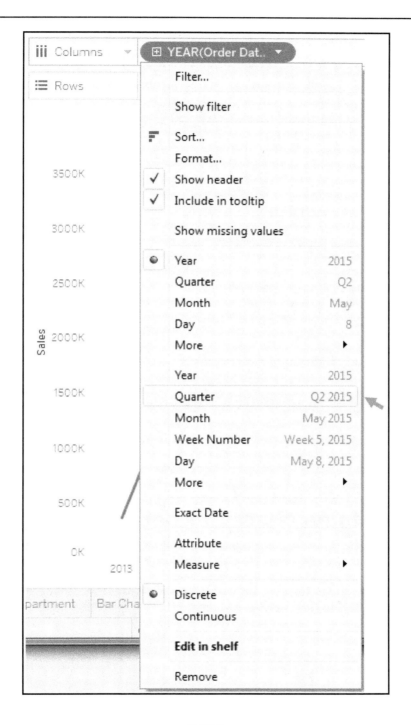

Observe the cyclical pattern that is quite evident when looking at the sales by quarter:

# Iterations of line charts for deeper analysis

Right now you are looking at the overall sales over time. Let's do some analysis at a slightly deeper level:

1. Navigate to the **Sales over time (overlapping lines)** sheet where you will find a view identical to the one you just created.

2.  Drag the **Region** field from **Dimensions** to **Color**. Now, you have a line per region with each line being a different color and a legend indicating which color is used for which region. As with the bars, adding a dimension to color splits the marks. However, unlike the bars where the segments were stacked, the lines are not stacked. Instead, the lines are drawn at the exact value for the sum of sales for each region and quarter. This allows for easy and accurate comparison. It is interesting to note that the cyclical pattern can be observed for each region, as shown:

With only four regions, it's fairly easy to keep the lines separate. What about dimensions that have more than four or five distinct values?

1. Navigate to the **Sales over time (multiple rows)** sheet, where you will find a view identical to the one you just created.

2. Drag the **Category** field from **Dimensions** and drop it directly on top of the **Region** field currently on the **Marks** card. This replaces the **Region** field with **Category**. You now have 17 overlapping lines. Often you'll want to avoid more than two to four overlapping lines. However, clicking an item in the color legend will highlight the associated line in the view. Highlighting can be a good way to pick out a single item and compare it to all others.

3. Drag the **Category** field from **Color** on the **Marks** card and drop it on **Rows**. You now have a line chart for each category. Now you have a way to compare each product over time without overwhelming the overlap function. You can still compare trends and patterns over time. This is the start of a sparklines visualization that will be developed fully in the *Advanced visualizations* section of Chapter 10, *Advanced Visualizations, Techniques, Tips, and Tricks*.

# Creating geographic visualizations

Tableau makes creating geographic visualizations very easy. The built-in geographic database recognizes geographic roles for fields, such as country, state, city, or zip code. Even if your data does not contain latitude and longitude values, you can simply use geographic fields to plot locations on a map. If your data contains latitude and longitude fields, you may use those instead of the generated values.

 Although most databases do not strictly define geographic roles for fields, Tableau will automatically assign geographic roles to the fields based on the field name and a sampling of values in the data. You can assign or re-assign geographic roles to any field by right-clicking on the field in the data pane and using the **Geographic Role** option. This is also a good way of seeing what built-in geographic roles are available.

The power and flexibility of Tableau's geographic capabilities, as well as the options for customization, will be covered in more detail in the *Mapping techniques* section of `Chapter 10`, *Advanced Visualizations, Techniques, Tips, and Tricks*. In the following examples, we'll consider some of the foundational concepts of geographic visualizing.

Geographic visualization is incredibly valuable when you need to understand where things happen and if there are any spatial relationships within the data. Tableau offers two basic forms of geographic visualization:

- Filled maps

- Symbol maps

# Filled maps

Filled maps, as the name implies, makes use of filled areas, such as country, state, county, or zip code, to show location. The color that fills the area can be used to encode values of measures or dimensions.

What if you want to understand sales for Superstore and see whether there are any patterns geographically? Let's take a look at some examples of how you can do this:

1. Navigate to the **Sales by State** sheet.
2. Double-click on the **State** field in the data pane. Tableau automatically creates a geographic visualization using the **Latitude (generated)**, **Longitude (generated)**, and **State** fields.

3. Drag the **Sales** field from the data pane and drop it on the **Color** shelf on the **Marks** card. Based on the fields and shelves you've used, Tableau has switched the automatic mark type to filled maps:

The filled map fills each state with a single color to indicate the relative sum of sales for each state. The color legend, now visible in the view, gives the range of values and indicates that the state with the least sales had a total of **$3,543** and the state with the most sales had a total of **$1,090,616**.

When you look at the number of marks displayed on the status bar on the lower-left side, you'll see that it is 49. Careful examination reveals that the marks consist of the lower 48 states and Washington DC. Hawaii and Alaska are not shown. Tableau will only draw a geographic mark, such as a filled state if it exists in the data and is not excluded by a filter.

Observe that the map does display Canada, Mexico, and other locations not included in the data. These are part of a background image retrieved from an online map service. The state marks are then drawn on top of the background image. We'll look at how you can customize the map and even use other map services in the *Mapping techniques* section of Chapter 10, *Advanced Visualizations, Techniques, Tips, and Tricks*.

Filled maps can work well in interactive dashboards and have quite a bit of aesthetic value. However, certain kinds of analysis are very difficult with filled maps. Unlike other visualization types, where size can be used to communicate facets of the data, the size of a filled geographic region only relates to the geographical size and can make comparisons difficult. For example, which state has the highest sales? You might be tempted to say Texas or California because they appear larger, but would you have guessed Massachusetts? Some locations may be small enough that they won't even show up compared to larger areas. Use filled maps with caution and consider pairing them with other visualizations on dashboards for clear communication.

# Symbol maps

Another standard type of geographic visualization available in Tableau is a symbol map. Marks on this map are not drawn as filled regions; rather, marks are shapes or symbols placed at specific geographic locations. Size, color, and shape may also be used to encode additional dimensions and measures.

Continue your analysis of Superstore sales, following these steps:

1. Navigate to the **Sales by Postal Code** sheet.
2. Double-click on **Postal Code** under **Dimensions**. Tableau automatically adds postal code to the **Detail** of the **Marks** card and **Longitude (generated)** and **Latitude (generated)** to **Columns** and **Rows**. The mark type is set to a circle by default and a single circle is drawn for each postal code at the correct latitude and longitude. You may also notice an indicator for **1 unknown** postal code. We'll take a look at how to handle this in the future chapters.
3. Drag **Sales** from **Measures** to the **Size** shelf on the **Marks** card. This causes each circle to be sized according to the sum of sales for that postal code.
4. Drag **Profit** from **Measures** to the **Color** shelf on the **Marks** card. This encodes the mark color to correspond to the sum of profit. You can now see the geographic location of profit and sales at the same time. This is useful because you will see some locations with high sales and low profit that may require some action.

The final view should look like this after making some slight adjustments to size and color details:

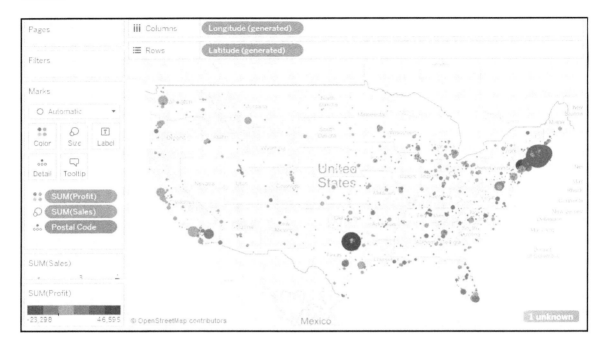

Sometimes you'll want to adjust the marks on a symbol map to make them more visible. Some of the options are:

- If marks are overlapping, click on the **Color** shelf and set transparency to somewhere between 50% and 75%. Additionally, add a dark border. This makes the marks stand out and you can often discern any overlapping marks much better.
- If marks are too small, click on the **Size** shelf and adjust the slider. You can also double-click on the **Size** legend and edit the details of how Tableau assigns size.
- If marks are too faint, double-click the **Color** legend and edit the details of how Tableau assigns a color. This is especially useful when you are using a continuous field that defines a color gradient.

A combination of tweaking the size and using **Stepped Color** and **Use Full Color Range**, as shown here, produced the final result for this example:

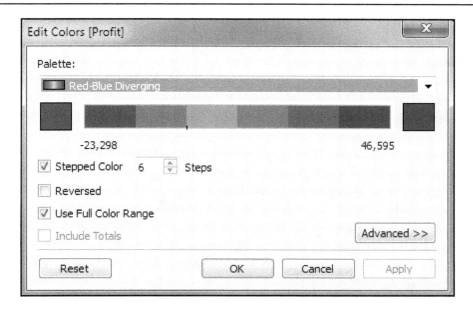

Unlike filled maps, symbol maps allow you to use size to visually encode aspects of the data. Symbol maps also allow for greater precision. In fact, if you have latitude and longitude in your data, you can very precisely plot marks at a street address level of detail. This type of visualization allows you to map locations that do not have clearly defined boundaries. Notice that if you were to change the mark type from **Automatic** to **Filled Map** in the preceding view, you would get an error message indicating that filled maps are not supported at the level of detail in the view.

# Using Show Me

**Show Me** is a powerful component of Tableau, which arranges selected and active fields into the arrangement required for the selected visualization type. The **Show Me** toolbar displays small thumbnail images of different types of visualizations, thus allowing you to create visualizations with a single-click. Based on the fields you select in the data pane and the fields that are already in the view, **Show Me** will enable possible visualizations and highlight a recommended visualization. Explore the features of **Show Me** by following these steps:

1. Navigate to the **Show Me** sheet.
2. If the **Show Me** pane is not expanded, click on the **Show Me** button in the upper-right corner of the toolbar to expand the pane.

3. Press and hold the *Ctrl* key while clicking on the **Postal Code**, **State**, and **Profit** fields in the data pane to select each of those fields. With those fields highlighted, **Show Me** should look similar to this:

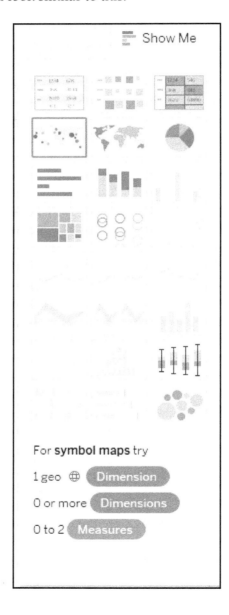

Observe that the **Show Me** window has enabled certain visualization types, such as text tables, heat maps, **symbol maps**, filled maps, and bar charts. These are the visualizations that are possible given the fields already in the view, in addition to any selected in the data pane. **Show Me** highlights the recommended visualization for the selected fields and also gives a description of what fields are required as you hover over each visualization type. Symbol maps, for example, require one geographic dimension and up to two measures.

Other visualizations are grayed out, such as line charts, and histograms. **Show Me** will not create these visualization types with the fields that are currently in the view and selected in the data pane. Hover over the grayed out line charts in **Show Me**. **Show Me** indicates that line charts require one or more measures, which you have selected, but also require a date field, which you have not selected.

Tableau will actually draw line charts with fields other than dates. **Show Me** gives you options for what is typically considered a good practice for visualizations. However, there may be times when you know a line chart would accurately show your data. Understanding how Tableau renders visualizations based on fields and shelves, instead of always relying on **Show Me**, will give you much greater flexibility in your visualizations and will allow you to rearrange things when **Show Me** doesn't give the exact results you want. At the same time, you will need to cultivate an awareness of good visualization practices.

**Show Me** can be a powerful way to quickly iterate through different visualization types as you search for insights into the data. But as a data explorer, analyst, and storyteller you should consider **Show Me** as a helpful guide that is giving suggestions. You may know that a certain visualization type will answer your questions more effectively than the suggestions of **Show Me**. You may also have a plan for a visualization type that will work well as part of a dashboard but isn't even included in **Show Me**.

You will be well on your way to learning and mastering Tableau when you can use **Show Me** effectively, but feel just as comfortable building visualizations without it. **Show Me** is powerful for quickly iterating through visualizations as you look for insights and raise new questions. It is useful for starting with a standard visualization that you will further customize. It is wonderful as a teaching and learning tool. Be careful not to use it as a crutch without understanding how visualizations are actually built from the data. Take time to evaluate why certain visualizations are or are not possible. Pause to see what fields and shelves were used when you selected a certain visualization type.

Conclude the **Show Me** example by experimenting with **Show Me,** clicking various visualization types and looking for insights into the data that may be more or less obvious based on the visualization type. Circle views and box and whisker plots show the distribution of postal codes for each state. Bar charts easily expose several postal codes with negative profit.

# Bringing everything together in a dashboard

Often you'll need more than a single visualization to communicate the full story of the data. In these cases, Tableau makes it very easy for you to use multiple visualizations together on a dashboard. In Tableau, a dashboard is a collection of views, filters, parameters, images, and other objects that work together to communicate a data story. Dashboards are often interactive and allow end users to explore different facets of the data.

Dashboards serve as a wide variety of purposes and can be tailored for a wide variety of audiences. Consider the following possible dashboards:

- A summary level view of profit and sales to allow executives to have a quick glimpse of the current status of the company
- An interactive dashboard allowing sales managers to drill into sales territories to identify threats or opportunities
- A dashboard allowing doctors to track patient read missions, diagnosis, and procedures in order to make better decisions about patient care
- A dashboard allowing executives of a real-estate company to identify trends and make decisions for various apartment complexes
- An interactive dashboard for loan officers to make lending decisions based on portfolios broken down by credit ratings and geographic location

Considerations for different audiences and advanced techniques will be covered in detail in Chapter 7, *Telling a Data Story with Dashboards*. For now, follow these steps for an example that introduces the foundational concepts:

1. Navigate to the **Superstore Sales** sheet, which is a blank dashboard. The sidebar on the left now shows options for building a dashboard, instead of the data pane that was visible in a worksheet:

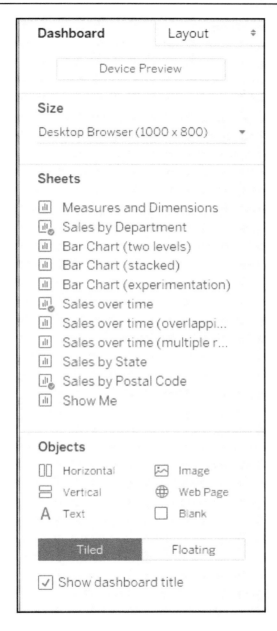

The dashboard window consists of several key components. Techniques for using these objects will be detailed in `Chapter 7`, *Telling a Data Story with Dashboards*. For now, focus on gaining some familiarity with the options that are available.

The left sidebar contains two tabs:

- A **Dashboard** tab for sizing options and adding sheets and objects to the dashboard
- A **Layout** tab for adjusting the layout of various objects on the dashboard

The **Dashboard** pane contains options for previewing based on the target device, sizing options, and a list of all visible sheets (views) in the dashboard. You can add these sheets to a dashboard by dragging and dropping. As you drag the view, a light grey shading will indicate the location of the sheet in the dashboard once it is dropped. You can also double-click any sheet and it will be added automatically.

The next section lists multiple additional objects that can be added to the dashboard. **Horizontal** and **Vertical** layout containers will give you finer control over the layout; **Text** allows you to add text labels and titles. **Images** and even embedded web content can be added. Finally, a **Blank** object allows you to preserve blank space in a dashboard or can serve as a placeholder.

Using the toggle, you can select whether new objects will be added as **Tiled** or **Floating**. Tiled objects will snap into a tiled layout next to other tiled objects or within layout containers. Floating objects will float on top of the dashboard in successive layers.

# Building your dashboard

Continue following these steps to build the dashboard:

1. Successively, Double-click each sheet listed in the **Dashboard** section on the left in turn: **Sales by Department**, **Sales over time**, and **Sales by Postal Code**. Notice that double-clicking the object adds it to the layout of the dashboard.

When a worksheet is first added to a dashboard, any legends, filters, or parameters that were visible in the worksheet view will be added to the dashboard. If you wish to add them at later point, select the sheet in the dashboard and click the little drop-down caret in the upper-right corner. Nearly every object has a drop down caret, providing many options for fine-tuning appearance and controlling behavior. Take note of the various UI elements that become visible for selected objects on the dashboard, as shown:

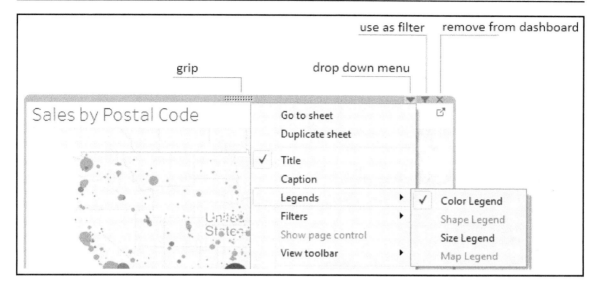

2. Add a title to the dashboard by checking **Show Title** in the lower-left corner of the sidebar. Make sure nothing is selected in the dashboard (such as a view or legend), otherwise the **Show Title** checkbox will likely apply to the selection. If necessary, click in a gray area off of the dashboard or a blank area in the left sidebar to clear any objects selections. You may edit the title by double-clicking it.

3. Select the **Sales by Department** sheet in the dashboard and click on the drop-down caret in the upper-right corner. Navigate to **Fit | Entire View**. The fit options describe how the visualization should fill any available space.

 Be careful when using various fit options. If you are using a dashboard with a size that has not been fixed, or if your view dynamically changes the number of items displayed based on interactivity, then what might have once looked good might not fit the view nearly as well.

4. Select the **Sales** size legend by clicking on it. Use the remove UI element to remove the legend from the dashboard.

5. Select the **Profit** color legend by clicking on it. Use the grip to drag the legend and place it under the map.

6. For each view, **Sales by Department, Sales by Postal Code,** and **Sales over time** select the view by clicking an empty area in the view. Then click on the use as filter UI element to make that view an interactive filter for the dashboard. Your dashboard should look similar to this:

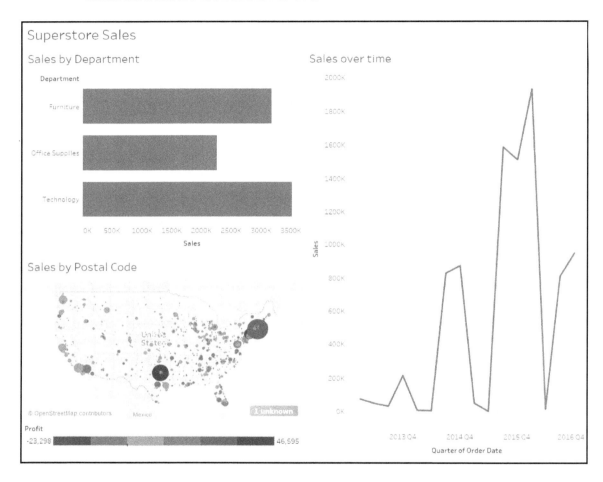

7. Take a moment to interact with your dashboard. Click on the various marks, such as the bars, states, and points of the line. Notice that each selection filters the rest of the dashboard. Clicking on a selected mark will deselect it and clear the filter. Notice that selecting marks in multiple views cause filters to work together. For example, selecting the bar for **Furniture** in **Sales by Department** and **2016 Q4** in **Sales over time**, allows you to see all the postal codes that had furniture sales in the last quarter of 2016:

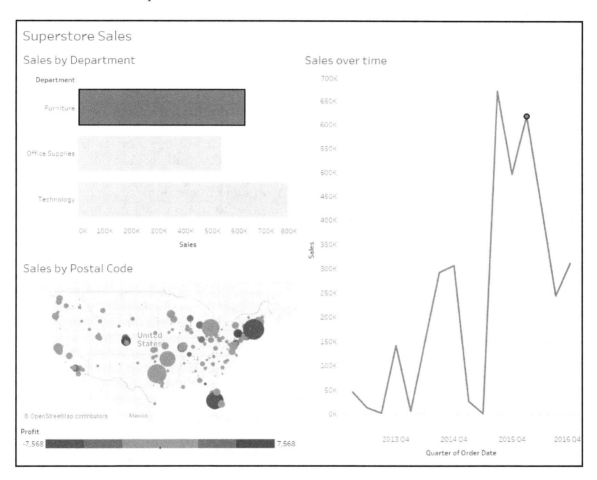

You have now created a dashboard that allows for interactive analysis. As an analyst for the Superstore chain, your visualizations allowed you to explore and analyze the data. The dashboard you created can be shared with management as a tool to help them see and understand the data in order to make better decisions. When a manager selects the **Furniture** department, it immediately becomes obvious that there are locations where sales are quite high but are actually making a loss. This may lead to decisions such as a change in marketing or a new sales focus for that location. Most likely it will require additional analysis to determine the best course of action. In that case, Tableau will empower you to continue the cycle of discovery, analysis, and storytelling.

# Summary

Tableau's visual environment allows for a rapid and iterative process of exploring and analyzing data visually. You've taken your first steps in understanding how to use the platform. You are connected to the data and then explore and analyze the data using some foundational visualization types such as bar charts, line charts, and geographic visualizations. Along the way, you focused on learning the techniques and understanding key concepts, such as the difference between measures and dimensions, and discrete and continuous fields. Finally, you put all the pieces together to create a fully functional dashboard that allows an end-user to understand your analysis and make discoveries of their own.

In the next chapter, we'll explore how Tableau works with data. You will be exposed to the fundamental concepts and practical examples of how to connect to various data sources. Combined with the foundational concepts you just learned about building visualizations, you will be well equipped to move on to more advanced visualizations, deeper analysis, and telling fully interactive data stories.

# Working with Data in Tableau

2

Tableau offers us the ability to connect to nearly any data source. It does so using a unique paradigm that allows it to leverage the power and efficiency of existing database engines with an option to extract data locally. This chapter focuses on the foundational concepts of how Tableau works with data; we will also cover the following topics:

- The Tableau paradigm
- Connecting to data
- Managing data source metadata
- Working with extracts instead of live connections
- Tableau file types
- Joins and blends
- Filtering data

## The Tableau paradigm

Tableau connects directly to native data engines and also includes the option to extract data locally. The unique experience of working with data in Tableau is a result of **Visual Query Language (VizQL)**.

VizQL was developed as a Stanford Research Project focusing on the natural ways by which humans visually perceive the world and how those ways can be applied to data visualization. We naturally perceive differences in size, shape, spatial location, and color. VizQL allows Tableau to translate your actions, as you drag and drop fields of data in a visual environment, into a query language that defines how the data encodes those visual elements. You will never need to read, write, or debug VizQL.

Tableau will generate the Visual Query Language behind the scenes as you drag and drop fields onto various shelves defining size, color, shape, and spatial location. This allows you to focus on visualizing data and not on writing code!

One of the benefits of VizQL is that it provides a common method to describe how the arrangement of various fields in a view defines a query of the data. This common baseline can then be translated into numerous flavors of **Structured Query Language** (**SQL**), **Multidimensional** Expressions (**MDX**), and **Tableau Query Language** (**TQL**),(used for extracted data). Tableau will automatically perform the translation of VizQL into a native query to be run natively by the source data engine.

At its simplest, the Tableau paradigm of working with data looks similar to the following diagram:

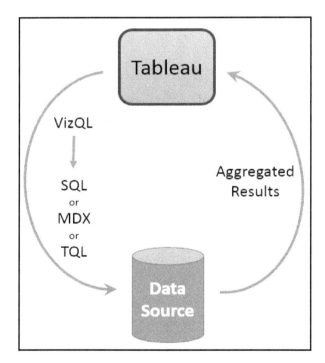

# A simple example

Go ahead and open the `Chapter 02 Starter.twbx` workbook located in the `\Learning Tableau\Chapter 02\` directory and navigate to the **Tableau Paradigm** sheet. Take a look at the view that was created by dropping the dimension **Region** on **Columns** and the measure **Sales** on **Rows**:

The **Region** field is used as a discrete (blue) field in the view and it defines the **Columns** headers. As a dimension, it defines the level of detail in the view and slices the measure. The **Sales** field is a measure that is being aggregated by summing up each sale within each market. As a continuous (green) field, **Sales** defines an axis.

You do not need to understand SQL or any kind of scripting to use Tableau. As you design data visualizations, you will most likely not be concerned with what scripts Tableau generates. The following example is simply to demonstrate what Tableau does behind the scenes, but you do not have to understand the script before moving on.

For this example, let's say that you were connected live to an SQL Server database with the Superstore data stored in a table called `SuperstoreData`. When you first create this view, Tableau generates a VizQL script which is translated into an SQL script and sent to the SQL Server. The SQL query will look similar to the following example:

```
SELECT [SuperstoreData].[Region] AS [none:Region:nk],
  SUM([SuperstoreData].[Sales]) AS [sum:Sales:ok]
FROM [dbo].[ SuperstoreData] [SuperstoreData]
GROUP BY [SuperstoreData].[Region]
```

This script selects the market and the sum of sales from the table and groups it according to the region. The script aliases the field names using naming conventions that are used by Tableau's engine when the data is returned.

On certain occasions, a database administrator may want to understand what scripts are running against a certain database to debug performance issues or determine a more efficient indexing or data structure. Many databases supply profiling utilities or log execution of queries. In addition to this, you can find SQL or MDX generated by Tableau in the logs located in the `\My Tableau Repository\Logs` directory. You can also use Tableau's built-in Performance Recorder. From the top menu, navigate to **Help** | **Settings and Performance** | **Start Performance Recording**, then interact with a view and finally stop the recording from the menu. Tableau will open a dashboard that will allow you to see tasks, performance, and queries that were executed during the recording session.

There may have been hundreds, thousands, or even millions of rows of sales data in SQL Server. However, it returns aggregate results when SQL Server processes the query. In this case, SQL Server returns only **4** aggregate rows of data to Tableau-one row for each region, as shown in the following screenshot. To see the aggregate data Tableau used to draw the view, press *Ctrl + A* to select all the bars, then right-click on one of them and select **View Data.** It is shown in the following figure:

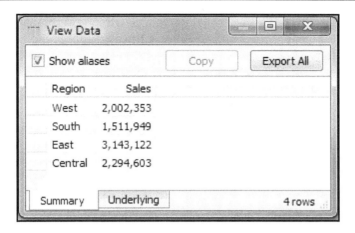

The **Summary** tab displays the aggregate level data that makes up the view. The **Sales** here is the sum of sales for each region. When you click on the **Underlying** tab, Tableau will query the data source to retrieve all the records that make up the aggregate records. In this case, there are **9,426** underlying records, as indicated on the status bar in the lower-right corner:

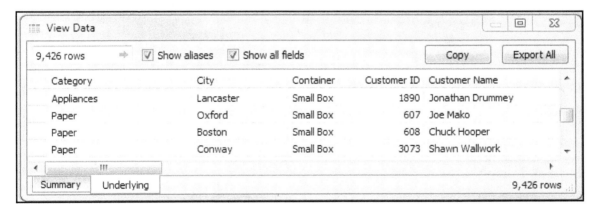

Tableau did not need **9,426** records to draw the view and did not request them from the data source until the **Underlying** data tab was clicked.

Database engines are optimized to perform aggregations on data. Typically, these database engines are also located on powerful servers. Tableau leverages the optimization and power of the underlying data source. In this way, Tableau can visualize massive data sets with relatively little local processing of the data.

Additionally, Tableau will only query the data source when you make changes requiring a new query or refresh a view. Otherwise, it will use the aggregate results stored in a local cache, as illustrated here:

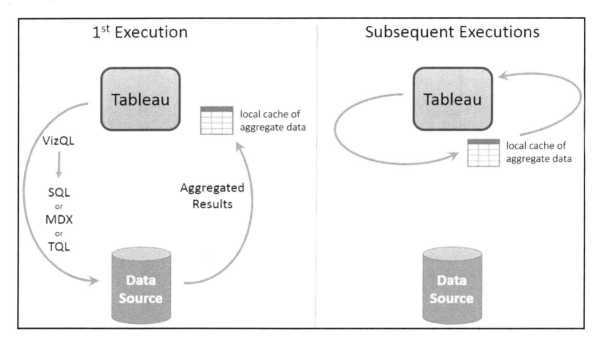

In the preceding example, the query based on the fields in the view (**Region** as a dimension and the sum of **Sales** as a measure) will only be issued once to the data source. When the four rows of aggregate results are returned, they are stored in the cache. Then, if you were to move **Region** to another visual encoding shelf, such as **Color**, or **Sales** to a different visual encoding shelf, such as **Size**, then Tableau will retrieve the aggregate rows from the cache and simply re-render the view.

You can force Tableau to bypass the cache and refresh the data from the data source by pressing *F5* or selecting your data source from the **Data** menu and selecting **Refresh**. Do this any time you want a view to reflect the most recent changes in a live data source.

Of course, if you were to introduce new fields into the view, which did not have cached results, then Tableau would send a new query to the data source, retrieve the aggregate results, and add those results to the cache.

# Connecting to data

There is virtually no limit to the data Tableau can visualize. Each successive version of Tableau adds new native connections. Tableau continues to add native connectors for cloud-based data and recently included the **Web Data Connector**, which allows you to custom-build a connector for any online data you wish to retrieve. Additionally, for any database without a native connection, Tableau gives you the ability to use a generic ODBC connection. The **Extract API** allows you to programmatically extract and combine any data source(s) for use in Tableau.

You may have multiple data source connections to different sources in the same workbook. Each connection will show up under the **Data** tab on the left sidebar.

This section will focus on a few practical examples of connecting to various data sources. We won't cover every possible connection, but we will cover several that are representative of others. You may or may not have access to some of the data sources in the following examples. Don't worry if you aren't able to follow each example. Merely observe the differences.

 In Tableau 10, a connection technically refers to the connection made to a single set of data, such as table(s) in a single database or file(s) in a directory. A **data source** may contain more than one connection which can be joined together, such as a table in SQL Server joined to an Excel table. You may often hear these terms used interchangeably.

# Connecting to data in a file

File-based data includes all sources of data where the data is stored in a file. File-based data sources include:

- **Tableau data extract**: A `.tde` file containing data that was extracted from an original source. When you connect to an extract, the connection retains information about the extract, but not about the original source.
- **Microsoft access**: A `.mdb` or `.accdb` database file created in Access.
- **Microsoft excel**: A `.xls`, `.xlsx`, or `.xlsm` spreadsheet created in Excel. Multiple Excel sheets or sub tables may be joined or unioned together in a single connection.
- **Text file**: A delimited text file, most commonly `.txt`, `.csv`, or `.tab`. Multiple text files in a single directory may be joined or unioned together in a single connection.

- **Statistical file**: A `.sav`, `.sas7bdat`, `.rda`, or `.rdata` file generated by statistical tools such as SAS or R.
- **Other files**: Select this option to connect to any file data source. In addition to those mentioned previously, you can connect to Tableau files to import connection you have saved in another Tableau workbook (`.twb` or `.twbx`). The connection will be imported and changes will only affect the current workbook.

Follow this example to see a connection to an Excel file:

1. Navigate to the **Connect to Excel** sheet in the `Chapter 02 Starter.twbx` workbook.
2. From the menu, navigate to **Data** | **Create new data source** and select **Excel** from the list of possible connections.
3. In the open dialogue, open the `Superstore.xlsx` file from the `\Learning Tableau\Chapter 02\` directory. Tableau will open the **Data Source** screen. You should see the two sheets of the Excel document listed on the left.
4. Double-click the **Orders** sheet and then the **Returns** sheet. Your Data Source screen should look similar to this:

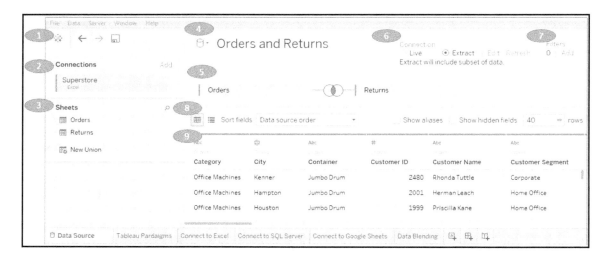

Take some time to familiarize yourself with the **Data Source** screen interface, which has the following features (numbered earlier):

1. **Toolbar**: The toolbar has a few of the familiar controls, including undo, redo, and save.

2. **Connections**: All the connections in the current data source. Click **Add** to add a new connection to the current data source. This allows you to join data across different connection types. Each connection will be color coded so you can distinguish which data is coming from which connection.

3. **Sheets (Tables):** This lists all the tables of data available for a given connection. This includes sheets, sub tables, and named ranges for Excel, tables, views, and stored procedures for relational databases, as well as other connection-dependent options such as **New Union** or **Custom SQL**.

4. **Data source name**: This is the name of the currently selected data source (in the dropdown). You may click this name to change it. You may also click the down arrow on the database icon to change which data source you wish to edit.

5. **Connection editor**: Drop sheets and tables from the left in this area to make them part of the connection. For many connections, you may add multiple tables, which will be joined or unioned together. We'll take a look at some advanced examples of options later in the chapter. For now, notice that you can hover over tables in this space and get options via a dropdown.

6. **Live or Extract options**: For many data sources, you may choose whether you would like to have a live connection or an extracted connection. We'll look at details later in the chapter.

7. **Data source filters**: You may add filters to the data source. These will be applied universally.

8. **Preview pane options**: These options allow you to specify whether you'd like to see a preview of the data or a list of metadata, and how you would like to preview the data (for example, with alias values, hidden fields shown, and how many rows you'd like to preview).

9. **Preview pane / Metadata view**: Depending on your selection in the options, this space either displays a preview of data or a list of all fields with additional metadata. Notice that these views give you a wide array of options such as changing data types, hiding or renaming fields, and applying various data transformation functions. We'll consider some of these options in this and later chapters.

Once you have created and configured your data source, you can click on any sheet to start using your data source.

Conclude this exercise with the following steps:

1. Click on the data source name to edit the text and rename the data source as `Orders and Returns`.
2. Navigate to the **Connect to Excel** sheet and use the **Orders and Returns** data source to create a time series showing **Profit by Quarter**.

If you need to edit the connection at any time, select **Data** from the menu, locate your connection, and then select **Edit DataSource...** Alternately, you can right-click on any data source under the **Data** tab on the left hand bar and select **Edit Data Source** or click on the **Data Source** tab in the lower-left corner.

Prior to version 8.2, Tableau used the Microsoft JET driver to connect to Access, Excel, and Text files. Tableau now uses a new connection that avoids limitations that were present in the JET driver, but also removes the option for writing custom SQL. If you need to use the legacy connection, you can select that option using the drop-down arrow on the **Open File** dialog:

When using legacy connections, you will lose support for some aggregations, functions, and cross-database joins. Additionally, this option is not available for the Mac version.

# Connecting to data on a server

Database servers, such as SQL Server, MySQL, Vertica, and Oracle, host data on one or more server machines and use powerful database engines to store, aggregate, sort, and serve data based on queries from client applications. Tableau can leverage the capabilities of these servers to retrieve data for visualization and analysis. Alternately, data can be extracted from these sources and stored in a Tableau Data Extract (`.tde`).

As an example of connecting to a server data source, we'll look at connecting to SQL Server. If you have access to a server-based data source, you may wish to create a new data source and explore the details. However, there is no specific example to follow in the `chapter 02` workbook. As soon as the Microsoft SQL Server connection is selected, the interface displays options for some initial configuration. These are shown in the following screenshot:

A connection to SQL Server requires the **Server** name, as well as authentication information. A database administrator can configure SQL Server to use Windows Authentication or a SQL Server username and password. With SQL Server, you can also allow for reading uncommitted data. This can potentially improve performance, but may also lead to unpredictable results if data is being inserted, updated, or deleted at the same time Tableau is querying. Additionally, you may specify SQL to be run at connect time using the **Initial SQL...** link in the lower-left corner.

In order to maintain high standards of security, Tableau will not save a password as a part of a data source connection. This means that if you share a workbook using a live connection with someone else, they will need to have credentials to access the data. This also means that when you first open the workbook, you will need to re-enter your password for any connections requiring a password.

Once you click the orange **Sign In** button, you will see a screen that is similar to the connection screen you saw for Excel. The main difference is on the left, where you have an option for selecting a database:

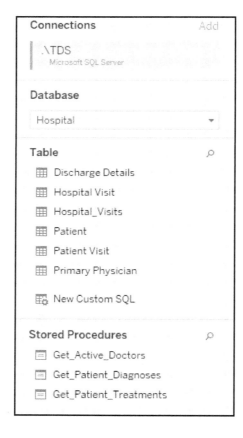

Once you have selected a database, you will see the following:

- **Tables**: Any data tables or views contained in the selected database.
- **New Custom SQL**: You may write your own custom SQL scripts and add them as tables. You may join these as you would for any other table or view.
- **Stored Procedures**: You may use a stored procedure that returns a table of data. You will be given the option of setting values for stored procedure parameters or using or creating a Tableau parameter to pass values.

Once you have finished configuring the connection, click on any sheet to begin visualizing the data.

# Connecting to data in the cloud

Certain data connections are made to data that is hosted in the cloud. These include **Amazon Redshift**, **Google Analytics**, **Google Sheets**, **Salesforce**, and many others. It is beyond the scope of this book to cover each connection in depth, but as an example of a cloud data source, we'll consider connecting to Google Sheets.

Google Sheets allows users to create and maintain spreadsheets of data online. Sheets may be shared and collaborated on by many different users. Here, we'll walk you through an example of connecting to a sheet that is shared via a link.

To follow the example, you'll need a free Google account. With your credentials, follow these steps:

1. Click on the **Add new data source** button on the toolbar:

2. Select **Google Sheets** from the list of possible data sources. You can use the search box to quickly narrow the list.

3. On the next screen, sign in to your Google account and allow Tableau Desktop the appropriate permissions. You will then be presented with a list of all your Google Sheets, along with preview and search capabilities:

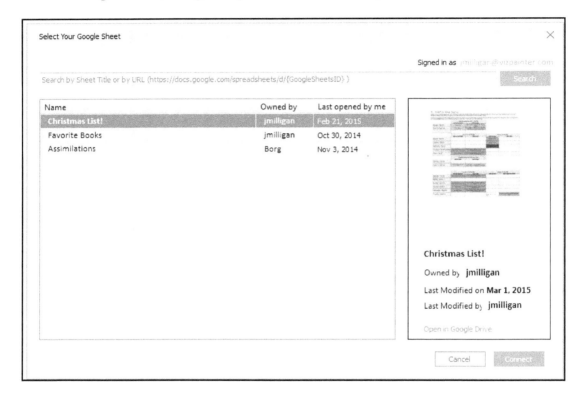

4. Enter this URL (for convenience it is included in the `Chapter 02 Starter` workbook and may be copied and pasted) into the search box and click the **Search** button: `https://docs.google.com/spreadsheets/d/171HdLYlQYSo66_VVbIe1R0UNbggXK6AHOD2gUB1Ce-0/edit?usp=sharing`.

5. Select the resulting Superstore sheet in the list and then click the **Connect** button. You should now see the **Datasource** screen.

6. Rename the data source as `Superstore (Google Sheets)`.

7. Switch the connection option from **Live** to **Extract**.

8. Navigate to the **Connect to Google Sheets** sheet. The data should be extracted within a few seconds.

9. Create a filled map of **Profit** by **State** with **Profit** defining the **Color** and the **Label**.

# Shortcuts for connecting to data

You can make certain connections quickly. These options will allow you to start doing analysis more quickly:

- **Paste data from the clipboard**: If you have copied data from a spreadsheet, a table on a webpage, or a text file, you can paste the data directly into Tableau. This can be done using *Ctrl + V* or **Data | Paste Data** from the menu. The data will be stored as a file and you will be alerted of its location when you save the workbook.
- **Select File | Open from the menu**: This will allow you to open any data file that Tableau supports, such as text files, Excel files, Access files (not available on Mac), and even offline cube (.cub) files.
- **Drag and drop a file from Windows Explorer onto the Tableau workspace**: Any valid file-based data source can be dropped onto the Tableau workspace or even the Tableau shortcut on your desktop or taskbar.
- **Duplicate an existing connection**: You can duplicate an existing data source connection by right-clicking and selecting **Duplicate**.

# Managing data source metadata

Data sources in Tableau are a definition of the connection(s). In addition to storing information about the connection (such as database server name, database, and/or file names), the data source also contains information about all the fields available (such as field name, data type, default format, comments, aliases, and so on). Often, this data about the data is referred to as **metadata**.

Right-clicking on a field in the data pane reveals a menu of metadata options. Some of these options will be demonstrated in the following exercise, others will be explained throughout the book. The following are some of the options available via right-click:

- Rename the field
- Hide the field
- Change aliases for values of a dimension (other than date fields)
- Create calculated fields, groups, or sets
- Split the field
- Change the default use of date or numeric field to either discrete or continuous

- Redefine the field as a dimension or a measure
- Change the data type of the field
- Assign a geographic role to the field
- Change defaults for how a field is displayed in a visualization, such as the default colors and shapes, number or date format, sort order (for dimensions), or type of aggregation (for measures)
- Add a default comment for a field (which will be shown as a tooltip when hovering over a field in the data pane, or shown as part of the description when **Describe...** is selected from the menu)
- Add or remove the field from a hierarchy

Metadata options that relate to the visual display of the field, such as default sort order or default number format, define the overall default for a field. However, you can override the defaults in any individual view by right-clicking on the active field on the shelf and selecting the desired options.

To see how this works, use the filled map view of **Profit** by **State** that you created in the **Connect to Google Sheets** view. If you did not create this view, you may use the **Orders and Returns** data source, though the resulting view will be slightly different. With the filled map in front of you, follow these steps:

1. Right-click on the **Profit** field in the data pane and navigate to **Default properties | Number Format...** The resulting dialog will give you many options for the numeric format.
2. Set the number format to **Currency (Custom)** with 0 decimal places. After clicking on **OK**, you will note that the labels on the map have been updated to include the currency notation.
3. Right-click on the **Profit** field again and select **Default properties | Color**. The resulting dialog gives you an option to select and customize the default color encoding of the **Profit** field:

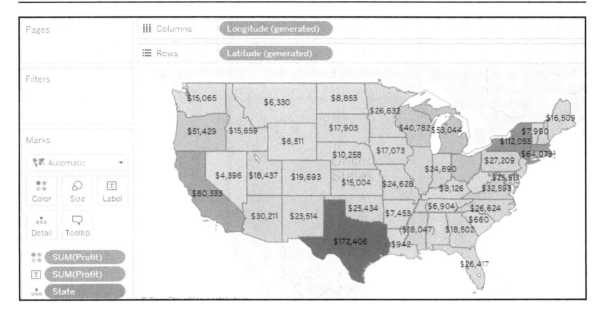

Because you have set the default format for the field at the data source level, any additional views you create using **Profit** will include the default formatting you specified.

 Consider using color-blind safe colors in your visualizations. Orange and blue are usually considered a color-blind safe alternative to red and green. Tableau also includes a discrete color-blind safe palette. Additionally, consider adjusting the intensity of colors.

# Working with extracts instead of live connections

Most data sources give the option of either connecting live or extracting the data; however, some cloud-based data sources do require an extract. Conversely, OLAP data sources cannot be extracted and require live connections.

When using a live connection, Tableau issues queries directly to the data source (or uses data in the cache if possible). When you extract the data, Tableau pulls some or all of the data from the original source and stores it in a Tableau Data Extract file (.tde). Extracts extend the way in which Tableau works with data. Consider the following diagram:

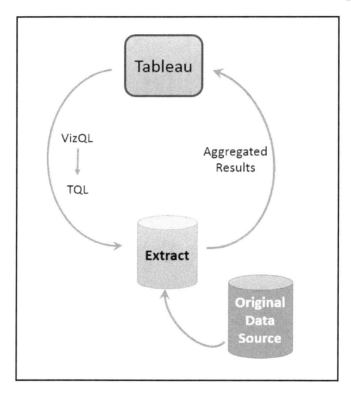

The fundamental paradigm of how Tableau works with data does not change, but you'll notice that Tableau is now querying and getting results from the extract. Data can be retrieved from the source again to refresh the extract. Thus, each extract is a snapshot of the data source at the time of the latest refresh. Extracts offer the benefit of being portable and extremely efficient.

# Creating extracts

Extracts can be created in multiple ways, such as:

1. Select **Extract** on the **Data Source** screen. The **Edit...** link will allow you to configure the extract:

2. Select the data source from the **Data** menu, or right-click on **Data Source** on the data pane, and select **Extract**. You will be given a chance to set configuration options for the extract:

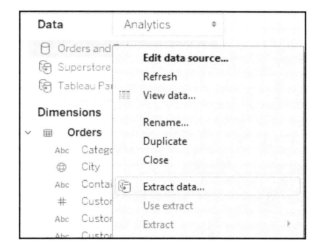

3. Developers may create an extract using the **Tableau Data Extract API**. This API allows you to use Python or C/C++ to programmatically create an extract file. The details of this approach are beyond the scope of this book, but the documentation is readily available on Tableau's website.

4. Certain analytics platforms, such as Alteryx, support the creation of Tableau extracts.

When you first create or subsequently configure an extract, you will be prompted to select certain options, as shown in the following screenshot:

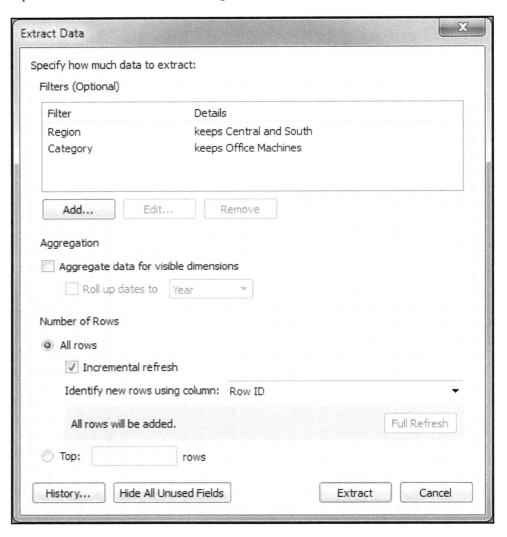

You have a great deal of control when configuring an extract. Here are the various options and the impact your choices will make on performance and flexibility:

- You may optionally add **Extract Filters,** which limit the extract to a subset of the original source. In this example, only records where **Region** is **Central** or **South** and where **Category** is **Office Machines** will be included in the extract.

- You may aggregate an extract by checking the box. This means that data will be rolled up to the level of visible dimensions and optionally to a specified date level, such as year or month.

Visible fields are those that are shown in the data pane. You may hide a field from the **Data Source** screen or from the data pane by right-clicking a field and selecting **Hide**. This option will be disabled if the field is used in any view in the workbook. Hidden fields are not available to be used in a view. Hidden fields are not included in an extract as long as they are hidden prior to creating or optimizing the extract.

- In the previous example, if only the **Region** and **Category** dimensions were visible, the resulting extract would only contain two rows of data (one row for **Central** and another for **South**). Additionally, any measures would be aggregated at the **Region/Category** level and would be done with respect to the **Extract Filters**. For example, **Sales** would be rolled up to the sum of sales in **Central/Office Machines** and **South/Office Machines**. All measures are aggregated according to their default aggregation.
- You may adjust the **Number of Rows** in the extract by including all rows or a sampling of the top *n* rows in the data set. If you select all rows, you can indicate an incremental refresh. If your source data incrementally adds records and you have a field, such as an identity column or date field, that can be used reliably to identify new records as they are added, an incremental extract can allow you to add those records to the extract without recreating the entire extract. In the previous example, any new rows where row ID is higher than the highest value of the previous extract refresh would be included in the next incremental refresh.

Incremental refreshes can be a great way to deal with large volumes of data that grow over time. However, use incremental refreshes with care, because the incremental refresh will only add new rows of data based on the field you specify. You won't get changes to existing rows, nor will rows be removed if they were deleted at the source. You will also miss any new rows if the value for the incremental field is less than the maximum value in the existing extract.

# Using extracts

Any data source that is using an extract will have a distinctive icon, which indicates that the data has been pulled from an original source into an extract:

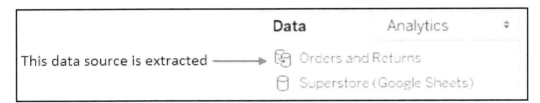

The first data connection in the preceding image is extracted, while the second is not. After an extract has been created, you may choose to use the extract or not. When you right-click on a data source (or select **Data** from the menu and then the data source) you will get a menu options as shown here:

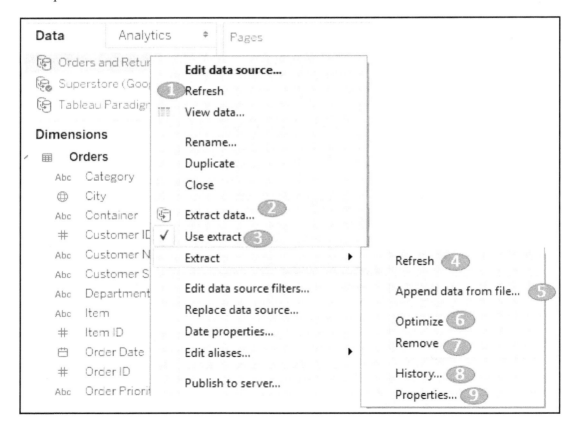

1. **Refresh**: The refresh option under the data source simply tells Tableau to refresh the local cache of data. This option does not update the extract from the original source. To do that, use **Refresh** under the **Extract** sub-menu.

2. **Extract data...**: This creates a new extract from the data source (replacing an existing extract if it exists).

3. **Use extract:** This option is enabled if there is an extract for a given data source. Unchecking the option will tell Tableau to use a live connection instead of the extract. The extract will not be removed and can be used again by checking this option at any time. If the original data source is not available for this workbook, then Tableau will ask where to find it.

4. **Refresh**: This option refreshes the extract with data from the original source. It does not optimize the extract for the changes you make, such as hiding fields or creating new calculations.

5. **Append data from file...**: This option allows you to append additional files to an existing extract, provided they have the same exact data structure as the original source. This adds rows to your existing extract; it will not add new columns.

6. **Optimize**: This option will restructure the extract, based on the changes you have made since originally creating the extract, to make it as efficient as possible. For example, certain calculated fields may be **materialized** (calculated once so that the resulting value can be stored) and newly hidden columns or deleted calculations will be removed from the extract.

7. **Remove**: This removes the definition of the extract, optionally deletes the extract file, and resumes a live connection to the original data source.

8. **History...**: This allows you to view the history of the extract and refreshes.

9. **Properties...**: This enables you to view the properties of the extract, such as the location, underlying source, filters, and row limits.

# Performance

Extracts are very efficient. In fact, extracts are generally faster than most live connections, except for a few extremely efficient columnar databases. This is a result of several factors, such as:

- Extracts are columnar and are extremely efficient for executing the query.

- Extracts are structured so that they can be loaded quickly into memory without additional processing and moved between memory and disk storage so the size is not limited to the amount of RAM available.

- Many calculated fields are materialized in the extract. The pre-calculated value stored in the extract can often be read faster than executing the calculation every time the query is executed.

You may choose to use the extracts to increase performance over traditional databases. To maximize your performance gain, consider the following:

- Prior to creating the extract, hide unused fields. If you have created all desired visualizations, you can click on the **Hide Unused Fields** button on the extract dialog to hide all the fields that are not used in any view or calculation.

- If possible, use a subset of data from the original source. For example, if you have historical data for the last 10 years, but only need the last two years for analysis, then filter the extract by the date field.

- Optimize an extract after creating or editing calculated fields, or deleting or hiding fields.

- Store extracts on solid state disks or drives that are defragmented regularly.

# Portability and security

Let's say that your data is hosted on an SQL Server accessible only from inside your office network. Normally, you'd have to be onsite or using a VPN to work with the data. With an extract, you can take the data with you and work offline.

A Tableau Data Extract (.tde) file contains data extracted from the source. When you save a workbook, you may save it as a Tableau Workbook (.twb) file or a Tableau Packaged Workbook (.twbx) file. A workbook (.twb) contains definitions for all the connections, fields, visualizations, and dashboards but does not contain any data or external files, such as images. When you save a packaged workbook (.twbx), any extracts and external files are packaged together in a single file with the workbook.

A packaged workbook using extracts can be opened with Tableau Desktop or Tableau Reader, and published to Tableau Public or Tableau Online.

A packaged workbook file (.twbx) is really just a compressed zip file. If you rename the extension from .twbx to .zip, you can access the contents as you would any other zip file. You may also consider associating the .twbx extension with your zip utility so you won't have to rename the files.

There are a couple of security considerations to keep in mind when using an extract:

- The extract is made using a single set of credentials. Any security layers that limit what data can be accessed according to the credentials used will not be effective after the extract is created. An extract does not require a username or password. All data in an extract can be read by anyone.
- Any data for visible (non-hidden) fields contained in an extract file (.tde) or in an extract contained a packaged workbook (.twbx) can be accessed even if the data is not shown in the visualization. Be very careful when distributing extracts or packaged workbooks containing sensitive or proprietary data.

A story is told of an employee who sent a packaged workbook containing HR data to others in the company. Even though none of his dashboards displayed sensitive data, the extract contained it. It wasn't long before everyone in the company knew everyone else's salary and the original individual was no longer an employee.

# When to use an extract

You should consider various factors when determining whether or not to use an extract. In some cases, you won't have an option (for example, OLAP requires a live connection and some cloud-based data sources require an extract). In other cases, you'll want to evaluate your options.

In general, use an extract when:

- You need a better performance than you can get with the live connection.
- You need the data to be portable.
- You are using legacy (JET driver) connections to Excel, Access, or text files and you need to use functions, such as COUNTD (count distinct), that are not supported by the JET driver but are supported when the data is extracted.

- You want to share a packaged workbook. This is especially true if you want to share a packaged workbook with someone who uses the free Tableau Reader, which can only read packaged workbooks with extracts.

In general, do not use an extract when:

- You have sensitive data. However, you may hide sensitive fields prior to creating the extract, in which case they are no longer part of the extract.
- You need to manage security based on the login credentials. (However, if you are using Tableau Server, you may still use extracted connections hosted on Tableau Server that are secured by login. We'll consider sharing your work with Tableau Server in Chapter 11, *Sharing Your Data Story*).
- You need to see changes in the source data updated in real-time.
- The volume of data makes the time required to build the extract impractical. The number of records that can be extracted in a reasonable amount of time will depend on factors, such as the data types of fields, the number of fields, the speed of the data source, and the network bandwidth.

# Tableau file types

In addition to the file types mentioned before, there are quite a few other file types associated with Tableau. The following are some of the Tableau file types (with commonly used ones in bold):

- .tbm: This stands for **Tableau Bookmark**. This is an XML file containing definitions of a static snapshot of a single view and associated data source(s). As sheets can now be copied and pasted from one workbook to another, this file type is largely not needed. You can create a bookmark and import it into other workbooks from the **Window** menu.

- .tde: This stands for **Tableau Data Extract**, which is a binary file containing data extracted from another source. The .tde file by itself does not contain information about the original data source.
- .tds: This stands for **Tableau Data Source**, which is an XML file containing the definition of a data source (server name, file path, and so on) but does not contain the data. You can export a data source as a .tds file by right-clicking on the data source and selecting **Add to Saved Data Sources**. Any .tds file in your \My Tableau Repository\Data Sources\ directory will show as a data connection shortcut on the Home Screen.

- `.tdsx`: This stands for **Tableau Data Source Extracted**, which is a compressed file containing the definition of the data source along with an extract of the data. You may create a packaged data sources in the same way you create `.tds` files, selecting `.tdsx` as the file type.
- `.tld`/`.tlf`/`.tlq`/`.tlr`: **Tableau License Disconnected/ File/ Request/ Return Response** file types are used for license activation.
- `.tms`: This stands for **Tableau Map Source**. This is an XML file type used to specify map services and configuration available to Tableau.
- `.tmsd`: This stands for **Tableau Map Source Defaults**. This is an XML file containing defaults for map services.
- `.tps`: This stands for **Tableau Preferences**. This is an XML file containing preference defaults for Tableau Desktop, including UI elements and color palettes.
- `.tsvc`: This stands for the **Tableau Atom Service** file type.
- `.twb`: This stands for **Tableau Workbook**. This is an XML file containing definitions for all sheets, data sources, preferences, and formatting. It does not contain any data.
- `.twbx`: This stands for **Tableau Packaged Workbook**. This is a compressed file containing the Tableau Workbook (`.twb`) file along with any data extract (`.tde`) and any other external files (such as images, or Text/Excel files for data sources that are not extracted).

# Joins and blends

Joining tables and blending data sources are two different ways to link related data together in Tableau. Joins are performed to link tables of data together on a row-by-row basis. Blends are performed to link together multiple data sources at an aggregate level.

# Joining tables

Most databases have multiple tables of data that are related in some way. Additionally, Tableau 10 even allows you to join together tables of data across various data connections for many data sources. As we'll see, Tableau makes it easy to join together tables of data relatively easy.

For example, consider tables such as the following:

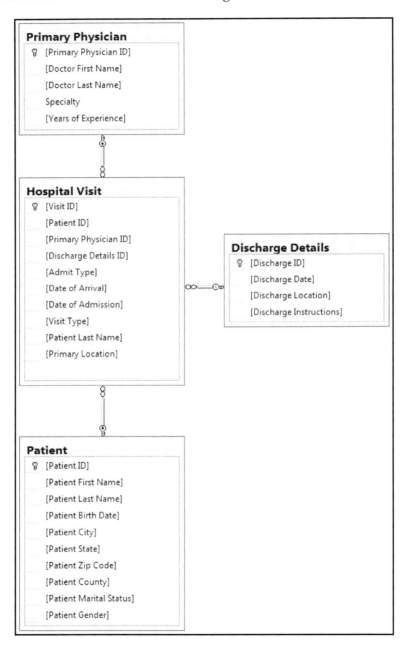

The primary table is the **Hospital Visit** table which has a record for every visit of a patient to the hospital and includes details, such as admission type (inpatient, outpatient, ER). It also contains key fields that link a visit to a **Primary Physician, Patient,** and **Discharge Details**.

When you connect to the database in Tableau, you'll see the tables listed on the left and will have the option to drag and drop them into the data source designer.

Typically, you'll want to start by dragging the primary table into the designer. In this case, **Hospital Visit** contains keys for joining additional tables. Those tables should be dragged and dropped after the primary table.

If key fields and relationships have been defined in the database, Tableau will automatically create the joins as you add additional tables. Otherwise, it will attempt to match field names. In any case, you may adjust the joins as needed. The preceding tables will look similar to this when dropped into the designer:

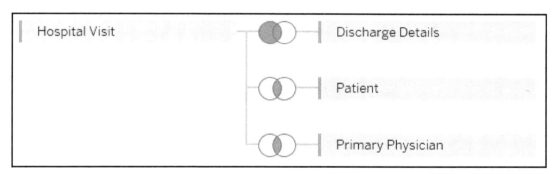

You may adjust the join by clicking on the small diagram between the tables. The diagram indicates what kind of join is used. For example, the join between **Hospital Visit** and **Patient** is an inner join because it is assumed that every visit will have a patient and every patient will have a visit. However, the join between **Hospital Visit** and **Discharge Details** is a left join because some records in **Hospital Visit** may be for patients still in the hospital (so they haven't been discharged).

Clicking on the diagram will allow you to select a different type of join and define which fields are a part of the join.

You may specify the following types of joins:

- **Inner**: Only records that match the join condition from both the table on the left and the table on the right will be kept. In this example, only the three matching rows are kept in the results:

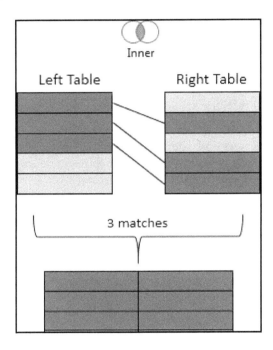

- **Left**: All records from the table on the left will be kept. Matching records from the table on the right will have values in the resulting table, while unmatched records will contain NULL values for all fields from the table on the right. In this example, the five rows from the left table are kept with NULL results for right values that were not matched:

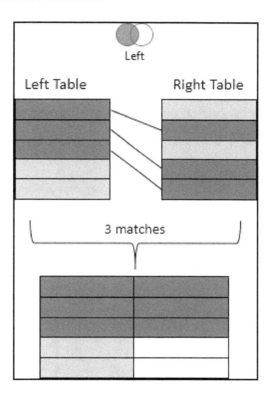

- **Right**: All records from the **Right Table** will be retained. Matching records from the table on the left will result in values, while unmatched records will contain NULL values for all fields from the table on the left. Not every data source supports a right join. If it is not supported, the option will be disabled. In this example, the five rows from the right table are kept with NULL results for left values that were not matched:

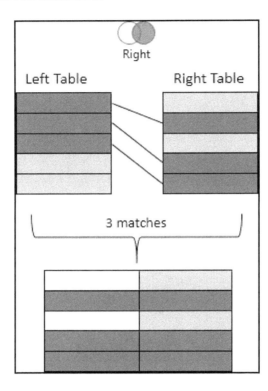

- **Full Outer**: All records from tables on both sides will be kept. Matching records will have values from the left and the right. Unmatched records will have NULL values where either the left or the right matching record was not found. Not every data source supports a full outer join. If it is not supported, the option will be disabled. In this example, all rows are kept from both sides with NULL values where matches were not found:

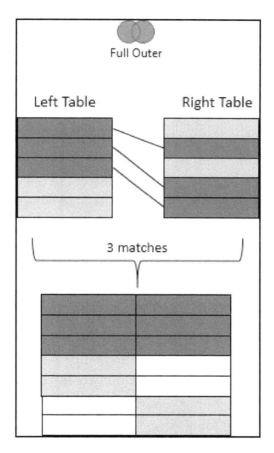

In the hospital example, an inner join was defined for patient and primary physician, because every hospital visit (left table) should find a match with a patient (right table) and primary physician (right table). However, every visit might not have a discharge if, for example, the patient is still in the hospital. So, a left join was used to ensure that every visit was kept in the results.

# Cross – database joins

Tableau 10 introduces the ability to join (at a row level) across multiple different data connections. These joins are referred to as **cross-database joins** or **cross-data connection joins**. For example, you can join SQL Server tables with text files or Excel files or tables in one database with tables in another. This opens all kinds of possibilities for supplementing your data or analyzing data from disparate sources.

With Tableau 10, you can add additional data sources to a connection and join tables from the different sources. Consider the hospital data mentioned previously. It would not be uncommon for billing data to be present in a system different from the patient care data. Let's say you had a file for patient billing that contained data you wanted to include in your analysis of hospital visits. You would be able to accomplish this by adding the text file as a data connection and then joining it to the existing tables, as shown:

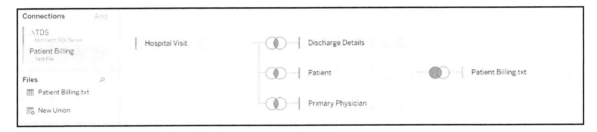

You'll see that the interface on the **Data Source** screen includes an **Add** link that allows you to add data connections to a data source. Clicking on each connection will allow you to drag and drop tables from that connection into the data source designer and specify the joins as you desire. Each data connection will be color-coded so that you can immediately identify the source of various tables in the designer.

In the preceding example, the text file `Patient Billing.txt` has been joined to the **Patient** table from SQL Server.

With all joins, including cross-data connection joins, you will need to make certain that you have the field(s) that is shared in common between the tables. For example, to join `Patient Billing.txt` to the **Patient** table, there needs to be some kind of patient ID or account number that can be matched. Cross-data connection joins also require that the data types be identical.

# Blending data sources

Data blending is a powerful and innovative feature in Tableau. It allows you to use data from multiple data sources in the same view. Often these sources may be of different types. For example, you can blend data from Oracle with data from Excel. You can blend Google Analytics data with Access. Data blending also allows you to compare data at different levels of detail. Some advanced uses of data blending will be covered in `Chapter 8`, *Deeper Analysis – Trends, Clustering, Distributions, and Forecasting*. For now, let's consider the basics and a simple example.

Data blending is done at an aggregate level and involves different queries sent to each data source, unlike joining which is done at a row level and involves a single query to a single data source. A simple data blending process involves several steps, as shown in the following diagram:

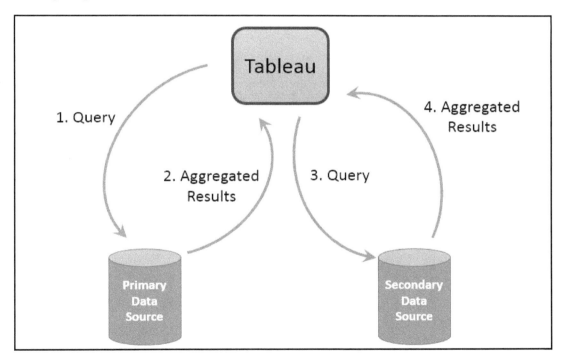

We can gather the following points from the preceding diagram:

1. Tableau issues a query to the **Primary Data Source**.
2. The underlying data engine returns aggregate results.
3. Tableau issues another query to the **Secondary Data Source**. This query is filtered based on the set of values returned from the **Primary Data Source** for dimensions that link the two data sources.
4. The underlying data engine returns aggregate results from the secondary data source.

Tableau then blends the results of the two queries together in the cache. It is important to note how data blending is different from joining. Joins are accomplished in a single query and results are matched row-by-row. Data blending occurs by issuing two separate queries and then blending together the aggregate results.

There can only be one primary source, but there can be as many secondary sources as you desire. Steps three and four will be repeated for each secondary source. When all aggregate results have been returned, Tableau will match the aggregate rows based on linking fields.

When you have more than one data source in Tableau workbook, whichever source you use first in a view becomes the primary source for that view. Blending is view specific. You can have one data source as primary in one view and the same data source as secondary in another. Any data source can be used in a blend, but OLAP cubes, such as SSAS, must be used as the primary source.

**Linking fields** are dimensions that are used to match data blended between primary and secondary data sources. Linking fields define the level of detail for the secondary source. Linking fields are automatically assigned if fields match by name and type between data sources. Otherwise, you can manually assign relationships between fields by navigating, from the menu to **Data | Edit Relationships**. This is illustrated in the following diagram:

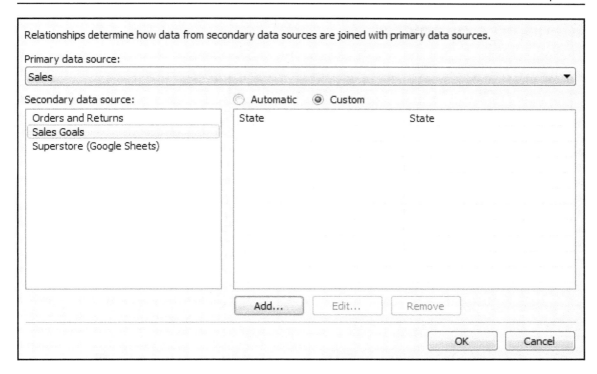

The **Relationships** window will display the relationships recognized between different data sources. You can switch from **Automatic** to **Custom** to define your own data sources.

Linking fields can be activated or deactivated for blending in a view. Linking fields used in the view will usually be active by default, while other fields will not. You can, however, change whether a linking field is active or not by clicking on the link icon next to a linking field in the data pane.

Additionally, use the **Edit Data Relationships** screen to define the fields that will be used for cross-data source filters, which are discussed here.

# Blending example

The following screenshot shows a simple example of data blending in action:

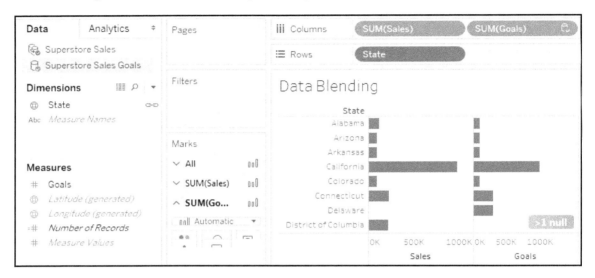

There are two data source connections defined in this workbook, one for the **Superstore** data and the other for **Superstore Sales Goals**. The **Superstore** data source is the primary data source in this view (indicated by the blue check mark) and **Superstore Sales Goals** is the secondary source (indicated by the orange checkmark). Active fields in the view, which are from the secondary data source, are also indicated with an orange checkmark icon.

The **Sales** measure has been used from the primary source and the **Goals** from the secondary sources. In both cases, the value is aggregated. The **State** dimension is an active linking field, indicated by the complete orange link icon next to the field in the data pane. Both measures are being aggregated at the level of **State** (**Sales** by **State** in **Superstore Sales** and **Goals** by **State** in **Superstore Sales Goals**) and then matched by Tableau based on the value of the linking field **State**.

Data blending will be done based on an exact match of the dimension values for the linking field(s). Be careful as this can lead to some matches being missed. You'll note that the indicator in the lower right of the previously viewed which indicates **> 1 null** (at least one null value).

An examination of the data reveals that the state value in **Superstore Sales** is **District of Columbia,** while it is **DC** in the **Superstore Sales Goals** data source. You'll either need to fix the values in the data source, create a calculated field to change values, or change the alias of the value in one data source to match the value in another. For example, you could right-click on **District of Columbia** in the row header, select **Edit alias...** and set the value to **DC**.

An **alias** is an alternate value for a dimension value that will be used for display and data blending. Aliases for dimensions can be changed by right-clicking on row headers, or using the menu on the field in the view or in the Data Pane, and selecting the option for editing aliases.

# Filtering data

Often you will want to filter data in Tableau in order to perform analysis on a subset of data, narrow your focus, or drill into detail. Tableau offers multiple ways to filter data.

If you want to limit the scope of your analysis to a subset of data, you can filter the data at the source:

- **Data source filters**: These filters are applied before all other filters and are useful when you want to limit your analysis to a subset of data. These filters are applied before any other filters.
- **Extract filters**: These filters limit the data that is stored in a Tableau Data Extract (`.tde`) file. Data source filters are often converted into extract filters if they are present when you extract the data.
- **Custom SQL filters**: These filters can be accomplished using a live connection with custom SQL that has a Tableau parameter in the `WHERE` clause. We'll examine parameters in `Chapter 4`, *Using Row-Level, Aggregate, and Level of Detail Calculations.*

Additionally, you can apply filters to one or more views using one of the following techniques:

1. Drag and drop fields from the data pane to the **Filters** shelf.
2. Select one or more marks or headers in a view and then select **Keep only** or **Exclude,** as shown in the following figure:

3. Right-click on any field in the data pane or in the view and select **Show Filter**. The filter will be shown as a control (such as drop-down list, checkbox, and so on) to allow the end-user of the view or dashboard the ability to change the filter.
4. Use an action filter. We'll look more at filters and action filters in the context of dashboards.

Each of these options adds one or more fields to the **Filters** shelf of a view. When you drop a field on the **Filters** shelf, you will be prompted with options to define the filter. The filter options will differ most noticeably based on whether the field is discrete or continuous. Whether a field is filtered as a dimension or as a measure will greatly impact how the filter is applied and the results.

# Filtering discrete fields

When you filter using a discrete field, you will be given options for selecting individual values to keep or exclude. For example, when you drop the discrete dimension **Department** onto the **Filters** shelf, Tableau will give you the following options:

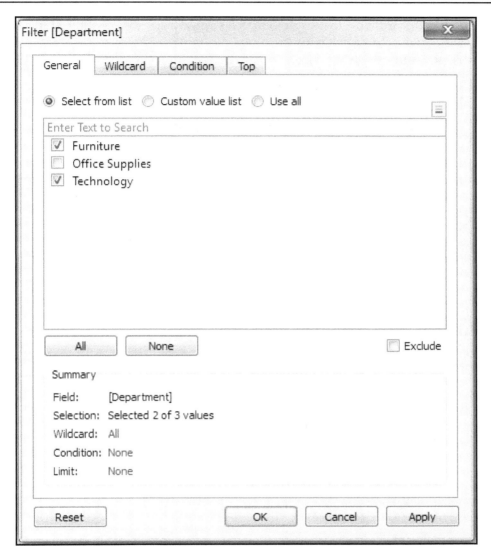

The filter options include **General**, **Wildcard**, **Condition**, and **Top** tabs. Your filter can include options from each tab. The **Summary** section on the **General** tab will show all the selected options:

- The **General** tab allows you to select items from a list (you can use the custom list add items manually if the dimension contains a large number of values that takes a long time to load.) You can use the **Exclude** option to exclude the selected items.

- The **Wildcard** tab allows you to match string values that contain, start with, end with, or exactly match a given value.
- The **Condition** tab allows you to specify conditions based on aggregations of other fields that meet conditions (such as keeping any **Departments** where the **Sum of Sales** was greater than $1,000,000). Additionally, you can write a custom calculation to form complex conditions. We'll cover calculations more in Chapters 4, *Using Row-Level, Aggregate, and Level of Detail Calculations* and Chapter 5, *Table Calculations*.
- The **Top** tab allows you to limit the filter to only the top or bottom items. For example, you might decide to keep only the top five items by the sum of Sales.

Discrete measures (except for calculated fields using table calculations) cannot be added to the **Filters** shelf. If the field is a date or numeric, you can convert it to a continuous field before filtering. Other data types will require the creation of a calculated field to convert values you wish to filter into continuous numeric values.

# Filtering continuous fields

If you drop a continuous dimension onto the **Filters** shelf, you'll get a different set of options. Often, you will first be prompted as to how you want to filter the field:

The options here are divided into two major categories:

- **All values**: The filter will be based on each individual value of the field. For example, an **All Values** filter keeping only **Sales** more than $100, will evaluate each record of underlying data and keep only individual sales more than $100.
- **Aggregation**: The filter will be based on the aggregation specified (such as **Sum**, **Average**, **Minimum**, **Maximum**, **Standarddeviation**, **Variance**, and so on) and the aggregation will be performed at the level of detail of the view. For example, a filter keeping only the **Sumof Sales** more than $100,000 on a view at the level of **Category** will keep only categories that had at least $100,000 in total sales.

Once you've made a selection (or if the selection wasn't applicable for the field selected), you will be given another interface for setting the actual filter:

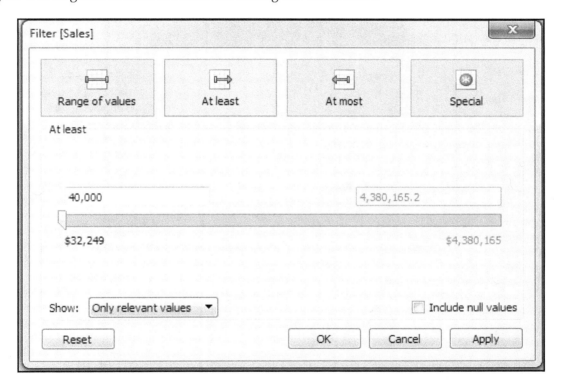

Here you'll see options for filtering continuous values based on a range with a start, end, or both. The **Special** tab gives options for showing all values, NULL values, or non-NULL values.

# Filtering dates

We'll take a look at the special way Tableau handles dates in the *Visualizing dates and times* section of Chapter 3, *Moving from Foundational to More Advanced Visualizations*. For now, consider the options available when you drop a date field onto the **Filters** shelf:

The options here include:

- **Relative date**: This option allows you to filter a date based on a specific date (such as keep the last 3 weeks from today or the last six months from first January)
- **Range of dates**: This option allows you to filter a date based on a range with a starting date, ending date, or both
- **Date Part**: This option allows you to filter based on discrete parts of dates such as **Years, Months, Days** or combinations of parts, such as **Month / Year** and **Month / Day / Year**
- **Individual dates**: This option allows you to filter based on each individual value of the date field in the data
- **Count** or **Count (Distinct)**: This option allows you to filter based on the count or distinct count of date values in the data

# Other filtering options

You will also want to be aware of the following options when it comes to filtering:

- You may display a filter control for nearly any field by right-clicking on it and selecting **Show Filter**. The type of control depends on the type of field, whether it is discrete or continuous, and may be customized using the little drop-down arrow at the upper-right corner of the filter control.
- Filters may be added to the **Context**. Any filter added to the context is evaluated first and results in what can be thought of as a subset of the data. Other filters and calculations (such as computed sets and Fixed LoD calculations) are based on the subset of the data. This can be useful if, for example, you want to filter to the top 5 customers but want to be able to first filter to a specific region. Making a **Region** a context filter ensures that the top 5 filter is calculated in the context of the **Region** filter.
- Filters may be set to show all values in the database, all values in the context, or only values that are relevant based on other filters. These options are available via the drop-down menu on the filter control.

- By default, any field placed on the **Filters** shelf defines a filter that is specific to the current view. However, you may specify the scope of a filter by using the menu for the field on the Filters shelf. Select **Apply to** and select one of the following options:
    - **All related data sources**: All data sources will be filtered by the value(s) specified. The relationships of fields are the same as blending (which is by default by name and type match or customized through the **Data | Edit Relationships...** menu option). All views using any of the related data sources will be affected by the filter. This option is sometimes referred to as cross-data source filtering.
    - **Current Data Source**: The data source for that field will be filtered. Any views using that data source will be affected by the filter.
    - **Selected Worksheets**: Any worksheets selected that uses the data source of the field will be affected by the filter.
    - **Current Worksheet**: Only the current view will be affected by the filter.
- When using Tableau Server, you may define user filters that allow you to provide row-level security by filtering based on user credentials.

# Summary

This chapter covered foundational concepts of how Tableau works with data. Although you will not usually be concerned with the queries Tableau generates to query underlying data engines, having a solid foundational understanding of Tableau's paradigm will greatly aid you as you to analyze data.

We looked at multiple examples of different connections to different data sources, considered the benefits and potential drawbacks of using data extracts, considered how to manage metadata, dived into details on joins and blends, and finally considered options for filtering data.

Working with data is fundamental to everything you do in Tableau. Having an understanding of connecting to various data sources, working with extracts, customizing metadata, and the difference between joins and blends will be the key as you begin deeper analysis and more complex visualizations, such as those covered in the next chapter.

# 3
# Moving from Foundational to More Advanced Visualizations

You are now ready to set out on a journey of building advanced visualizations. Advanced does not necessarily mean difficult. Tableau makes it easy to create them. Advanced also does not necessarily mean complex. The goal is to communicate the data, not obscure it with needless complexity.

Instead, these visualizations are advanced in the sense that you will need to understand when they should be used, why they are useful, and how to leverage the capabilities of Tableau to create them. Additionally, many of the examples introduce some advanced techniques, such as calculations, to extend the usefulness of foundational visualizations. Many of these techniques will be developed more in future chapters, so don't worry about trying to absorb every detail.

Most of the examples in this chapter are designed so that you can follow along. However, don't simply memorize a set of instructions. Instead, take time to understand how the combinations of different field types that you place on different shelves change the way headers, axes, and marks are rendered. Experiment and even deviate from the instructions from time to time just to see what else is possible. You can always use Tableau's back button to return to following the example.

Visualizations in this chapter will fall under the following major categories:

- Comparing values across different dimensions
- Visualizing dates and times
- Relating parts of the data to the whole
- Visualizing distributions
- Visualizing multiple axes to compare different measures

You will notice the lack of a spatial location or geographic category in the preceding list. Mapping was introduced in Chapter 1, *Creating Your First Virtualizations and Dashboards* and we'll cover some advanced geographic capabilities in Chapter 10, *Advanced Visualizations, Techniques, Tips, and Tricks*.

The complete examples are included in the Chapter 03 workbook. You can also use the data sources in that workbook to work through the examples on your own.

# Comparing values across different dimensions

More often than not, you will want to compare the differences of measured values across different categories. You might find yourself asking questions like this:

- How much profit did we generate in each department?
- How many views did each web page get?
- How many patients did each doctor see?

In each case, you are looking to make a comparison (among departments, websites, or doctors) in terms of some quantitative measurement (profit, number of views, and count of patients).

## Bar charts

The following figure is a simple bar chart, similar to the one we built in Chapter 1, *Creating Your First Visualizations and Dashboards*:

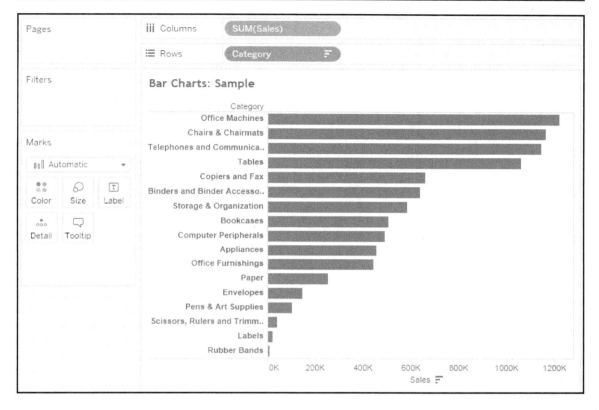

The sum of sales is compared for each category of item sold in the chain of stores. **Category** is used as a discrete dimension in the view, which defines row headers (because it is discrete) and slices the sum of sales for each category (because it is a dimension). **Sales** defines an axis (because it is continuous) and is summed (because it is a measure) for each category.

Note that the bar chart is sorted with the category with the highest sum of sales at the top and the lowest at the bottom. Sorting a bar chart often adds a lot of value to the analysis because it makes it easier to make comparisons and see rank order. For example, it is easy to see that **Bookcases** have more total sales than **Computer Peripherals,** even though the bar lengths are close. Were the chart not sorted, it may not have been as obvious.

You can sort a view in multiple ways:

- **Click on one of the sort icons on the toolbar**: This results in an automatic sorting of the dimension based on the measure that defined the axis. Changes in data or filtering that result in a new order will be reflected in the view, as shown:

- **Click on the sort icon on the axis**: The option icon will become visible when you hover over the axis and then remain in place when you enable the sort. This will also result in an automatic sort:

- **Use the drop-down menu on the active dimension field** and select **Sort** to view and edit sorting options. You can also select **Clear sort** to remove any sorting:

- **Drag and drop row headers** to manually rearrange them. This results in a manual sort that does not get updated with data refreshes.

Any of these sorting methods are specific to the view and will override any default sort you defined in the metadata.

# Bar chart variations

A basic bar chart can be extended in many ways to accomplish various objectives. Consider the following variations:

- Bullet chart to show progress toward a goal or target
- Bars in a bar chart to show the progress towards a target
- Highlighting categories of interest

## Bullet chart – showing progress toward a goal

Let's say that you are an enterprise manager and you've set the following profit targets for your regional managers:

| Region | Profit Target |
|--------|---------------|
| Central | 600,000 |
| East | 350,000 |
| South | 100,000 |
| West | 300,000 |

You maintain these goals in a spreadsheet and would like to see a visualization that tells you how the actual profit compares with your goals.

A **bullet graph** (sometimes also called a **bullet chart**) is a great way to visually compare a primary measure (in this case, Profit) with a secondary measure (in this case, Profit Target). We'll build an example using the Chapter 03 workbook, which contains the **Superstore Sales** and the **Profit Targets** spreadsheet data sources. We'll use these two data sources to visualize the relationship between actual and target profit, as you complete the following steps:

1. Navigate to the **Bullet Chart: Progress toward a goal** sheet.

2. Using the **Superstore Sales** connection, create a basic bar chart of the sum of **Profit** per **Region**:

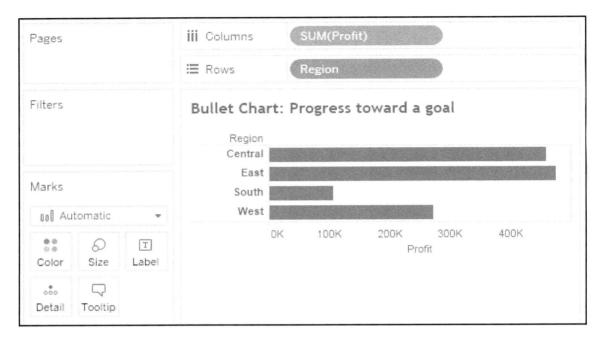

3. In the left data pane, select the **Profit Targets** connection and click to highlight the **Profit Target** field in the data pane.
4. Open **Show Me** and select the bullet graph. At this point, Tableau has already created a bullet graph using the fields in the view and the **Profit Target** field you had selected. You'll observe that the **Region** field has been used in the data blend to link the two data sources and it is already enabled because the **Region** field was used in the view, as shown in the following screenshot:

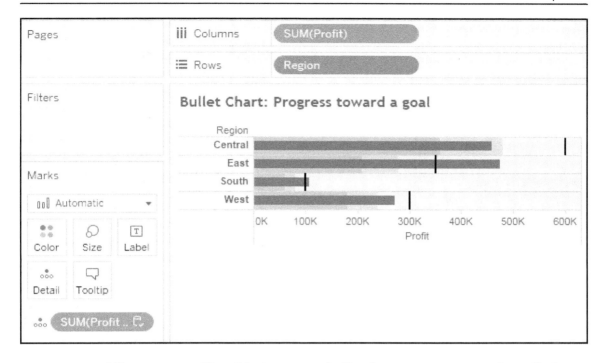

 When you use **ShowMe** to create a bullet chart, you may sometimes find that Tableau uses the fields in reverse order from what you intend (with the wrong measure defining the axis and bars and the other defining the reference line). If this happens, simply right-click on the axis and select **Swap reference line fields**.

You can now clearly see that the **Central** and **West** regional managers are falling short of the goal you set. Bullet graphs make use of reference lines, which will be more thoroughly covered in later chapters. (If you are interested, right-click the axis and select **Edit Reference Line** to explore the reference lines Tableau created).

# Bar in bar chart

Another possibility for showing progress toward a goal is to use **bar in bar charts**, such as this:

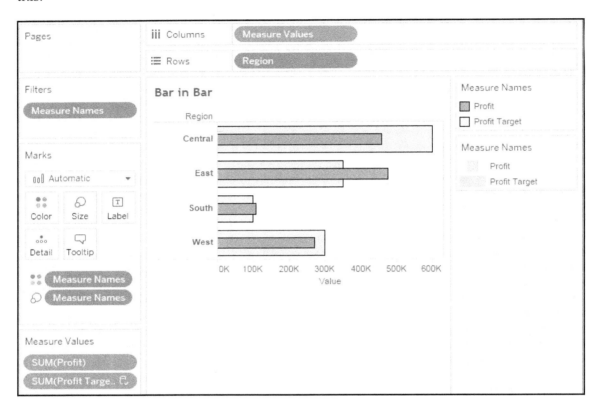

To create this view, continue in the same workbook and follow these steps:

1. Navigate to the **Bar in Bar** sheet.
2. Drag and drop **Profit** from the **Superstore Sales** data source onto the horizontal axis in the view (which is the same as dropping onto the **Columns** shelf).
3. Drag and drop **Region** onto **Rows**.
4. Drag the **Profit Target** field from the **Profit Targets** data source and drop it directly onto the horizontal axis. Since you are dropping one measure (**ProfitTarget**) onto the same space (in this case, an axis) that was being used by another measure (**Profit**), Tableau substituted the special fields **Measure Names** and **Measure Values**.

Any time you want two or more measures to share the same space within a view, you can use Measure Names and Measure Values.

**Measure Names** is a special dimension field that Tableau adds to every data source that is a placeholder for the names of measures. You can place it in the view anywhere you would place another dimension.

**Measure Values** is a special measure field that Tableau adds to every data source that is a placeholder for the values of other measures. You can use it in almost any way you would use any other measure. When these special fields are in use, you will see a new **Measure Values** shelf in the workspace. This shelf contains all the measures that are referenced by **Measure Names** and **Measure Values**.

You can add and remove measures from this shelf as well as rearrange the order of any on the shelf. You can drag and drop the **Measure Names** and **Measure Values** fields directly from the data pane into the view. Many times it is easier to remember that if you want two or more measures to share the same space, all you have to do is, simply drag and drop the second onto the same space that is occupied by first. For example, if you want multiple measures to define a single axis, drag and drop the second measure onto the axis. If you want two or more measures to occupy the pane, drop the second onto the pane.

5. Move the **Measure Names** field from the **Rows** shelf to the **Color** shelf and edit the colors in the legend (double-click on the legend or use the drop-down arrow on the legend) and set **Profit** to orange and **Profit Target** to light gray). You now have a stacked bar chart with a different color for each measure name being used:

6. Copy the **Measure Names** field from **Color** to the **Size** shelf (hold Ctrl while you drag a field in the view and drop it on another shelf in the view). This creates different sizes for each bar segment.
7. Tableau's default is to stack marks. In this case, you do not want the bars to be stacked. Instead, you want them to overlap. To change the default behavior, from the menu navigate to **Analysis | Stack Marks | Off**.

The order of the measures in the **Measure Values** shelf will determine which marks appear on top. If the gray bars are on top of the orange bars, switch the order of the fields. Your view should now look like the bar chart similar to the first image in this section. You can further enhance the visualization by:

- Adding a border to the bars. Accomplish this by clicking on the **Color** shelf and using the **Border** option.

- Adjusting the size range to reduce the difference between the large and small extremes. Accomplish this by double-clicking on the **Size** legend (or using the caret dropdown and selecting **Edit** from the menu).
- Adjusting the sizing of the view. Accomplish this by hovering over the canvas, just over the bottom border, until the mouse cursor changes to a sizing cursor, then click and drag to resize the view.

# Highlighting categories of interest

Let's say one of your primary responsibilities at the Superstore is to monitor the sales of **Tables** and **Bookcases**. You don't necessarily care about the details of other categories, but you do want to keep a track of how tables and bookcases compare with other categories. You might design something similar to the following screenshot:

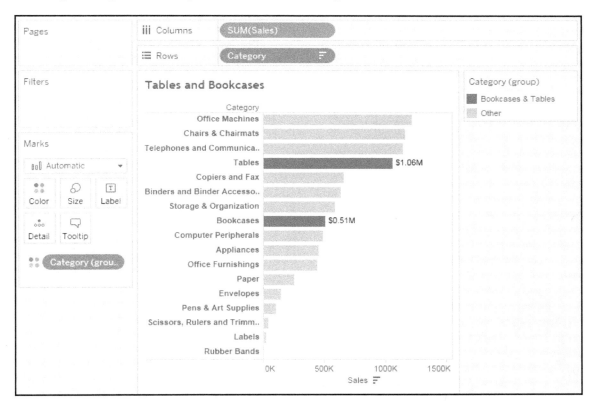

Now you will be able to immediately see where **Tables** and **Bookcases** are compared to other categories as sales figures change day by day. To create this view, follow these steps:

1. Navigate to the **Tables and Bookcases** sheet.
2. Place **Category** on **Rows** and **Sales** on **Columns**. Sort the bar chart in descending order.
3. Click on the bar mark in the view for **Tables** and, while holding the *Ctrl* key, click on the bar for **Bookcases**.
4. Hover over one of the selected bars and from the **Tooltip** menu click on the **Create Group** button (which looks like a paperclip). It is shown in the following figure:

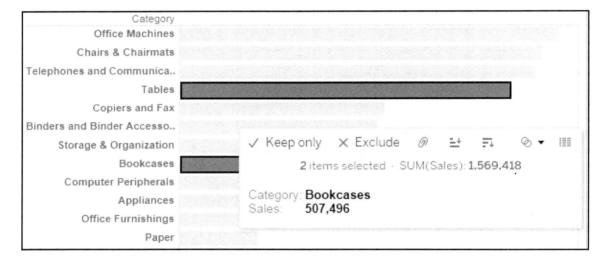

5. This will create a group, which results in a new dimension, named **Category (group)**, in the data pane. Tableau automatically assigns this field to **Color**.

**Ad hoc groups** are powerful in Tableau. You can create groups in the view (as you did here) or using the menu for a dimension in the data pane and navigating to **Create | Group**. Unlike previous versions, Tableau 10 allows you to use groups in calculations.

6. To add a label, only to the **Tables** and **Bookcases** bars, right-click on each bar and navigate to **Mark label | Always show**. The label for the mark will always be shown, even if other labels are turned off for the view or the label overlaps marks or other labels.

7. We'll look at formatting in `Chapter 6`, *Formatting a Visualization to Look Great and Work Well*, but for now you might want to format the label using the drop-down menu on the **Sales** field on **Columns**, selecting **Format**. Switch to the left formatting pane and under **Default | Numbers**, select **Currency (Custom)** and set the **Units** to **Millions (M)**.

As an alternative to labels, you can add annotations to **Views** in Tableau.

**Annotations** Annotations can be used to display values of data and freeform text to draw attention or give explanation. There are three kinds of annotations in Tableau: Mark, Point, and Area.

**Mark** Mark annotations are associated with a specific mark (such as bar or shape) in the view. The annotation can display any data associated with the mark. It will be shown in the view as long as that mark is visible.

**Point** Point annotations are associated with a specific point as defined by one or more axes in the view. The annotation can display values, which define the X and/or Y location of the point. It will be shown in the view as long as the point is visible.

**Area** Area annotations are associated with an area in the view. They are typically shown when at least part of the area defined is visible.

# Visualizing dates and times

Often in your analysis, you will want to understand when something happened. You'll ask questions like:

- When did we gain the newest customers?
- What times of day have the highest call volume?
- What kinds of seasonal trends do we see in sales and profit?

Fortunately, Tableau makes this kind of visual discovery and analysis easy.

# The built-in date hierarchy

When you are connected to a flat file, relational, or extracted data source, Tableau provides a robust built-in date hierarchy for any date field.

Cubes/OLAP connections do not allow for Tableau hierarchies. You will want to ensure that all the date hierarchies and date values that you need are defined in the cube.

To see this in action, continue with the Chapter 03 workbook, navigate to the **Built-in Date Hierarchy** sheet, and create a view similar to the one shown here by dragging and dropping **SUM(Sales)** to **Rows** and **YEAR(Order Date)** to **Columns**:

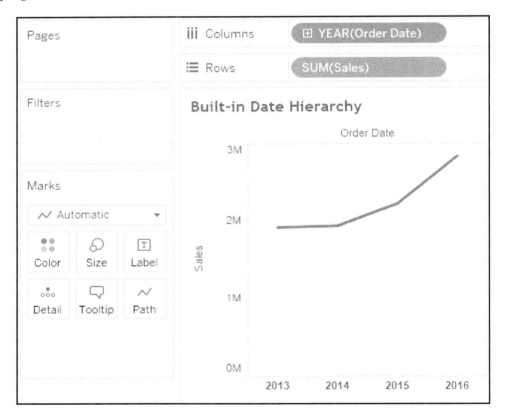

Note that even though the **Order Date** field is a date, Tableau defaulted to showing sales by **YEAR**. Additionally, the field in **Columns** has a + icon indicating that the field is a part of a hierarchy which can be expanded. When you click the + icon, additional levels of the hierarchy are added to the view. Starting with **Year**, this includes Year | **Quarter** | **Month** | **Day**. When the date and time is selected in the field, you can further drill down into **Hour** | **Minute** | **Second**. Any part of the hierarchy can be moved within the view or removed from the view completely.

You can specify how a date field should be used in the view, by right-clicking the date field or using the drop-down menu and selecting various date options.

 As a shortcut, you can right-click, drag, and drop a date field into the view to get a menu of options for how the date field should be used prior to the view being drawn.

The options for a date field look similar to the following screenshot:

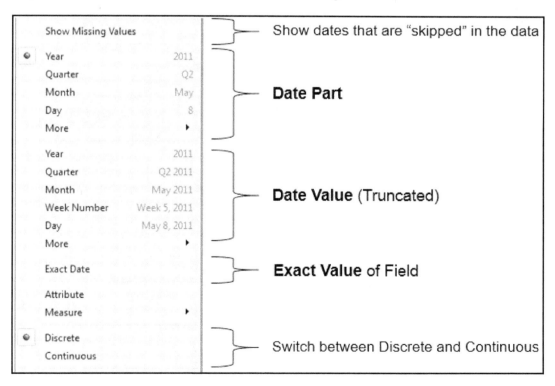

The three major ways in which a date field can be used are as follows:

- **Date Part**: The field will represent a specific part of the date, such as the **Quarter** or **Month**. The part of the date is used by itself and without reference to any other part of the date. That means that date of November 8, 1980, when used as a Month date part, is simply November:

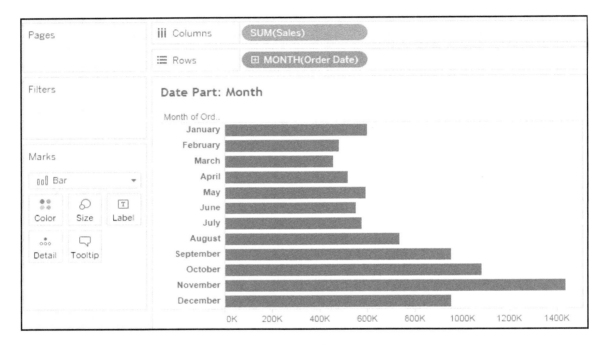

In this **Date Part** view, the bar for November represents the sum of sales for all Novembers, regardless of the year or day.

- **Date Value**: The field will represent a date value, but rolled-up or truncated to the level you select. For example, if you select a **date value** of Month, then November 8, 1980, gets truncated to the month and year and is November 1980:

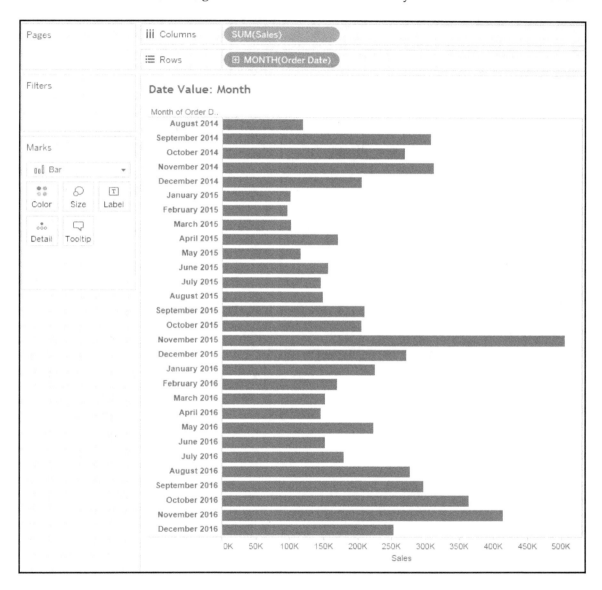

The preceding view includes a bar for the sum of sales November 2012 and another bar for November 2013. All individual dates within the month have been rolled up, so sales for November 1, 2013, and November 11, 2013, are all summed under November 2013.

- **ExactDate**: The field represents the **exact date** value (including time if applicable) in the data. This means that November 8, 1980 2:01 am is treated different from November 8, 1980, 3:08 pm.

It is important to note that any of the preceding options can be used as discrete or continuous fields. Date parts are discrete by default. Date values and exact dates are continuous by default. However, you can switch them between discrete and continuous as needed to allow for flexibility in the visualization.

For example, you must have an axis (requiring a continuous field) to create a reference line. Also, Tableau will only connect lines at the lowest level of row or column headers. Using a continuous date value instead of multiple discrete date parts will allow you to connect lines across multiple years, quarters, and months.

# Variations of date and time visualizations

The ability to use various parts and values of dates, and even mixing and matching them, gives you a lot of flexibility in creating unique and useful visualizations.

For example, using the month and date part for columns and the year date part for color gives a time series that makes year over year analysis quite easy. The year date part has been copied to the label, so the lines could be labeled in the following screenshot:

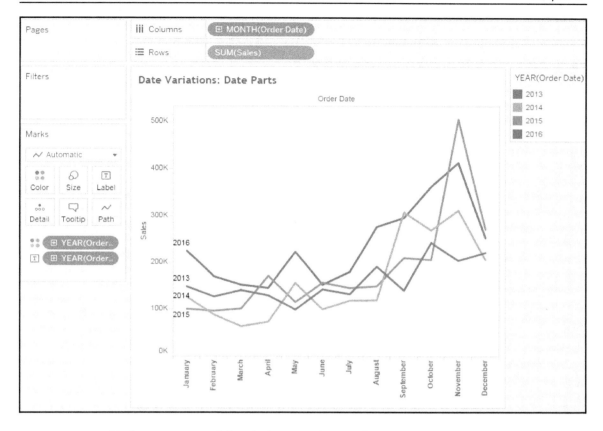

**Date Variations: Date Parts**

 Clicking on any of the shelves on the **Marks** card will give you a menu of options. Here, **Label** has been clicked and the label was adjusted to show only at the start of each line.

The following screenshot is another example of using date parts on different shelves to achieve useful analysis. This kind of visualization can be useful when looking at patterns across different units of time, such as hours in a day or weeks in a month:

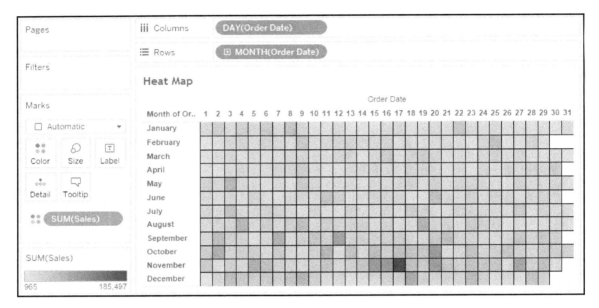

The **Heat Map** view shows the sum of sales for the intersection of each day and each month. Year has not been included in the view, so this is an analysis of all years in the data and allows us to see if there are any seasonal patterns or **hot spots**. Observe that placing a continuous field on the **Color** shelf resulted in Tableau completely filling each intersection of **Row** and **Columns** with the shade of color that encoded the sum of sales. Clicking on the **Color** shelf gives some fine-tuning options, including the option to add borders to marks. Here, a black border has been added to help distinguish each cell.

# Gantt charts

**Gantt charts** can be incredibly useful for understanding any series of events with duration, especially if those events have some kind of relationship. Visually, they are very useful for determining if certain events overlap, have dependency, or take longer or shorter than other events. For example, here is a Gantt chart that shows a series of processes, some of which are clearly dependent on others:

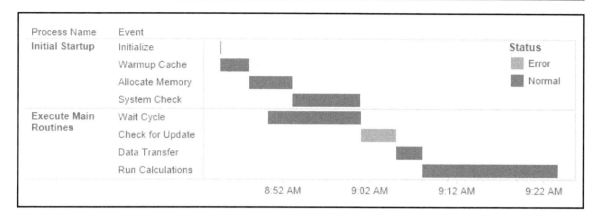

Gantt charts can be created fairly easily in Tableau. Tableau uses the Gantt mark type that places a Gantt bar starting at the value defined by the field defining the axis. The length of the Gantt bar is set by the field on the **Size** card.

Let's say, you want to visualize the time it takes from an order being placed to the time the order is shipped. You might follow steps similar to these:

1. Place **Order Date** on **Columns** as a continuous **Exact Date** or as a **Day** value (not day part). Note that Tableau's automatic default for the mark type is Gantt bars:

2. Place **Order ID** on **Rows**. The result is a row for each order and the Gantt bar shows the date of the order.
3. Filter the view for October 2016. Accomplish this by dragging and dropping the **Order Date** field on the **Filters** shelf. Select the **Month/Year** option and then choose the single month and year from the list.

4. The length of the Gantt bar is set by placing a field with a value of duration on the **Size** shelf. There is no such field in this data set. However, we have the **Ship Date** and we can create a calculated field for the duration. We'll cover calculations in more detail in the next chapter. For now, select **Analysis** from the menu and click **Create Calculated Field...**. Name the field Days to Ship and enter the following code:

```
DATEDIFF('day', [Order Date], [Ship Date])
```

When plotted on a date axis, the field defining the length of Gantt bars always needs to be in terms of days. If you want to visualize events with durations that are measured in hours or seconds, avoid using the 'day' argument for DATEDIFF because it computes whole days and loses precision of hours and seconds.

Instead, calculate the difference in hours or seconds and then convert back to days. The following code converts the number of seconds between a start and end date and then divides it by 86,400 to convert the result into days (including fractional parts of the day):

```
DATEDIFF('second', [Start Date], [End Date]) / 86400
```

5. The new calculated field will appear under **Measures** in the data pane. Drag and drop the field onto the **Size** shelf. You now have a Gantt chart showing when orders were placed. There is, however, one problem. Some orders include more than one item and you are showing the sum of days to ship. This means that if one item took 5 days to ship and another item in the same order took 7 days, the length of the bar shows 12 days for the order. If both items took 5 days and were shipped at the exact same time, the length of the bar indicates 10 even though the order really only took five days.

6. To correct this, decide whether you want to show the minimum number of days or the maximum number of days for each order, right-click on the **Days to Ship** field on the **Marks** card or use the drop-down menu, and select **Measure | Minimum** or **Measure | Maximum**. Alternately, you might decide to add RowID, ItemID, or Item to the **Detail** of the **Marks** card.

Your final view should look similar to the following screenshot:

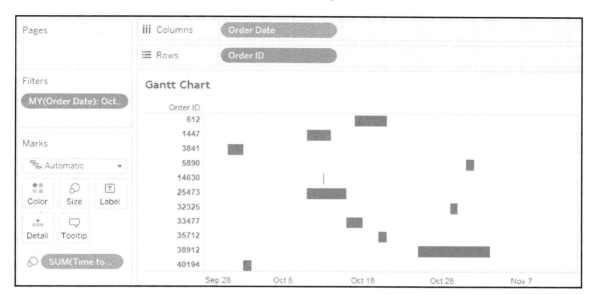

Often, you'll want to sort a Gantt chart so the earliest start dates appear first. Do this via the drop-down menu of the dimension on rows and select **Sort**. Sort it in ascending order by the minimum of the date field.

# Relating parts of the data to the whole

As you explore and analyze data, you'll often want to understand how various parts add up to a whole. For example, you'll ask questions such as:

- How many patients with different admission statuses (in-patient, out-patient, observation, ER) make up the entire population of patients in the hospital?
- What percentage of total national sales is made in each state?
- How much space does each file, sub-directory, and directory take up on my hard disk?

These types of questions are asked about the relationship between the part (patient type, state, and file/directory) and the whole (entire patient population, national sales, and hard disk). There are several types of visualizations and variations that can aid you in your analysis.

# Stacked bars

We took a look at stacked bars in Chapter 1, *Creating Your First Visualizations and Dashboard* where we noted one significant drawback: it is difficult to compare values across categories for any bar other than the bottom-most bar (for vertical bars) or left-most bar (for horizontal bars). The other bar segments have different starting points, so lengths are difficult to compare.

In this case, however, we are using stacked bars to visually understand the makeup of the whole. We are less concerned with visually comparing across categories.

Say a bank manager wants to understand the makeup of her lending portfolios. She might start with a visualization similar to the following screenshot:

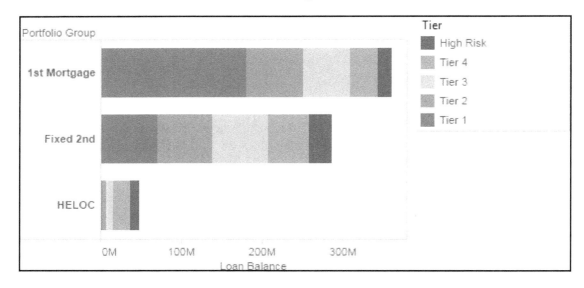

This gives a decent view of the makeup of each portfolio. However, in this case, the bank manager already knows that the bank has more balance in first mortgage loans than fixed second loans. But she wants to understand if the relative makeup of the portfolios is similar. And specifically, do the **High Risk** balances constitute a higher percentage of balances in any portfolio?

Consider this alternative:

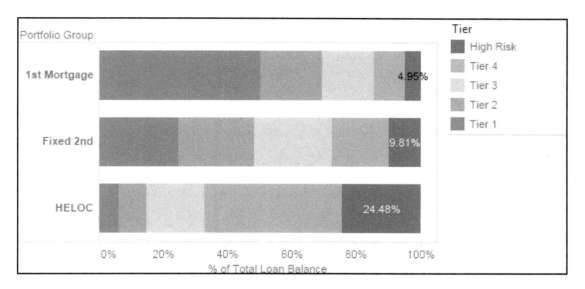

None of the data has changed, but the bars now represent the percentage of the total of each portfolio. You can no longer compare the absolute values, but comparing the relative breakdown of each portfolio has been made much easier. The bank manager may find it alarming that nearly 25% of the balance of **HELOC** loans is in the high risk category when the bar segment looked fairly small in the first visualization.

Creating this visualization involved using quick table calculations. We'll consider table calculations which will be covered in depth in `Chapter 5`, *Table Calculations*. Here, it only takes a few clicks to implement.

Continuing with the Chapter 03 workbook, follow these steps:

1. Create a stacked bar chart by placing **Department** on **Rows**, **SUM(Shipping Cost)** on **Columns**, and **Ship Mode** on **Color**.

2. Duplicate the **SUM(Shipping Cost)** field on **Columns** by either holding *Ctrl* key while dragging the **Shipping Cost** field to a spot on **Columns** immediately to the right of its current location or by dragging and dropping it from the data pane to **Columns**. At this point, you have two Shipping Cost axes which, in effect, duplicate the view:

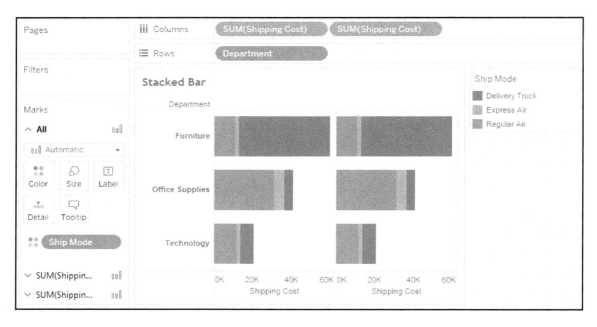

3. Using the drop-down menu of the second **Shipping Cost** field, navigate to **Quick Table Calculation | Percent of Total**. This table calculation runs a secondary calculation on the values returned from the data source to compute a percentage of the total. You will need to further specify how that total should be computed.

4. Using the same drop-down menu, navigate to **Compute Using | Ship Mode**. This tells Tableau to compute the percentage of the total along **Ship Mode** within a given department. This means that the values will add up to 100% for each department.

5. Turn on labels, by clicking the **Abc** button on the top toolbar. This turns on the default labels for each mark:

6. Right-click on the second axis, which is now labeled **% of Total Shipping Cost**, and select Edit Axis... Then set the range as fixed, with fixed a start at 0 and a fixed end at 1. Since you know the totals will add up to 100%, this fixes the axis in such a way that, allows Tableau to draw the bar all the way across:

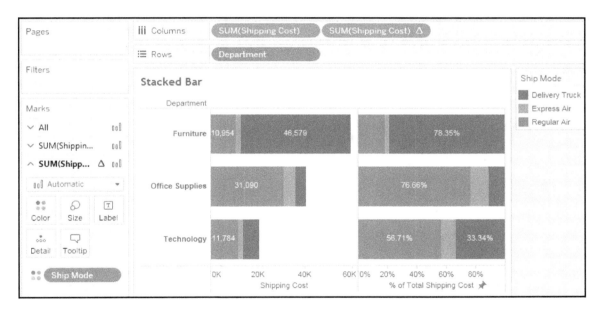

# Treemaps

**Treemaps** use a series of nested rectangles to represent hierarchical relationships of parts to the whole. Treemaps are particularly useful when you have hierarchies and dimensions with high cardinality (a high number of distinct values).

Here is an example of a treemap that shows how sales of each **Item** add up to give total sales by **Category**, then **Department**, and finally total sales overall. **Profit** has been encoded by **Color** to add additional analytical value to the visualization. It is now easy to pick out items with the negative profit that have relatively high sales when placed in the context of the whole:

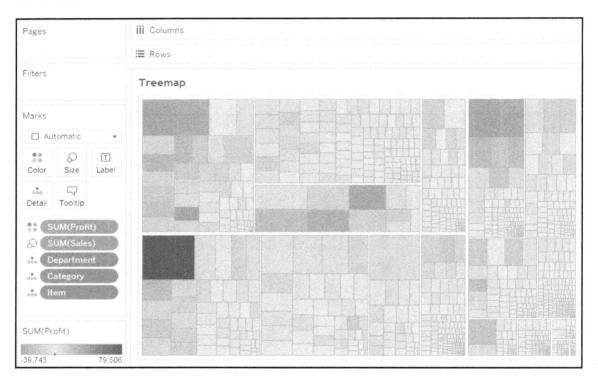

To create a treemap, you simply need to place a measure on the **Size** shelf and a dimension on the **Detail** shelf. You can add additional dimensions to the level of detail to increase the detail of the view. Tableau will add borders of varying thickness to separate the levels of detail created by multiple dimensions. Note that in the previous view you can easily see the division of departments, categories, and items. You can adjust the border of the lowest level by clicking on the **Color** shelf.

The order of the dimensions on the **Marks** card defines the way the treemap groups the rectangles. Additionally, you can add dimensions to rows or columns to slice the treemap into multiple treemaps. The end result is effectively a bar chart of treemaps:

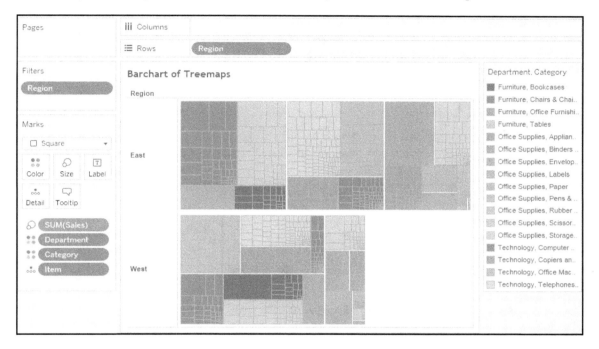

The preceding treemap not only demonstrates the ability to have multiple rows (or columns) of treemaps, it demonstrates the technique of placing multiple fields on the **Color** shelf. This can only be done with discrete fields. You can assign two or more colors by holding the *Shift* key while dropping the second field on **Color**. Alternately, the icon or space to the left of each field on the **Marks** card can be clicked to change which shelf is used for the field:

Treemaps, along with packed bubbles, word clouds, and a few other chart types, are called non-Cartesian chart types. This means they are drawn without an X or Y axis and do not even require row or column headers. To create any of these chart types, make sure no continuous fields are used on **Rows** or **Columns**. Use any field as a measure on **Size**. Change the mark type based on the desired chart type: square for treemap, circle for packed bubbles or text for word cloud (with the desired field on Label).

# Area charts

Think of a line chart and then fill in the area beneath the line. If you have multiple lines, stack the filled areas on top of each other. That's how you might think of an **area chart**.

As an example, consider a visualization of delinquent loan balances being analyzed by the bank manager:

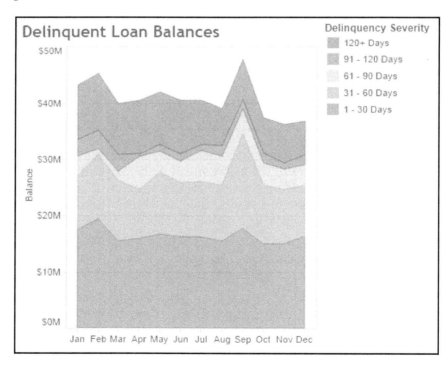

This area chart shows delinquent balances over time. Each band represents a different severity of delinquency. In many ways, the view is aesthetically pleasing, but it suffers from some of the same weaknesses as the stacked bar chart. Since all but the bottom band have different starting locations from month to month, it is difficult to compare the bands between months. For example, it is obvious that there is a spike in delinquent balances in September. But is it in all bands? Or is one of the lower bands pushing the higher bands up? Which band has the most significant spike?

Now consider this similar view:

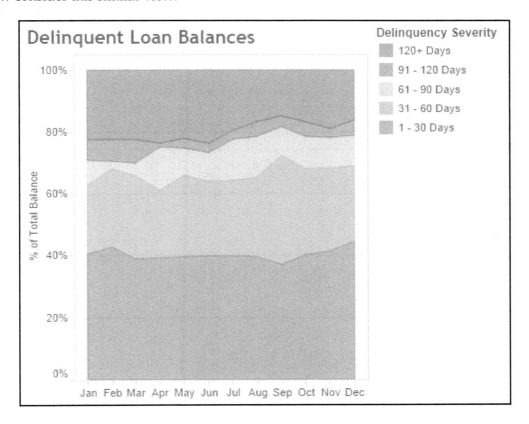

This view uses a quick table calculation similar to the stacked bars. It makes it clear that the percent of balances within the **31 - 60 Days** delinquent range increased in September. However, it is no longer clear that September represents a spike in balances. If you were telling a story with this data, you would want to carefully consider what either visualization might represent or misrepresent.

To create an area chart, simply create a line chart or time series as you have done previously and then change the mark type on the **Marks** card to **Area**. Any dimensions on **Color**, **Label**, or **Detail** shelves will create slices of area that will be stacked on top of each other. The **Size** shelf is not applicable to an area chart.

 You can define the order in which the areas are stacked by changing the sort order of the dimensions on the shelves of the **Marks** card. If you have multiple dimensions defining slices of area, you can additionally re-arrange them on the **Marks** card or in the **Color** shelf to further adjust the order.

# Pie charts

To create a **pie chart**, change the mark type to **Pie**. This will give you an **Angle** shelf which you can use to encode a measure. Whatever dimension(s) you place on the **Marks** card (typically on the **Color** shelf) will define the slices of the pie:

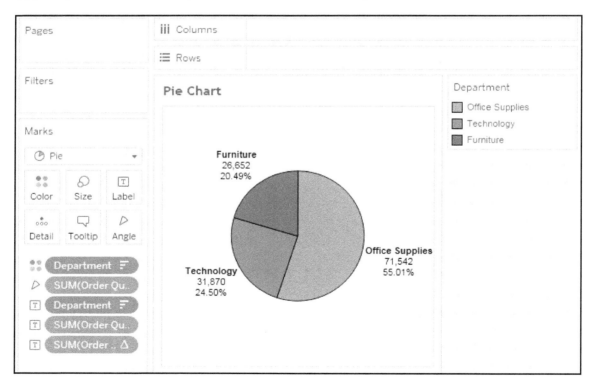

Observe that the preceding pie chart uses the sum of the order quantity to define the angle of each slice; the higher the sum of the order quantity, the wider the slice. The **Department** dimension is slicing the measure and defining slices of the pie. This view also demonstrates the ability to place multiple fields on the **Label** shelf. The second **SUM(Order Quantity)** field is the percentage of total table calculation you have seen earlier.

Before using a pie chart, consider a better alternative (such as a bar chart) if it exists. If you choose to use pie charts, try to limit the number of slices to two or three. Any more than that and pie charts become difficult to understand. Also, as a good practice, sort the slices by sorting the dimension that defines the slices. In the previous example, the **Department** dimension has been sorted by the sum of order quantity descending, using the drop-down menu option. This causes slices to be ordered from largest to smallest and gives anyone reading the chart the ability to easily see which slices are larger, even when the size and angles are nearly identical.

# Visualizing distributions

Often, simply understanding totals, sums, and even the breakdown of the part to whole only gives a piece of the overall picture. Many times, you'll want to understand where individual items fall within a distribution of all similar items.

You might find yourself asking questions such as:

- How long do most of our patients stay in the hospital? Which patients fall outside the normal range?
- What's the average life expectancy for components in a machine and which components fall above or below that average? Are there any components with extremely long or extremely short lives?
- How far above or below the average score were most students' test scores?

These questions all have similarities. In each case, you seek an understanding of where individuals (patients, components, students) were in relation to the group. In each case, you most likely have a relatively high number of individuals. In data terms, you have a dimension (patient, components, and student) with high **cardinality** (a high number of distinct individual values) and some measure (length of stay, life expectancy, and test score) you'd like to compare. Using one or more of the following visualizations might be a good way to do this.

# Circle charts

**Circle charts** are one way to visualize a distribution. Consider the following view, which shows how each state compares to other states within the same region in terms of total profit:

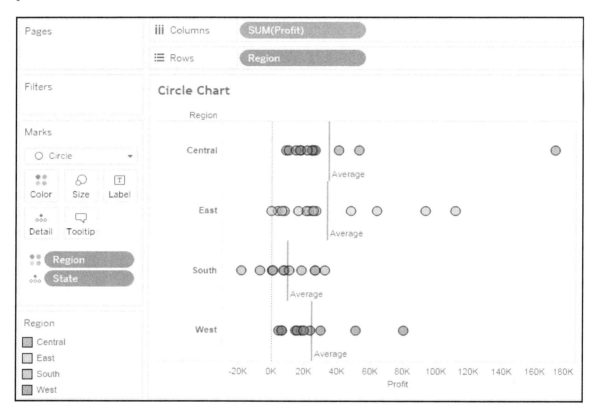

Here you can easily see that certain states do far better or far worse than others in terms of profit. More than that, you can see whether the state has made or lost money and how much above or below the regional average the state was.

After placing the fields on shelves shown in the preceding image, simply change the mark type from **Automatic** (which was a **Bar** mark) to **Circle**. **Region** defines the rows and each circle is drawn at the level of the state, which is in the **Level of Detail** on the **Marks** card. Finally, to add the average lines, simply switch to the **Analytics** tab of the left sidebar and drag the **Average Line** to the view, specifically dropping it on the **Cell** option, as shown:

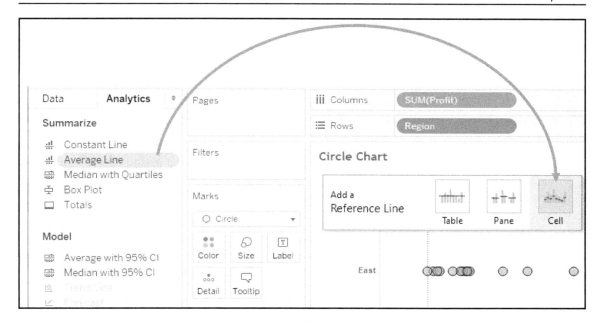

You can additionally click on one of the resulting average lines and select **Edit** to find fine-tuning options such as labeling.

# Jittering

When using views such as circle plots (or other similar visualization types), you'll often see that marks overlap, which can lead to obscuring of the true story. Do you know for certain, just by looking, that there are only two states in the **South** region that are unprofitable? Or could there be two or more circles exactly overlapping? One way of minimizing this potential issue is to click on the **Color** shelf and add some transparency and a border to each circle. Another approach is a technique called jittering.

Jittering is a common technique in data visualization that involves adding a bit of intentional noise to visualization to avoid overlap without harming the integrity of what is communicated. Alan Eldridge and Steve Wexler are among those who pioneered techniques for jittering in Tableau. Various jittering techniques, such as using Index() or Random() functions, can be found by searching for *jittering* on the Tableau forums or for *Tableau jittering* using a search engine.

Here, for example, is one approach that uses the `Index()` function, computed along **State**, as a continuous field on **Rows**. Since `Index()` is continuous (green), it defines an axis and causes the circles to spread out vertically. Now you can see each individual mark more clearly and have a higher level of confidence that overlap is not obscuring the true picture of the data. You can use jittering techniques on many different kinds of visualizations:

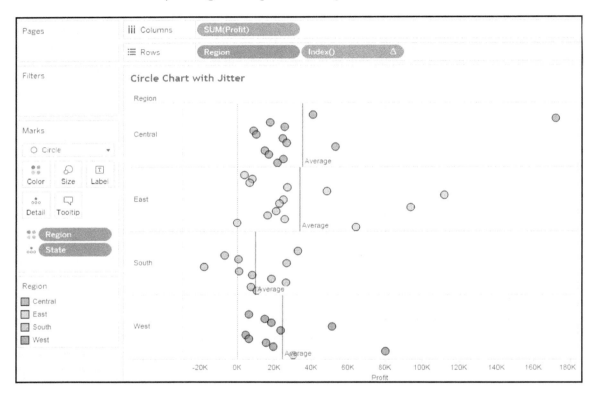

 In the previous view, the vertical axis created by the `Index()` field is hidden. You can hide an axis or header by using the drop-down menu of the field defining the axis or header and unchecking **Show Header**. Alternately, you can right-click on any axis or header in the view and select the same option.

# Box and whisker plots

**Box and whisker** plots add additional information and context to distributions. They show the upper and lower quartile and whiskers, which extend to either 1.5 times the upper/lower quartile or to the maximum/minimum values in the data. This allows you to see which data points are close to normal and which are outliers.

The following is the original circle chart from the preceding section, with the addition of box and whiskers:

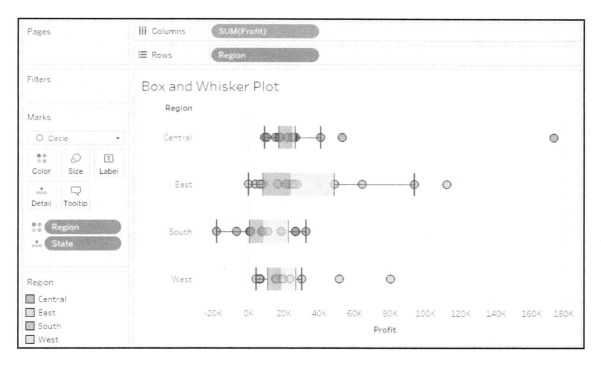

To add **Box and Whisker plots**, use the **Analytics** tab on the left sidebar and drag **Box Plot** to the view.

# Histograms

Another way of showing a distribution is to use a histogram. A **histogram** looks similar to a bar chart, but the bars are showing the count of occurrences of a value. For example, standardized test auditors looking for evidence of grade tampering might construct a histogram of student test scores. Typically, a distribution might look similar to this:

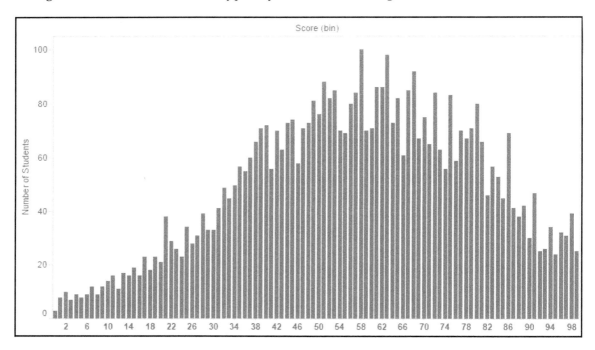

The test scores are shown on the X-axis and the height of each bar shows the **Number of Students** that made that particular score. A typical distribution should have a fairly recognizable bell curve with some students doing poorly, some doing extremely well, and most falling towards somewhere in the middle.

What if auditors saw something similar to this?

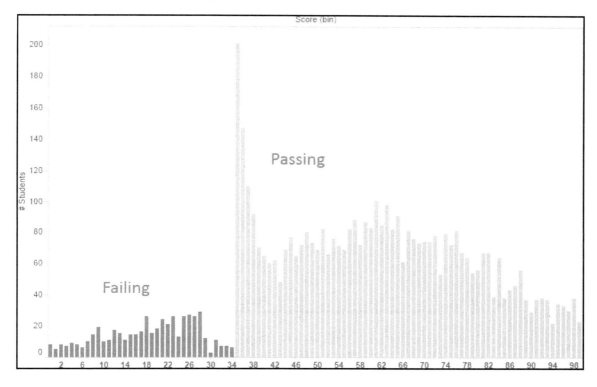

Something is clearly wrong. It appears that graders may have bumped up students who were just shy of passing to barely passing. Histograms are very useful in catching anomalies similar to this.

Let's say you'd like to create a histogram to show you a distribution of items according to the number of days it took to ship the item. Tableau includes the ability to easily create bins that makes creating histograms easy.

**Bins** are ranges of measure values that can be used as dimensions to slice the data. You can think of bins as buckets. For example, you might look at test scores by 0-5%, 5-10%, and so on or people's ages by 0-10, 10-20, and so on. You can also set the size or range of the bin when it is created and edit it at any point. Tableau will also suggest a size for the bin based on an algorithm that looks at the values present in the data. Tableau will use uniform bin sizes for all bins.

Create bins using steps similar to these:

1.  Decide the numeric field for which you'd like to see a distribution. In this case, use the drop-down menu for the **Days to Ship** calculated measure we created earlier and select **Create Bins**. Set the size of the bin to **1** in the resulting dialog box and click on **OK**:

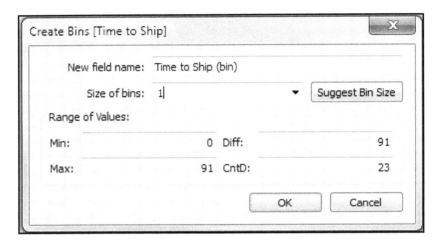

2.  This creates a bin field, named **Days to Ship (bin),** under **Dimensions** in the data pane. Drag and drop this field on **Columns**. This gives you a column for each possible value of the number of days to ship.
3.  You'll need to decide what you want to count for each bucket and place that on **Rows**. Do you want to know how many distinct customers fell into each bucket? Then you'd use customer ID or customer name aggregated as **COUNTD**. If you want to know how many total items fell into each bucket (and not just the unique ones) you could use a **Count of Item ID** or the **Number of Records** field.

Here is an example of a histogram showing the number of days to ship and how many items took that long:

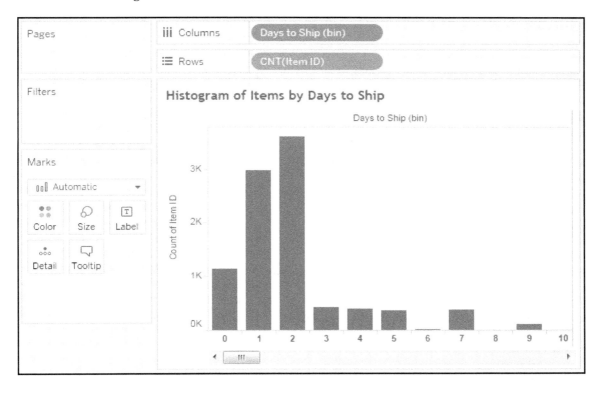

Most items took anywhere from 0 to 2 days to ship, with a sharp decline in the number of items that took 3 or more days to ship.

Just like dates, the bin field in the view has a drop-down menu that includes an option for **Show Missing Values**. This option is on by default. In the previous view, you'll note that there are no items that took **8** days to ship, but **8** is still shown. This can be very useful to avoid distorting the visualization and for identifying what values don't occur in the data.

Histograms can be created very easily using **Show Me**. Simply select a single measure and then select **Histogram** from **Show Me**. It will create the bin and place the required fields on the view. You can adjust the size of a bin using the Edit option from the drop-down menu in the data pane.

# Visualizing multiple axes to compare different measures

Often, you'll need to use more than one axis to compare different measures, understand the correlation, or analyze the same measure at different levels of detail. In these cases, you'll use the visualizations with more than one axis.

## Scatterplot

A **scatterplot** is an essential visualization type for understanding the relationship between the two measures. Consider a scatterplot when you find yourself asking questions such as:

- Does how much I spend on marketing really make a difference in sales?
- How much does power consumption go up with each degree of heating/cooling?
- Is there any correlation between hours of study and test performance?

Each of these questions seeks to understand the correlation (if any) between two measures. Scatterplots are great for seeing these relationships and also for locating outliers.

Consider the following scatterplot that looks at the relationship between the measures: the sum of **Sales** (on the X axis) and the sum of **Profit** (on the Y-axis):

The dimensions of **Department** and **Category** on the **Marks** card define the **view level of detail**. **Color** has been used to make it easy to see the department where the category belongs. Each mark in this preceding view represents the total sales and total profit for a particular **Category** in a particular **Department**. The **Size** of each circle indicates the number of distinct orders for that category/department. The scatterplot points out an issue with Tables. They have high sales but are unprofitable. Telephones, on the other hand, have high sales and high profit.

# Dual axis

One very important feature in Tableau is referred to as a **dual-axis** chart. Scatterplots use two axes, X and Y. You've already seen using **Measure Names** and **Measure Values** to show more than one measure on a single axis. You saw in the stacked bar example that placing multiple continuous (green) fields next to each other on **Rows** or **Columns** results in multiple side-by-side axes. Dual axis, on the other hand, means that a view is using two axes that are opposite each other with a common pane.

For example, this view is using a dual axis of **Sales** and **Profit**:

Observe several key features of the view:

- The **Sales** and **Profit** fields on **Rows** indicate that they have a dual axis by sharing a flattened side.
- The **Marks** card is now an accordion-like control with an **All** section and a section for **Sales** and **Profit**. You can use this to customize marks for all measures or specifically customize marks for either **Sales** or **Profit**.
- **Sales** and **Profit** both define Y axes that are on opposite sides of the view.

Note that the peaks of the lines might lead me to believe that **Sales** and **Profit** were roughly equal in value at certain points. That is hardly likely to be the case. Indeed, it is not. Instead, the axes are not in sync. Sales of $1,000,000 roughly align with the profit of just over $200,000. To fix this, right-click on the **Profit** axis and select **Synchronize Axis**.

You must set the synchronize option using the secondary axis (**Profit** in the preceding example). If the **Synchronize Axis** option is ever disabled on the secondary axis, it is likely that the two fields defining the axes are different numeric types.

For example, one may be an integer, while the other may be a decimal. To enable the synchronize option, you'll need to force a match of the types by either changing the data type of one of the fields (using the drop-down menu of the field) or by creating a calculated field that specifically casts one of the fields to the matching type, using conversion function, such as INT() or FLOAT().

To create a dual axis, drag and drop two continuous (green) fields next to each other on **Rows** or **Columns**, then use the drop-down menu on the second and select **Dual Axis**. Alternately, you can drop the second field onto the canvas, opposite the existing axis.

Dual axis can be used with any continuous field that defines an axis. This includes numeric fields, date fields, and latitude or longitude fields that define a geographic visualization. In the case of latitude or longitude, simply copy one of the fields and place it immediately next to itself on the **Rows** or **Columns** shelf. Then select **Dual Axis** using the drop-down menu.

# Combination charts

**Combination charts** extend the use of dual axes to overlay different mark types. This is possible because the Marks card will give options for editing all marks or customizing marks for each individual axis.

 Multiple mark types are available any time two or more continuous fields are located beside each other on **Rows** or **Columns**. This means that you can create views with multiple mark types, even when you are not using a dual axis.

As an example of a combination dual-axis chart, consider the following visualization:

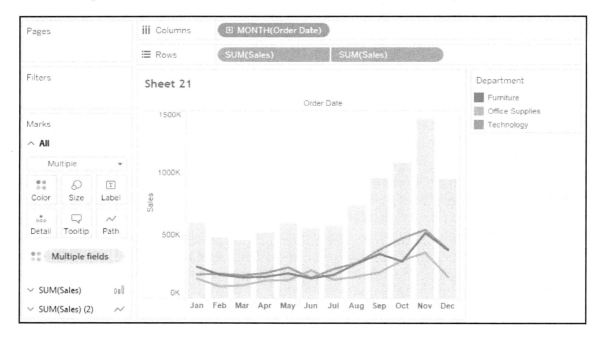

This chart uses a combination of bars and lines to show the total sales over time (using bars) and the breakdown of sales by the department over time (using lines). This kind of visualization can be quite effective for giving additional context in detail.

There are several things to note about this view:

- The field on the **Color** shelf is listed as **Multiple Fields** and is gray on the **Marks** card. This indicates that different fields have been used for **Color** for each axis on **Marks**. You can see different fields used by selecting the corresponding section of the **Marks** card.
- The view demonstrates the ability to mix levels of detail in the same view. The bars are drawn at the highest level (total sales for each month) while the lines have been drawn at a lower level (department sales for each month).
- The view demonstrates the ability to use the same field (**Sales**, in this case) multiple times on the same shelf (**Rows**, in this case).
- The second axis (the **Sales** field on the right) has the header hidden to remove redundancy from the view. You can do this by unchecking **Show Header** from the drop-down menu on the field in the view or right-clicking the axis or header you wish to hide.
- The months have been formatted to show abbreviations. This was done via the drop-down menu of the **Month(Order Date)** field on **Columns**, selecting **Format** and selecting the desired format of the field for headers.

Dual axis and combination charts open a wide range of possibilities for mixing mark types and levels of detail and are very useful for generating unique insights. We'll see a few more examples throughout the book, but definitely experiment with this feature and let your imagination run wild with all that can be done.

# Summary

We've covered quite a bit of ground in this chapter! You should now have a good grasp of when to use certain types of visualizations. The types of questions you ask of the data will often lead you to a certain type of view. You've explored how to create these various types and how to extend basic visualizations using a variety of advanced techniques such as calculated fields, jittering, multiple mark types, and dual axis. Along the way, we've also covered some details on how dates work in Tableau and using the special **Measure Names** / **Measure Values** fields.

Hopefully, the examples using calculations in this chapter have to whet your appetite for learning more about calculated fields. The ability to create calculations in Tableau opens up endless possibilities for extending the analysis of the data, calculating results, customizing visualizations, and creating rich user interactivity. We'll dive deep into row level, aggregate, level of detail, and table calculations in the next two chapters to see how they work and what amazing things they can do.

# 4
# Using Row-Level, Aggregate, and Level of Detail Calculations

One of the most incredible things about Tableau is that it is intuitive to use. We have already seen what amazing discovery, analysis, and data storytelling is possible in Tableau by simply connecting to data and dragging and dropping fields. As we'll see, Tableau allows much more depth beyond simple drag and drop.

Calculations significantly extend the possibilities for analysis, design, and interactivity in Tableau. In this chapter, we'll see how calculations can be used in many ways. We will examine how calculations can be used to fix common problems with data, extend the data by adding new dimensions and measures, and provide additional flexibility in interactivity.

At the same time, while calculations provide additional power and flexibility, they also introduce a level of complexity and sophistication. As you work through this chapter, try to understand the key concepts behind calculations and how they work in Tableau. As usual, follow along with the examples, but feel free to explore and experiment. The goal is not to merely have a list of calculations you can copy, but to gain knowledge of how calculations can be used to solve problems and add creative functionality to your views and dashboards.

The first half of the chapter focuses on some foundational concepts, while the second half gives quite a few practical examples. The topics we'll examine include:

- Creating and editing calculations
- Overview of the three main types of calculations
- Level of Detail calculations
- Parameters
- Practical examples
- Ad hoc calculations
- Performance considerations

We'll examine table calculations in the next chapter.

Most of the examples in this chapter will use the following dataset. It's simple and small so that we can easily see how the calculations are being done. This dataset is included as `Apartment Rentals.xlsx` in the `\Learning Tableau\Chapter 04` directory of the book resources and is also included in the `Chapter 4 workbook` as a data source named `Apartment Rentals`:

| Apartment | Occupant first name | Occupant last name | Start date | End date | Area | Price |
|-----------|---------------------|---------------------|------------|----------|------|-------|
| A-1 | Dwight | Moody | May 01 | Dec 31 | 1000 | 2000 |
| A-2 | Mary | Slessor | Aug 01 | Dec 02 | 800 | 1600 |
| A-3 | Charles | Ryrie | Feb 16 | Mar 02 | 1200 | 800 |
| A-4 | Hudson | Taylor | May 21 | June 03 | 1500 | 1500 |
| B-1 | Amy | Carmichael | Jan 18 | Sep 18 | 3000 | 3000 |
| B-2 | John | Walvoord | May 01 | Dec 20 | 800 | 2400 |

The dataset describes six apartments, the occupant, the start and end dates of the rental period, the area (in square feet), and the monthly rental price.

# Creating and editing calculations

A calculation is often referred to as a calculated field in Tableau. This is because, when you create a calculation, it will either show up as a new measure or a dimension in the data pane (unless it is an ad hoc calculation). Calculations consist of code that references other fields, parameters, constants, groups, or sets, and use combinations of functions and operations to achieve a result. Sometimes this result is per row of data and sometimes it is done at an aggregate level. We'll consider the difference shortly.

There are multiple ways to create a calculated field in Tableau:

1. Navigate to **Analysis** | **Create Calculated Field...** from the menu.
2. Use the drop-down menu next to **Dimensions** in the data pane:

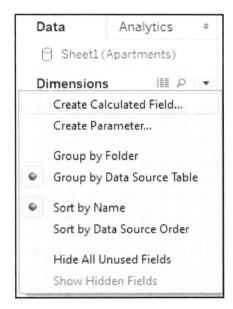

3. Right-click an empty area in the data pane and select **Create Calculated Field**.
4. Use the drop-down menu on a field, set, or parameter in the data pane and select **Create** | **Calculated Field...**.
5. In Tableau 9.0 or later, double-click an empty area on the **Rows**, **Columns**, or **Measure Values** shelves or in the empty area on the **Marks** card to create an ad hoc calculation.

The calculated field you create will be part of the data source that is currently selected at the time you create it.

You can edit an existing calculated field in the data pane by using the drop-down menu and selecting **Edit**.

When you create a calculation using the drop-down menu of an existing field or parameter, the calculation starts as a reference to that field.

The interface for creating and editing calculations looks like this:

The window has several key features:

1. Once created, the calculated field will show up as a field in the data pane with the name you enter in this text box.
2. The code editor allows you to type in the code for the calculation. The editor includes autocomplete for recognized fields and functions. Additionally, you may drag fields, sets, and parameters from the data pane or view into the code editor to insert them into your code.

You may also select snippets of your code in the code editor and then drag and drop the selected text into the data pane to create additional calculated fields. You may also drag and drop selected code snippets from the code window onto shelves in the view to create ad-hoc calculations. This is an effective way to test portions of complex calculations.

3. An indicator at the bottom of the editor will alert you to errors in your code. Additionally, you can use the **Sheets Affected** dropdown to see the sheets that will be affected by changes to the calculation.

4. Use the **Apply** button to save changes to the calculation and apply. Then, the **OK** button will apply changes and close the editor. Changes to a calculation apply anywhere the calculation is used. Use the **X** button in the upper, right corner to close the editor without applying the changes.

5. The functions list contains all the various functions available to be used in your code. Many of these functions will be used in examples or discussed in this chapter. Tableau defaults to showing a list of all available functions. But Tableau also groups various functions according to how they are used:

   - **Number**: Mathematical functions such as rounding, absolute value, trig functions, square roots, exponents, and so on.
   - **String**: Functions useful for string manipulation, such as getting a substring, finding a match within a string, replacing parts of a string, converting a string value to the upper or lower case, and so on.
   - **Date**: Functions useful for working with dates, such as finding the difference between two dates, adding an interval to date, getting the current date, and transforming strings with non-standard formats into dates.
   - **Type conversion**: Functions useful for converting one type of field to another, such as converting integers to strings, floating point decimals to integers, or strings into dates, and so on.
   - **Logical**: These are the decision-making functions, such as `if then else` logic or `case` statements. This category also includes functions, such as `IFNULL`, `ISNULL`, `IIF`; and some basic logical operators, such as `NOT`, `AND`, `OR`, and so on.
   - **Aggregate**: Functions used for aggregating, such as summing, counting, getting the minimum or maximum values, or calculating standard deviations or variances.
   - **User**: Functions used to obtain usernames and check whether the current user is a member of a group. These functions are often used in combination with logical functions to customize the user's experience or to implement user-based security when publishing to the Tableau Server or Tableau Online.
   - **Table calculation**: These functions are different from the others. They operate on the aggregate data after it is returned from the underlying data source and just prior to the rendering of the view. These are some of the most powerful functions in Tableau. They are also some of the most complicated and misunderstood functions in Tableau. We'll devote an entire chapter to covering them.

6. Selecting a function in the list or clicking on a field, parameter, or function in the code will reveal details about the selection in the expanded space on the right. This is helpful when nesting other calculated fields in your code and you want to see the code for that particular calculated field, or when you want to understand the syntax for a function.

Tableau supports numerous functions and operators. In addition to the functions listed on the calculation screen, Tableau supports the following operators, keywords, and syntax conventions:

- AND: Logical "and" between two Boolean (true/false) values or statements
- OR: Logical "or" between two Boolean values or statements
- NOT: Logical "not" to negate a Boolean values or statements
- = or ==: Logical "equals" to the test equality of two statements or values
- +: Addition of numeric or date values, or concatenation of strings
- −: Subtraction of numeric or date values
- *: Multiplication of numeric values
- /: Division of numeric values
- ^: Raise to power with numeric values
- (): Parentheses to define the order of operations
- []: Square brackets to enclose field names
- {}: Curly braces to enclose level of detail calculations
- //: Double slash to start a comment

 Field names that are a single word may optionally be enclosed in brackets when used in calculations. Field names with spaces, special characters, or from secondary data sources, must be enclosed in brackets.

# Overview of the three main types of calculations

The groupings of functions mentioned in the preceding section are important for understanding what kind of functionality is possible. However, the most fundamental way to understand calculations in Tableau is to think of the three different levels of calculations:

- **Row Level calculations**: These calculations are performed for every row of underlying data. For example, you might calculate the number of days between the start date and end date. The resulting value would be calculated and available for each row of data.
- **Aggregate Level calculations**: These calculations are performed at an aggregate level. The view level of detail is defined by fields used as dimensions in the view. You might add or change the dimension in the view, and the Aggregate calculation will be re-calculated to give the result at the new view level of detail.
- **Table calculations**: These calculations are performed at an aggregate level on the table of aggregate data, which has been returned by the data source to Tableau. They are not calculated as a part of the query to the data source.

The Row Level and Aggregate Level calculations are processed as part of the query executed by the underlying source data engine. When the aggregated results of the query are returned, those results are stored in the cache. Table calculations are applied in the cache just prior to the view being rendered.

Level of Detail calculations combines features of row level (you get a result per row of data) and aggregate (you perform aggregate functions). Although we won't treat them as a separate type of calculation, we will devote quite a bit of time later in this chapter to considering how and when to use them.

Understanding the three main types of calculations will make working with calculations much more pleasant. Let's consider some basic examples using the renter data introduced in the preceding table. Here we'll take a close look at two of the three main types of calculations in Tableau: Row Level and Aggregate calculations, along with the closely related level of detail calculations. We'll examine *Table Calculations* in detail in the next chapter.

# Row Level examples

Consider the `Apartment Rental` data source. Let's say the naming convention of the apartment actually has the building and the unit number; for example, the apartment named A-2 is unit 2 in building A.

In the `Chapter 03` workbook, create a couple of calculated fields. Name the first building with the following code:

```
SPLIT([Apartment], "-", 1)
```

Then create another calculated field named `Unit` with the following code:

```
SPLIT([Apartment], "-", 2)
```

Both of these functions use the `Split()` function, which splits a string into multiple values and keeps one based on a delimiter and a token number. The function takes three arguments: the `string`, the `delimiter` (value separator), and the token number (which value to keep from the split: 1st, 2nd, 3rd, and so on). Using the `"-"` (dash) as the delimiter, **Building** is the first value and **Unit** is the second.

Using the two calculated fields, create a bar chart of **Price per Building and Unit**, similar to the following screenshot:

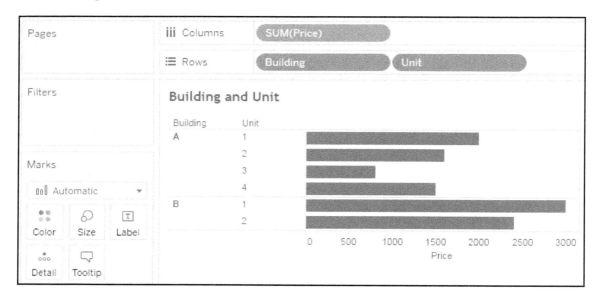

The **Building** and **Unit** fields show up in the data pane, under **Dimensions**. The calculated dimensions can be used just like any other dimension. They can slice the data, define the level of detail, and group measures.

The row-level calculations can be dimensions, but they can be defined or used as measures as well. For example, you could aggregate to find the maximum unit or count the distinct number of units. In fact, if the result of a row-level calculation is numeric, Tableau will often place the resulting field under **Measures** by default. As we've seen before, the default use of a field can be changed from a measure to a dimension, or vice versa, by dragging and dropping it within the data pane.

Note that Tableau adds a small equals sign to the icon of the fields in the data pane to indicate that they are calculated fields:

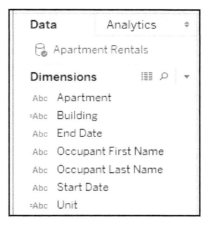

The code for both calculated fields is executed for every row of data and returns a row-level value. We can verify that the code is operating on a row level by examining the source data. Simply click on the **View Data** icon next to dimensions to see the row-level detail (it's next to the magnifying glass icon in the preceding image). In the following figure, the new fields of **Building** and **Unit** are seen clearly, along with the row-level values:

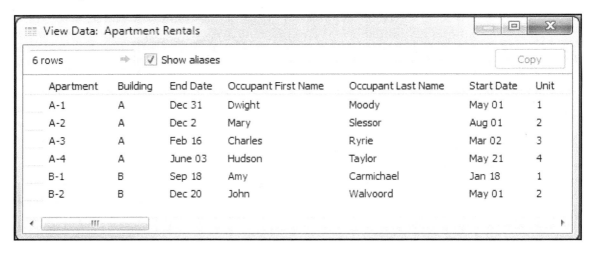

Tableau actually provides a shortcut for splitting a field. You can use the drop down menu on a field in the data pane and navigate to **Transform** | **Split** or **Transform** | **Custom Split** (if you have a non-standard delimiter).The results are calculated similarly to those you created in the preceding figure, but with some additional logic around determining data types. Transform functionality, such as split, is also available for fields in the **Preview** or **Metadata** views on the **Data Source** screen.

You can also build calculations that use other calculations. This is referred to as nesting and the resulting calculations are called nested calculations.

For example, let's say that you know that any unit numbered 1 or 2 is downstairs, while 3 or 4 are upstairs. You'd like to have that information available for analysis.

We could potentially add this attribute to the source data, but there are times when this may not be an option. We may not have permission to change the source data, or the source might be a spreadsheet that is automatically generated every day and any changes would be overwritten.

Instead, we can create a row-level calculation in Tableau to extend the data. To do so, create a calculated field named `Floor` with the following code:

```
IF INT([Unit]) > 2
THEN "Upstairs"
ELSE "Downstairs"
END
```

This code uses an `IF THEN ELSE` conditional statement and returns a string result. Since `Unit` was calculated as a `string` value, it is necessary to convert the `Unit` field to an integer in order to allow comparison to another integer.

A good question to ask yourself whenever you write a calculation in Tableau is: What happens if the data changes? Right now, for example, we only have apartments 1 through 4 in the data. But what happens if additional apartments are added in the future? Or what if bad data shows up tomorrow with an apartment marked as 0? The preceding calculation will only work as long as 1 and 2 are the only apartments downstairs and everything else is upstairs. Consider this alternative code:

```
IF INT([Unit]) = 1 OR INT([Unit]) = 2
  THEN "Downstairs"
ELSEIF INT([Unit]) = 3 OR INT([Unit]) = 4
  THEN "Upstairs"
ELSE "Unknown"
END
```

This code explicitly defines a case for 1 or 2 and also for 3 or 4, and defaults to `"Unknown"` for anything else. When `"Unknown"` shows up as a result in data visualization, you will immediately recognize that you have a new apartment.

# Aggregate Level example

One thing you might want for analysis is the `Price per Square Foot`. This does not exist in the data. This really couldn't have been stored at the source, because the value changes based on the level of detail present in the view (for example, the average price per square foot per building will be different than the average price per square foot per apartment). Rather, it must be calculated at an aggregate level.

Let's create a calculation named `Price per Square Foot` with the following code:

```
SUM([Price]) / SUM([Area])
```

This code indicates that the sum of `Price` should be divided by the sum of `Area`. That is, all values for `Price` will be added, all values for `Area` will be added, and then the division will take place.

Once you click **OK** in the **Calculated Field** dialog box, you'll note that Tableau places the new field under measures. Tableau will place any calculation with a numeric result under **Measures** by default. But in this case, there is an additional reason. Tableau will treat every Aggregate calculation as a measure, no matter what data type is returned. This is because an Aggregate calculation depends on dimensions to define the level of detail at which the calculation is performed. So, an Aggregate calculation cannot itself be a dimension. Note that you are not even able to redefine the new field as a dimension.

Now create a couple of views to see how the calculation returns different results depending on the level of detail in the view. First, take a look at the **Price per Square Foot** by **Building** and **Floor:**

Now notice how the values change when you add in the **Unit** field:

| Building | Floor | Unit | |
| --- | --- | --- | --- |
| A | Downstairs | 1 | 2.000 |
| | | 2 | 2.000 |
| | Upstairs | 3 | 0.667 |
| | | 4 | 1.000 |
| B | Downstairs | 1 | 1.000 |
| | | 2 | 3.000 |

Why did the values change? Because aggregations, including calculated aggregations, depend on what dimensions are defining the level of detail of the view. In the first case, **Building** and **Floor** defined the level of detail in the view, so the calculation added up all the prices for each floor and all the areas for each floor and then divided. In the second case, **Unit** redefines the level of detail, so the calculation added up all the prices for each unit/floor/building and all the areas for each unit/floor/building and then divided.

# Row Level or Aggregate – why does it matter?

What if you create a calculated field named **Price per Square Foot (Row Level)** with the following code:

```
[Price] / [Area]
```

The code differs from the calculated field named **Price per Square Foot (Aggregate)**:

```
SUM([Price]) / SUM([Area])
```

And here is the dramatic difference in results:

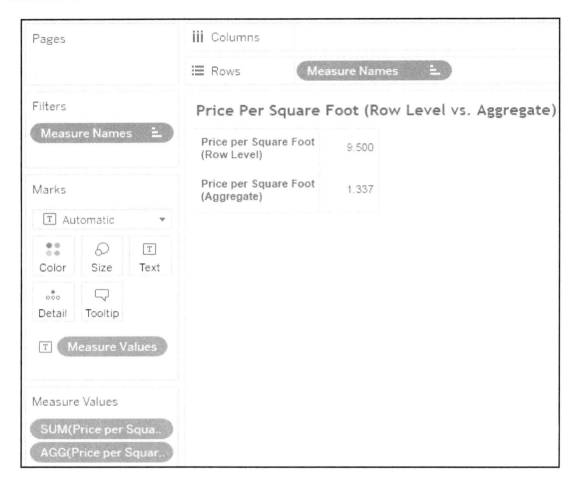

Why is there such a difference in the results? It's a result of the way the calculations are performed.

Note that the first measure in the preceding view is the **SUM (Price per Square Foot (Row Level))**. That's because the calculation is a Row Level calculation, so it gets calculated row-by-row and then aggregated as a measure after all row-level values have been determined.

The calculation and the final aggregation is performed, as shown:

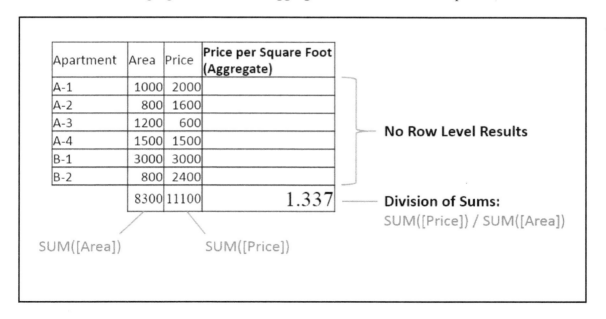

Contrast that to the way the Aggregate Level calculation is performed. Note that the aggregation listed on the active field in the view is **AGG** and not **SUM**. This indicates that you have defined the aggregation in the calculation. Tableau is not further aggregating the results. The following figure is how the Aggregate Level calculation is performed:

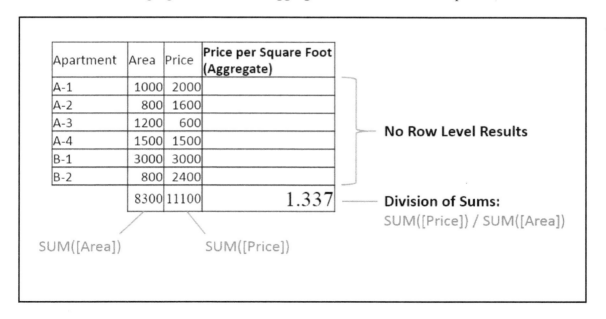

It is vital to understand the difference between the Row Level and Aggregate Level calculations. In general, use the Row Level calculations when you are certain that either you will use the value as a dimension, or that an aggregation of the Row Level values will make sense. Use Aggregate calculations if aggregations must be performed prior to other operations.

# Level of Detail calculations

**Level of Detail calculations** (sometimes abbreviated as **LoD calcs** or **LoD expressions**) is a special kind of calculation that allows you to perform aggregations at a specified level of detail, which may be different from the level of detail defined in the view, and then work with the resulting value at a row level. In this way, you can think of LoD calculations as a hybrid between Row Level calculations and Aggregate Row Level calculations.

## Level of Detail syntax

Level of Detail calculations follow this basic pattern of syntax:

```
{[TYPE] [Dimension 1],[Dimension 2] : AGG([Measure])}
```

The parts of the preceding declaration are as follows:

- **TYPE**: Is the type of LoD calculation (FIXED, INCLUDE, or EXCLUDE), which are described in detail in the following section.
- **Dimension 1, Dimension 2**: Is a comma-separated list of dimension fields that define the level of detail at which the calculation will be performed. You may use any number of dimensions to define the level of detail.
- **AGG**: Is the aggregate function you wish to perform (such as SUM, AVG, MIN, MAX, and so on)
- **Measure**: Is the field that will be aggregated by the aggregate function.

The types of level of detail calculations are as follows:

- **FIXED**: Aggregates at the level of detail specified by the list of dimensions in the code regardless of what dimensions are in the view. For example, the following code returns the average price per `Floor`:

```
{FIXED [Floor] : AVG([Price])}
```

Either of the following two snippets of code represents a fixed calculation of the average price for the entire data source (or the subset defined by a context filter):

```
{FIXED : AVG([Price])}
or
{AVG([Price])}
```

- **INCLUDE**: Aggregates at the level of detail determined by the dimensions in the view and the dimensions listed in the code. For example, the following code calculates the average price at the level of detail defined by dimensions in the view, but includes the dimension `Occupant Last Name`, even if `Occupant Last Name` is not in the view:

```
{INCLUDE [Occupant Last Name] : AVG([Price])}
```

- **EXCLUDE**: Aggregates at the level of detail determined by the dimensions in the view, excluding any listed in the code. For example, the following code calculates the average price at the level of detail defined in the view, but does not include the `Apartment` dimension as a part of the level of detail, even if `Apartment` is in the view:

```
{EXCLUDE [Apartment] : AVG([Price])}
```

# Level of Detail example

As an example with the apartment rentals data, let's say that you want to compare the area (size in square feet) of all apartments with the average size of an apartment for the building. It's fairly easy to get the area per apartment:

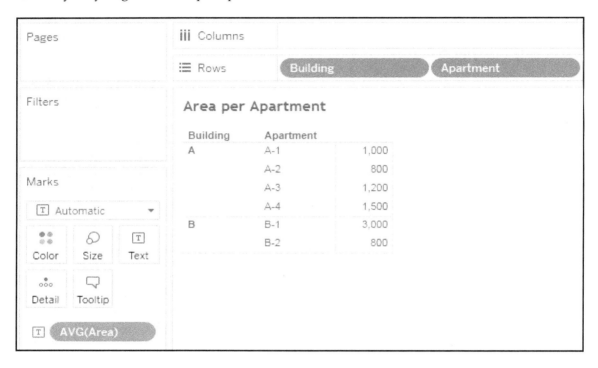

In the preceding figure, the **view level of detail** (the level of detail defined for the view) is **Building** and **Apartment** because those are the dimensions in the view. So, the average area is calculated per apartment, per building.

It's also fairly easy to get the average area per building, by simply removing the apartment dimension from the view, like this:

But what if you want to work with both the average area per apartment and average area per building in the same view? This is where level of detail calculations come in.

There are several ways to approach the solution, but you might consider using an EXCLUDE level of detail calculation named Average Area (exclude apartment), with codes such as the following:

```
{EXCLUDE [Apartment] : AVG(Area) }
```

When you use the calculation in a view that includes **Apartment** in the view level of detail, you get results similar to this:

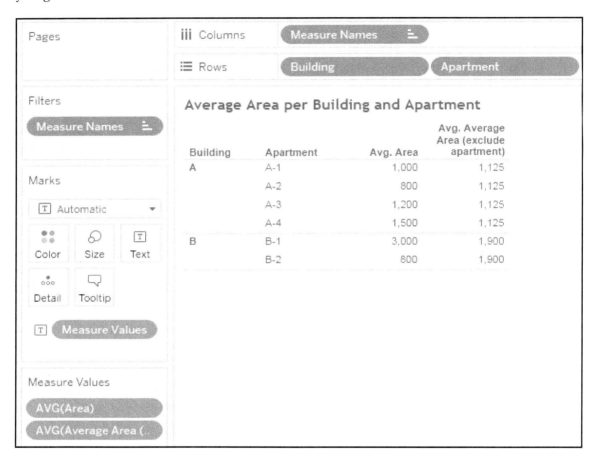

The **AVG(Area)** field on the **Measure Values** shelf is the standard aggregation of **Area** and is done at the view level of detail, so we are getting the average for every apartment for every building.

However, the `Average Area (exclude apartment)` field used on measures is calculated excluding the **Apartment** dimension, so it is calculated per building (the only other dimension in the view). The resulting value of the average area per building is available for every row of data. This is why you can see the values repeated for every row, for each building in the preceding figure. (It is also why it has to be aggregated again; in this case, we used **AVG**, but could have used **MIN** or **MAX** to achieve the same result.)

Additionally, we can use the value as a row-level value in addition to row-level calculations. For example, we could create a calculation to determine which apartments were higher or lower than the average for the building. Here is one such calculation, named `Above or Below Average Size`. The code for the calculation is as follows:

```
IF [Area] > [Average Area (exclude apartment)]
THEN "Above"
ELSE "Below"
END
```

When used in the view, it allows us to see which apartments are **Above** or **Below** the average for the building:

# Parameters

Before moving to some additional examples of Row Level and Aggregate Level calculations, let's take a little side trip to examine parameters, as they can be used in incredible ways in calculations.

A **parameter** in Tableau is a place-holder for a single global value, such as a number, date, or string. Parameters may be shown as controls (such as sliders, drop-down lists, or type-in text boxes) to end users of dashboards or views, giving them the ability to change the current value of the parameter. The value of a parameter is global so that if the value is changed, every view and calculation in the workbook that references the parameter will use the new value. Parameters provide another way to provide rich interactivity to end-users of your dashboards and visualizations.

Parameters can be used to allow anyone interacting with your view or dashboard to dynamically do many things, including the following:

- Alter the results of a calculation
- Change the size of bins
- Change the number of top or bottom items in a **Top N Filter** or **Top N Set**
- Set the value of a reference line or band
- Change the size of bins
- Pass values to a custom SQL statement used in a data source

Since parameters can be used in calculations, and since calculated fields can be used to define any aspect of visualization (from filters to colors, to rows and columns), the change of a parameter value can have dramatic results. We'll see some following examples.

# Creating parameters

Creating a parameter is similar to creating a calculated field.

There are multiple ways to create a parameter in Tableau:

1. Use the drop-down menu next to **Dimensions** in the data pane.
2. Right-click on an empty area in the data pane and select **Create Parameter Field**.
3. Use the drop-down menu on a field, set, or parameter in the data pane and select **Create | Parameter...**

In the last case, Tableau will create a parameter with a list of potential values based on the **domain** (distinct values) of the field. For fields in the data pane that are discrete (blue) by default, Tableau will create a parameter with a list of values matching the discrete values of the field. For fields in the data pane that are continuous (green), Tableau will create a parameter with a range set to the minimum and maximum values of the field present in the data.

Parameters created from fields will only contain the values or range defined by the field at the time they are created. The list or range will not dynamically update to reflect changes in the data.

When you first create a parameter (or subsequently edit an existing parameter), Tableau will present an interface, as shown:

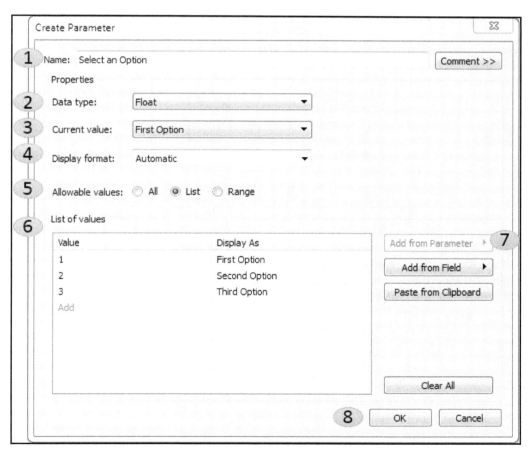

The interface contains the following features:

1. The **Name** will show as the default title for parameter controls and will also be the reference in calculations. You can also add a **Comment** to describe the use of the parameter.

2. The **Data type** defines the type of data that is allowed for the value of the parameter. The options include integer, float (floating point decimal), string, Boolean, date, or date with time.

3. The **Current value** defines what the initial default value of the parameter will be. Changing this value in this screen or on a dashboard or visualization where the parameter control is shown will change the current value.

4. The **Display format** defines how the values will be displayed. For example, you might want to show an integer value as a dollar amount, a decimal as a percentage, or display a date in a specific format.

5. The **Allowable values** option gives us the ability to restrict the scope of values that are permissible. There are three options for **Allowable Values**:

    - **All** allows any input from the user that matches the data type of the parameter.
    - **List** allows us to define a list of values from which the user must select a single option. The list can be entered manually, pasted from the clipboard, or loaded from a dimension of the same data type. Adding from a field is a one-time operation. If the data changes and new values are added, they will not appear automatically in the parameter list.
    - **Range** allows us to define a range of possible values, including an optional upper and lower-limit as well as a step size. This can also be set from a field or another parameter.

6. In the preceding screenshot, the **List of values** allows us to enter all possible values. In this example, a list of three items has been entered. Note that the value must match the data type, but the display value can be any string value. This list is static and must be manually updated. Even if you base the parameter on the values present in a field, the list will not change, even if new values appear in the data. You can drag and drop values in the list to record the list.

If you are using a list of options, consider an integer data type with display values that are easily understood by your end users. The values can be easily referenced in calculations to determine what selection was made and you can easily change the display value without breaking your calculations. This can also lead to increased performance, as comparisons of numeric values are more efficient than string comparisons. However, you'll want to balance the flexibility and performance of integers with readability in calculations.

7. With allowable values of **List** or **Range**, you'll get a series of buttons that allow you to obtain the list of values or range from various sources. **Add from Parameter** copies the list of values or range from an existing parameter; **Add from Field** copies the list of distinct values or range from a field in the data; **Paste from Clipboard** creates the list of values from the anything you have copied to the system clipboard. **Clear All** will clear the list of values.

8. Click **OK** to save changes to the parameter or **Cancel** to revert.

When the parameter is created, it appears in the data pane under the **Parameters** section. The drop-down menu for a parameter reveals an option to **Show Parameter Control,** which adds the parameter control to the view. The little drop-down caret in the upper-right corner of the parameter control reveals a menu for customizing the appearance and behavior of the parameter control. Here is the parameter control, shown as a Single Value List, for the parameter created previously:

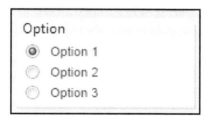

This control can be shown on any sheet or dashboard and allows the end-user to select a single value. When the value is changed, any calculations, filters, sets, or bins that use the parameter will be re-evaluated and any views that are affected will be redrawn.

# Practical examples of calculations and parameters

Let's turn our attention to some practical examples of calculations. These will be examples of Row Level and Aggregate Level calculations. These are merely examples. The goal is to learn and understand some of what is possible with calculations. You will be able to build on these examples as you embark on your analysis and visualization.

 A great place to find help and suggestions for calculations is the official Tableau forums at `https://community.tableau.com/community/forums`

# Fixing data issues

Often, data is not entirely clean. That is, it has problems that need to be corrected before meaningful analysis can be accomplished. For example, dates may be incorrectly formatted or fields may contain a mix of numeric values and character codes that need to be separated into multiple fields. We'll look in depth in many ways of working with messy data in `Chapter 9`, *Making Data Work for You.* Here, we'll consider how calculated fields can often be used to fix these kinds of issues.

We'll continue working with the Apartment Rentals data. You'll recall that the start and end dates looked something similar to this:

| Start date | End date |
|------------|----------|
| May 01     | Dec 31   |
| Aug 01     | Dec 2    |
| Feb 16     | Mar 02   |
| ...        | ...      |

Without the year, Tableau does not recognize the `Start Date` or `End Date` fields as dates. Instead, Tableau recognizes them as strings. Using the drop-down menu on the fields to change the data type to `Date` results in Tableau incorrectly parsing the string value (because it uses the day value as a year). This is a case where we'll need to use a calculation to fix the issue.

Assuming you are confident that the year should be 2016 in each case, you might create a calculated field named `Start Date` (fixed) with code:

```
DATE([Start Date] + ", 2016")
```

and another field named `End Date` (fixed) with the code:

```
DATE([End Date] + ", 2016")
```

What these calculated fields do is concatenate the year onto the existing string and then use the `DATE()` function to convert the string into a date value. Indeed, Tableau recognizes the resulting fields as dates (with all the features of a date field, such as built-in hierarchies). A quick check in Tableau reveals the expected results:

# Extending the data

Often, there will be dimensions or measures you'd like to have in your data, but which are not present in the source. Many times, you will be able to extend your dataset using calculated fields.

For example, you might want to be able to display the full name of the renter in the format Last Name, First Name. Create a calculated field named Occupant Full Name with the following code:

```
[Occupant Last Name] + ", " + [Occupant First Name]
```

Additionally, you might want to know the length of each rental. You have the start and end dates, but you do not have the length of time between those two dates. Fortunately, this is easy to calculate.

Create a calculated field named Length of Rental (days) with the following code:

```
DATEDIFF('day', [Start Date (fixed)], [End Date (fixed)])
```

 Tableau employs intelligent code completion. It will offer suggestions for functions and field names as you type in the code editor. Pressing the Tab key will autocomplete what you have started to type, based on the current suggestion:

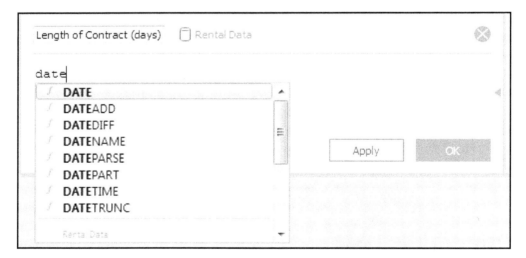

The DATEDIFF() function takes a date-part description, a start, and end date, and returns a numeric value for the difference between the two dates. We now have a new measure, which wasn't available previously. We can use the new measure in our visualizations, such as the following Gantt chart of rentals:

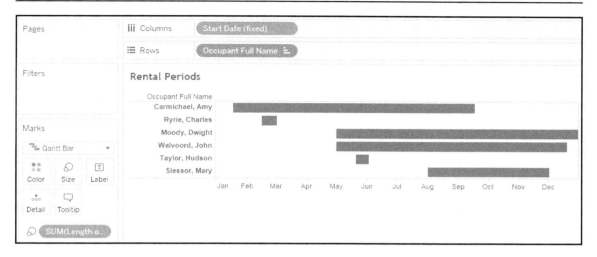

# Enhancing user experience, analysis, and visualizations

Calculations and parameters can greatly enhance the user experience, the analysis, and the visualizations.

Let's say we want to give the apartment manager the ability to do some what-if analysis. Every year, she offers a promotional month where any new renter gets a steep discount on rent. This rental manager would love to have a dashboard that gave the ability to pick an arbitrary date and then see how many renters would have gotten the discount.

To accomplish this, follow these steps:

1. If you have not done so, create the Gantt chart shown previously.
2. Create a parameter called `Promotional Month Start` with a data type of `Date` and a starting value of 5/1/2016. This will allow the manager to set and adjust the starting date for the promotional month. Show the parameter control on the view by selecting **Show Parameter Control** from the drop-down menu on the parameter in the data pane.
3. Create a calculated field called `Promotional Month End` that adds a month to the starting month set via the parameter. The code would be:

```
DATEADD('month', 1, [Promotional Month Start]).
```

4. Add the `Promotional Month End` field to the **Detail** shelf on the **Marks** card. Make sure that the field is set to **Exact Date** and is **Continuous**. This makes it available for use as a reference line or band. Parameters are globally available without explicitly adding them to the view.

5. Now add a band to the view to show the promotional month. Do this by switching to the **Analytics** tab in the left sidebar. Drag **Reference Band** to the view and drop it on **Table**:

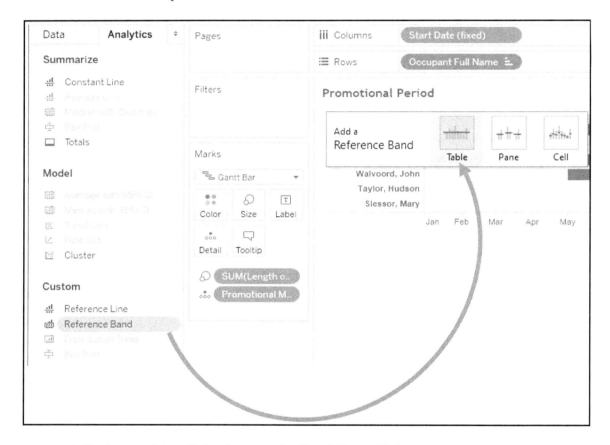

6. In the resulting dialog box, set the **Band From: Value** to `Promotional Month Start` and the **Band To: Value** to `Promotional Month End`. You may wish to set the **Label** for both the **Band From** and **Band To** to **None**.

7. Create an additional row-level calculation named `Started in Promotional Period?` that evaluates each start date to determine if it is in the promotional period. One possibility, which simply returns true or false based on whether the start date falls between the start and end dates as follows is:

```
[Start Date] >= [Promotional Month Start] AND
[Start Date] < [Promotional Month End]
```

8. Place this new calculated field on the **Color** shelf.

We now have a view that allows the apartment manager to change the date and see a dynamically changing view that makes it obvious which renters would have fallen within a given promotional period. Experiment with changing the value of the `Promotional Month Start` parameter to see how the view updates:

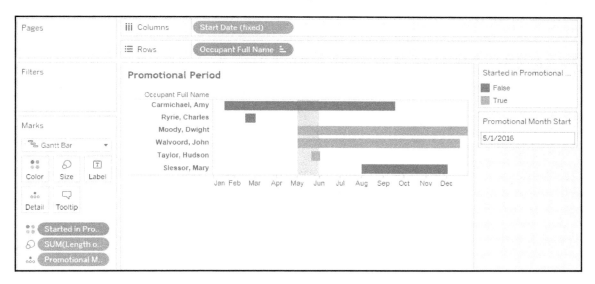

The preceding view shows the proposed promotional month as a band and highlights which rental periods would have started during the month. The band and shading color will change as the apartment manager adjusts the promotional start date.

# Achieving flexibility with data blends

Data blending, which we examined in detail in `Chapter 2`, *Working with Data in Tableau*, is a powerful feature in which Tableau can combine two different data sources in a single view. In order for a blend to work, Tableau requires at least one dimension in each data set that can be linked together (either automatically, when the name and data type matches, or manually, when you define a relationship via the menu **Data | Edit Relationships**). Sometimes, you may not have the required dimensions in one of the datasets, or the values may not match. You can use calculated fields as dimensions for blending.

In addition to the renter data we've been using, let's say we have another data source that gives us the discount given to some renters based on the apartment they rented. The discount indicates the percentage by which the rental price is reduced. Ultimately, the goal is to determine the actual price paid by all renters, including the discount if applicable:

| Apartment | Discount |
|-----------|----------|
| A1 | .05 |
| A2 | .02 |
| B2 | .01 |

This dataset is part of the `Apartment Rentals.xlsx` spreadsheet, and the connection is named `Discount` and is included in the `chapter 04 workbook`.

The `Apartment Rentals` and `Discount` data sources both contain a field called **Apartment**, but the original dataset contained dashes in the value, while this new dataset does not. How can we blend these sources together?

As you'll recall, whichever data source you start building a view with is the primary. Using **Apartment Rental** as the primary data source and **Discount** as the secondary, this is what happens when we accept the default blending on the **Renter** field:

Both **Apartment** and **Discount** from the secondary source are NULL. This is because the values of **Apartment** never exactly match.

Data blending occurs on the aliases of fields, so one option is to simply change the aliases for one of the fields to match the values in the other. For example, if you were to use the drop-down menu of the **Apartment** field in the primary source, and select **Aliases...**, you could change all the aliases to remove the dash. At that point, the data blend works.

However, if any new renters are added to the data, you'll need to edit the aliases again. That could become tedious, or even be un-maintainable, for a large, constantly changing data source.

Let's consider solving the data blending issue using a calculated field. Create a calculation in the primary data source called Apartment (Blend) with the following code:

```
REPLACE([Apartment], "-", "")
```

This code replaces the dashes in **Apartment** with blanks. The value of this new calculated field will now exactly match the value in the secondary source.

Now we need to tell Tableau to blend on the new calculated field **Renter Last Name**. Manually edit the data relationships (from the menu select **Data | Edit Relationships**) and manually match the **Apartment (blend)** field from the primary data source to the **Apartment** field in the secondary. At this point, the blend works and we can create a view similar to this (**Discount** has been given a default number format of percentage):

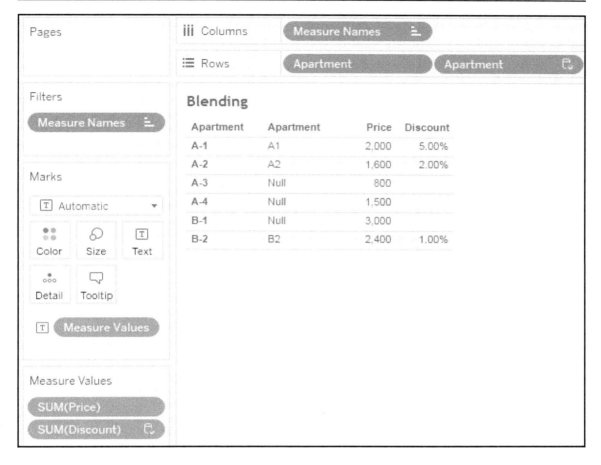

Note that **Discount** is still blank in several cases. This is because the secondary data source did not have records that matched values from the primary data source. In these cases, the value from the secondary source will be NULL.

We started out with a goal of determining the actual rental price, including any discount, for all renters. We're nearly there. What we'll need to do is create another calculation that takes the initial price and multiplies it by 1 minus the discount. That is, if the discount is .05 (5%), we'll multiply the price by .95 (95%) to get the actual price.

In order to calculate the actual rental price, we might start with a calculation in the primary source, as shown:

Note that we can reference fields from the secondary source in calculations. Also, you must reference them as aggregates. In this case, we used SUM, because we knew we'd keep our view at the level of individual apartments and so the SUM of the discount would be correct. However, Tableau indicates that the calculation has an error.

The drop down menu gives the detail, Cannot mix aggregate and non-aggregate arguments with this function. This is a common error that indicates that we've tried to mix Row Level calculations with Aggregate Level calculations. To fix this, we need to identify which elements of the calculation are row-level, which are aggregate, and what function is trying to use both. In this case, we are trying to multiply the row-level field **Price** by the aggregate-level field **Discount**. We know **Discount** has to be aggregate, since it is from a secondary data source. So, we fix the problem by making **Price** an aggregate.

Our new, valid function looks similar to the following screenshot:

When you find and double-click on a secondary field in the fields list to add it to the code, Tableau will automatically insert it with a default aggregation.

However, even though we have an indication of valid syntax, our view indicates that something is still wrong:

We wanted to get the actual price for all apartments, not just the ones that had a match in the secondary data source. The reason we're not is because the calculation returns a NULL when **Discount** is NULL because there is no match in the blend. To resolve this, we'll need to adjust the calculation. Edit the code of Actual Price to the following:

```
SUM([Price]) * (1 - ZN(SUM([Discount].[Discount])))
```

Here, we've wrapped the aggregation of the secondary **Discount** field in ZN(). This function (which stands for Zero if Null) evaluates the expression inside the parentheses and returns a 0 if the expression is NULL, or simply the expression if it's not NULL. So, in this case, any NULL value for the sum of **Discount** is converted to 0 and we get the sum of price multiplied by one, which means we get the original price with no discount:

| Apartment | Apartment | Price | Discount | Actual Price |
|---|---|---|---|---|
| A-1 | A1 | 2,000 | 5.00% | 1,900 |
| A-2 | A2 | 1,600 | 2.00% | 1,568 |
| A-3 | Null | 800 | | 800 |
| A-4 | Null | 1,500 | | 1,500 |
| B-1 | Null | 3,000 | | 3,000 |
| B-2 | B2 | 2,400 | 1.00% | 2,376 |

The final result is just what we wanted!

With Tableau 10.0, you have the ability to join together different data sources, which gives you some options to consider. The preceding example could might have been solved using a join because both data sources had one record per apartment. But imagine a data source that had multiple records for a single apartment. Joining would give you the discount value repeated for each row. Blending in such a case might be a more straightforward solution. A good understanding of data blending gives you additional options for working with your data.

# Ad hoc calculations

Ad hoc calculations add calculated fields to shelves in a single view without adding fields to the data pane.

Let's say that you have a simple view, which shows the **Price per Renter**, as shown:

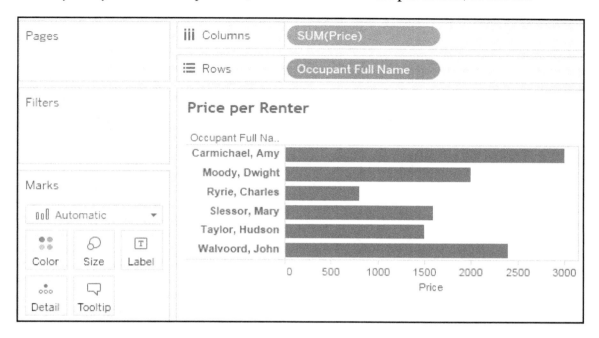

What if you want to quickly highlight any renters who had a contract of at least $**2000**? One option would be to create an ad hoc calculation. To do so, simply double-click on an empty area of the **Columns**, **Rows**, or **Measure Values** cards, or on the empty space of the **Marks** shelf, and then start typing the code for a calculation. In this example, we've double-clicked on the empty space on the **Marks** shelf:

Here, we've entered the code that will return `True` if the sum of **Price** is at least $**2000** and `False` otherwise. Pressing *Enter* or clicking outside the text box will reveal a new ad hoc field that can be dragged and dropped anywhere within the view. Here, we've added it to the **Color** shelf:

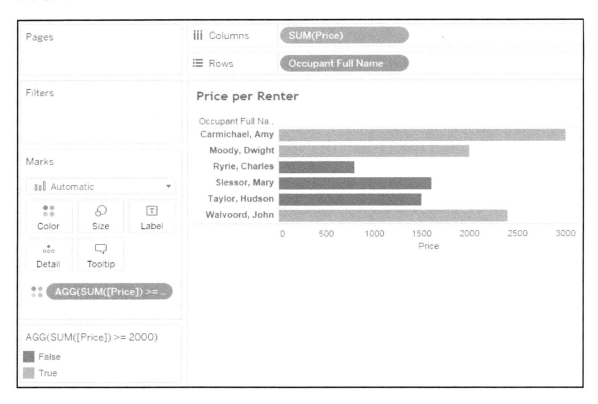

The ad hoc field is only available within the view and does not show up in the data pane. You can double-click on the field to edit the code.

Dragging and dropping an ad hoc field into the data pane transforms it into a regular calculated field that will be available for other views using that data source.

# Performance considerations

When working with a small dataset and an efficient database, you often won't notice inefficient calculations. With larger datasets, the efficiency of your calculations can start to make a fairly dramatic difference to the speed at which a view is rendered.

Here are some tips for getting the most efficiency in your calculations:

- Boolean and numeric calculations are faster than string calculations. If possible, avoid string manipulation and use aliasing or formatting to provide user-friendly labels. For example, don't write this code: IF [value] == 1 THEN "Yes" ELSE "No" END. Instead, simply write [value] == 1 and then edit the aliases of the field and set True to "Yes" and False to "No".

- Always look for ways to increase the efficiency of a calculation. If you find yourself writing a long IF...ELSEIF statement with lots of conditions, see if there are one or two conditions that you can check first to eliminate checks of all the other conditions. For example, let's consider simplifying the following code:

```
IF [Type] = "Dog" AND [Age] < 1 THEN "Puppy"
ELSEIF [Type] = "Cat" AND [Age] < 1 THEN "Kitten"
END
```

The preceding code snippet can also be written as shown:

```
IF [Age] < 1 THEN
  IF [Type] = "Dog" THEN "Puppy"
  ELSEIF [Type] = "Cat" THEN "Kitten"
  END
END
```

Note how the check of Type doesn't have to be done for any records where the age was less than 1. There can be a very high percentage of records in the dataset.

- Row Level calculations have to be performed for every row of data. Try to minimize the complexity of Row Level calculations. However, if that is not possible or doesn't solve a performance issue, consider the next option.

- When you create a data extract, certain Row Level calculations are **materialized**. This means that the calculation is performed once when the extract is created and the results are then stored in the extract. This means that the data engine does not have to execute the calculation over and over. Instead, the value is simply read from the extract. Calculations that use any user functions or parameters, or TODAY() or NOW(), will not be materialized in an extract, as the value necessarily changes according to the current user, parameter selection, and system time. Tableau's optimizer may also decide not to materialize certain calculations that are more efficiently performed in memory.

> When you use an extract to materialize Row Level calculations, only the calculations that were created at the time of the extract are materialized. If you edit calculated fields or create new ones after creating the extract, you will need to optimize the extract (use the drop-down menu on the data source or select it from the Data menu and then select **Extract** | **Optimize**.

# Summary

Calculations open up amazing possibilities in Tableau. You are no longer confined to the fields in the source data. With calculations, you can extend the data by adding new dimensions and measures, fix bad or poorly, formatted data, enhance the user experience with parameters for user input and calculations that enhance the visualizations, and you can achieve flexibility that makes data blending work in situations where the data might have made it difficult or impossible otherwise.

The key to using calculated fields is an understanding of the three levels of calculations in Tableau. The Row Level calculations are performed for every row of source data. These calculated fields can be used as dimensions or they can be further aggregated as measures. Aggregate Level calculations are performed at the level of detail defined by the dimensions present in a view. They are especially helpful, and even necessary when you must first aggregate components of the calculation before performing additional operations. Level of Detail calculations allows you to perform aggregations at any level of detail, even if it doesn't match that of the view.

In the next chapter, we'll explore the third main type of calculations: Table Calculations. These are some of the most powerful calculations in terms of their ability to solve problems and open up incredible possibilities for in-depth analysis. In practice, they range from very easy to exceptionally complex.

# 5
# Table Calculations

Table calculations are one of the most powerful features in Tableau. They enable solutions that cannot be achieved in any other way (short of writing a custom application or complex custom SQL scripts!):

- Table calculations make it possible to use data that isn't structured well and still get quick results without waiting for someone to fix the data at the source
- They make it possible to compare and perform calculations on aggregate values across the rows of the resulting table
- They open incredible possibilities for analysis and creative approaches to solving problems

Table calculations range in complexity from incredibly easy to create (a couple of clicks) to extremely complex (requiring an understanding of addressing, partitioning, and data densification). In this chapter, we will start off simple and move toward complexity. The goal is to gain a solid foundation for creating and using table calculations, understanding how they work, and to see some examples of how they can be used. In this chapter, we'll consider the following topics:

- Overview of table calculations
- Quick table calculations
- Relative versus fixed
- Scope and direction
- Addressing and partitioning
- Custom table calculations
- Practical examples
- Data densification

Most of the examples here will use the sample **Superstore** data we've used in previous chapters. To follow along with the examples, use the Chapter 05 Starter.twbx workbook.

# Overview of table calculations

Table calculations are different from all other calculations in Tableau. Row-Level, Aggregate calculations and LoD expressions, which we considered in the previous chapter, are performed at the data-source layer. If you were to examine the queries sent to the data source by Tableau, you'd find the code for your calculations translated into whatever flavor of SQL the data source used.

Table calculations, on the other hand, are performed after the initial query. Here's an extended diagram, which shows how aggregated results are stored in Tableau's cache:

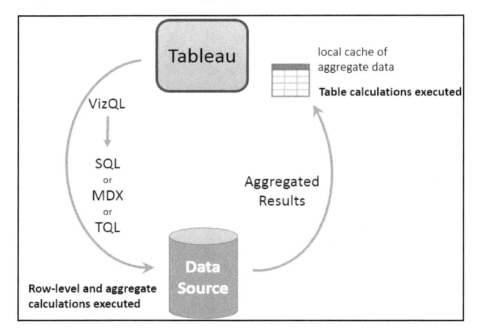

Table calculations are performed on the aggregate table of data in Tableau's cache right before the data visualization is rendered. It's very important to understand this, for various reasons, including the following:

- **Aggregation**: Table calculations operate on aggregate data. You cannot reference a field in a table calculation without referencing it as an aggregate.
- **Filtering**: Regular filters will be applied prior to table calculations. This means that table calculations will only be applied to data returned from the source to the cache. You'll need to determine whether you have allowed all the data necessary for table calculations to work as desired.
- **Late filtering**: Table calculations, used as filters, will be applied after the aggregate results are returned from the data source. The order becomes important. Row-level and aggregate filters are applied first, the aggregate data is returned to the cache, and then the table calculation is applied as a filter that effectively hides data from the view. This allows us to take some creative approaches to solve certain kinds of problems which we'll consider in some of the examples.
- **Performance**: If you are using a live connection to connect to an enterprise database server, then row-level and aggregate-level calculations will be taking advantage of enterprise-level hardware. Table calculations are performed in the cache, which means that they will be performed on the machine that is running Tableau. Most often, you will not need to be concerned if your table calculations are operating on a dozen, or even hundreds of, rows of aggregate data. However, if you are getting back several hundred-thousand rows of aggregate data, then you'll need to consider the performance of your table calculations.

# Creating and editing table calculations

There are several ways to create Table calculations in Tableau:

- Using the drop-down menu for any active field, used as a numeric aggregate in the view, select **Quick Table Calculation** and then the desired calculation
- Using the drop-down menu for any active field, used as a numeric aggregate in the view, select **Add Table Calculation** and then select the calculation type and adjust the desired settings, if any
- Create a calculated field and use one or more table calculation functions to write your own custom table calculations

The first two options create a quick table calculation, which can be edited or removed using the drop-down menu on the field and selecting **Edit Table Calculation** or **Clear Table Calculation**. The third option creates a calculated field, which can be edited or deleted like any other calculated field.

A field on a shelf in the view that is using a table calculation, or which is a calculated field using the table calculation function, will have a delta symbol icon.

Active field is shown in the following figure:

Active field with table calculation is shown in the following figure:

Table calculations can be used in any type of visualization. However, when building a view that uses table calculations, especially more complex ones, try to use a table with all dimensions on the **Rows** shelf, and then add table calculations as discrete values on **Rows** to the right of the dimensions. This most closely approximates the table present in the cache and makes it a bit easier to see how the Table calculations are working. Once you have all the table calculations working as desired, you can rearrange the fields in the view to give you the appropriate visualization.

# Quick table calculations

Quick table calculations are predefined table calculations that can be applied to any field used as a measure in the view. These calculations include common and useful calculations such as **Running Total, Difference, Percent Difference, Percent of Total, Rank, Percentile, Moving Average, YTD total, Compound Growth Rate, Year Over Year Growth,** and **YTD Growth**. You'll find applicable options on the dropdown on a field used as a measure in the view:

Consider the following example using the sample Superstore sales data:

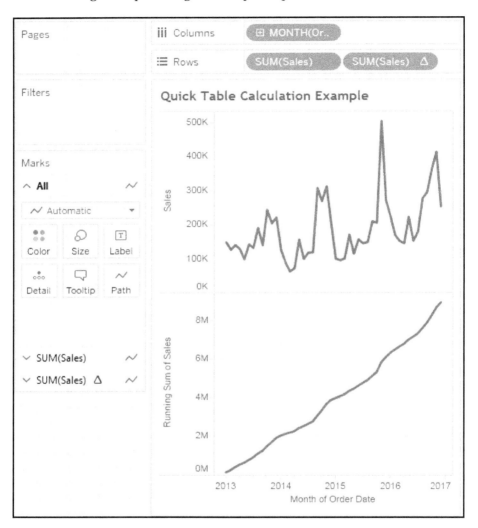

Here, **Sales over time** is shown. **Sales** has been duplicated on the **Rows** shelf and the another **SUM(Sales)** field has the running total quick table calculation that is applied. Using the quick table calculation we can avoid writing any code.

You can actually see the code that the quick table calculations use by double-clicking on the table calculation field in the view. This turns it into an ad hoc calculation. You can also drag an active field with a quick table calculation applied to the data pane, which will turn it into a calculated field, available to reuse in other views.

The following table demonstrates the quick table calculations available:

| Year of Order Date | Quarter of Order .. | Sales | Running Total | Difference | % Difference | % of Total | Rank | Percentile | Moving Average | YTD | Compound Growth Rate | Year over year Growth | YTD Growth |
|---|---|---|---|---|---|---|---|---|---|---|---|---|---|
| 2012 | Q1 | 415,886 | 415,886 | | | 4.65% | 12 | 31.25% | 415,886 | 415,886 | 0.00% | | |
| | Q2 | 352,779 | 768,665 | -63,107 | -15.17% | 3.94% | 13 | 25.00% | 384,333 | 768,665 | -15.17% | | |
| | Q3 | 456,694 | 1,225,359 | 103,915 | 29.46% | 5.10% | 10 | 43.75% | 408,453 | 1,225,359 | 4.79% | | |
| | Q4 | 698,986 | 1,924,345 | 242,292 | 53.05% | 7.81% | 5 | 75.00% | 502,820 | 1,924,345 | 18.90% | | |
| 2013 | Q1 | 272,065 | 2,196,410 | -426,921 | -61.08% | 3.04% | 16 | 6.25% | 475,915 | 272,065 | -10.07% | -34.58% | -34.58% |
| | Q2 | 337,352 | 2,533,762 | 65,287 | 24.00% | 3.77% | 14 | 18.75% | 436,134 | 609,417 | -4.10% | -4.37% | -20.72% |
| | Q3 | 546,388 | 3,080,150 | 209,036 | 61.96% | 6.10% | 6 | 68.75% | 385,268 | 1,155,805 | 4.65% | 19.64% | -5.68% |
| | Q4 | 788,742 | 3,868,892 | 242,354 | 44.36% | 8.81% | 3 | 87.50% | 557,494 | 1,944,547 | 9.57% | 12.84% | 1.05% |
| 2014 | Q1 | 294,067 | 4,162,959 | -494,675 | -62.72% | 3.28% | 15 | 12.50% | 543,066 | 294,067 | -4.24% | 8.09% | 8.09% |
| | Q2 | 428,267 | 4,591,226 | 134,200 | 45.64% | 4.78% | 11 | 37.50% | 503,692 | 722,334 | 0.33% | 26.95% | 18.53% |
| | Q3 | 508,189 | 5,099,415 | 79,922 | 18.66% | 5.68% | 9 | 50.00% | 410,174 | 1,230,523 | 2.02% | -6.99% | 8.46% |
| | Q4 | 1,000,217 | 6,099,632 | 492,028 | 96.82% | 11.17% | 2 | 93.75% | 645,558 | 2,230,740 | 8.30% | 26.81% | 14.72% |
| 2015 | Q1 | 536,158 | 6,635,790 | -464,059 | -46.40% | 5.99% | 7 | 62.50% | 681,521 | 536,158 | 2.14% | 82.33% | 82.33% |
| | Q2 | 518,601 | 7,154,391 | -17,557 | -3.27% | 5.79% | 8 | 56.25% | 684,992 | 1,054,759 | 1.71% | 21.09% | 46.02% |
| | Q3 | 722,674 | 7,877,065 | 204,073 | 39.35% | 8.07% | 4 | 81.25% | 592,478 | 1,777,433 | 4.03% | 42.21% | 44.45% |
| | Q4 | 1,074,962 | 8,952,027 | 352,268 | 48.75% | 12.01% | 1 | 100.00% | 772,079 | 2,852,395 | 6.54% | 7.47% | 27.87% |

# Relative versus fixed

You can compute table calculations in one of the following two ways:

- **Relative**: The table calculation will be computed relative to the layout of the table. They might move across or down the table. As we'll see, the key for relative table calculations is **scope** and **direction**. When you set a table calculation to use a relative computation, it will continue to use the same relative scope and direction, even if you rearrange the view.
- **Fixed**: The table calculation will be computed using one or more dimensions. Rearranging those dimensions may change whether the table calculation is moving across or down the table (or even in a more complex pattern). Here, the scope and direction remain fixed to one or more dimensions, no matter where they are moved within the view. When we talk about fixed table calculations, we'll focus on the concepts of **partitioning** and **addressing**.

# Scope and direction

Scope and direction are terms that describe how a table calculation is computed relative to the table. When a table calculation is relative to the layout of the table, rearranging the fields in the view will not change the scope and direction.

- **Scope**: The scope defines the boundaries within which a given table calculation can reference other values
- **Direction**: The direction defines how the table calculation moves within the scope

You've already seen table calculations being calculated Table (across) (for example, the running sum of Sales over time) and Table (down) (for example, the preceding table ). In these cases, the scope was the entire table and the direction was either across or down. You may recall that the running total calculation ran across the entire table, adding subsequent values as it moved.

To define scope and direction for a table calculation, use the drop-down menu for the field in the view and select **Compute Using**. You will get a list of options that will vary slightly depending on the dimensions present in the view. The first few options that are listed allow you to define the scope and direction relative to the table. After the option for Cells, you will see a list of dimensions present in the view; we'll take a look at those in the next section.

Options for scope and direction relative to the table: **Scope options**: Table, Panes, and Cells**Direction options**: Down, across, down then across, and across then down

In order to understand these options, consider the following example:

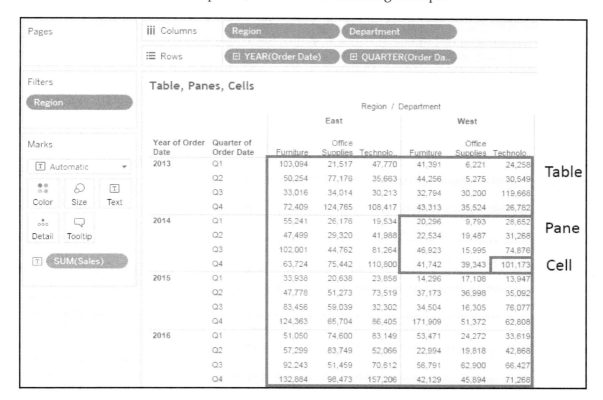

When it comes to the scope of table calculations, Tableau makes the following distinctions:

- The Table is the entire set of aggregate data.
- The Pane is defined by the next-to-second lowest level of the table (that is, the next-to-last dimension on the **Rows** and/or **Columns** shelf). In the preceding screenshot, you can see that the intersection of **Year** on **Rows** and **Region** on **Columns** defines the panes (one is highlighted, but there are actually eight in the view).
- The cell is defined by the lowest level of the table. In this view, the intersection of one **Department** within a **Region** and one **Quarter** within a **Year** is a single cell (one is highlighted, but there are actually 96 in the view).

# Working with scope and direction

In order to see how scope and direction work together, let's work through a few examples. We'll start by creating our own custom table calculation. Create a new calculated field named `Index` with the code `Index()`.

 Index is a table calculation function that starts with the value 1 and increments by one as it moves along a given direction and within a given scope. There are many practical uses for Index, but we'll use it here because it is easy to see how it is moving for a given scope and direction.

Create the table shown previously with **YEAR(Order Date)** and **QUARTER(Order Date)** on **Rows** and **Region**, and **Department** on **Columns**. Instead of placing **Sales** in the view, add the newly created **Index** field to the **Text** shelf. Then experiment, using the drop-down menu on the **Index** field, and select **Compute Using** to cycle through various scope and direction combinations. In the following examples, we've only kept the **East** and **West** regions and two years:

- **Table (across)**: By default, Tableau uses table (across). In the following example, note how **Index** increments across the entire table:

|      |    |           | East              |            |           | West              |            |
|------|----|-----------|-------------------|------------|-----------|-------------------|------------|
|      |    |           | Office            |            |           | Office            |            |
|      |    | Furniture | Supplies | Technolo.. | Furniture | Supplies | Technolo.. |
| 2015 | Q1 | 1 | 2 | 3 | 4 | 5 | 6 |
|      | Q2 | 1 | 2 | 3 | 4 | 5 | 6 |
|      | Q3 | 1 | 2 | 3 | 4 | 5 | 6 |
|      | Q4 | 1 | 2 | 3 | 4 | 5 | 6 |
| 2016 | Q1 | 1 | 2 | 3 | 4 | 5 | 6 |
|      | Q2 | 1 | 2 | 3 | 4 | 5 | 6 |
|      | Q3 | 1 | 2 | 3 | 4 | 5 | 6 |
|      | Q4 | 1 | 2 | 3 | 4 | 5 | 6 |

- **Table (down)**: When using table (down), index increments down the entire table, as shown:

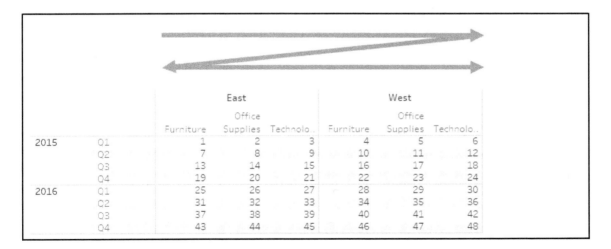

|  |  | East | | | West | | |
|--|--|--|--|--|--|--|--|
|  |  | Furniture | Office Supplies | Technolo.. | Furniture | Office Supplies | Technolo.. |
| 2015 | Q1 | 1 | 1 | 1 | 1 | 1 | 1 |
|  | Q2 | 2 | 2 | 2 | 2 | 2 | 2 |
|  | Q3 | 3 | 3 | 3 | 3 | 3 | 3 |
|  | Q4 | 4 | 4 | 4 | 4 | 4 | 4 |
| 2016 | Q1 | 5 | 5 | 5 | 5 | 5 | 5 |
|  | Q2 | 6 | 6 | 6 | 6 | 6 | 6 |
|  | Q3 | 7 | 7 | 7 | 7 | 7 | 7 |
|  | Q4 | 8 | 8 | 8 | 8 | 8 | 8 |

- **Table (across then down)**: This increments index across the table, then steps down and continues to increment across and repeats for the entire table, as shown:

|  |  | East | | | West | | |
|--|--|--|--|--|--|--|--|
|  |  | Furniture | Office Supplies | Technolo.. | Furniture | Office Supplies | Technolo.. |
| 2015 | Q1 | 1 | 2 | 3 | 4 | 5 | 6 |
|  | Q2 | 7 | 8 | 9 | 10 | 11 | 12 |
|  | Q3 | 13 | 14 | 15 | 16 | 17 | 18 |
|  | Q4 | 19 | 20 | 21 | 22 | 23 | 24 |
| 2016 | Q1 | 25 | 26 | 27 | 28 | 29 | 30 |
|  | Q2 | 31 | 32 | 33 | 34 | 35 | 36 |
|  | Q3 | 37 | 38 | 39 | 40 | 41 | 42 |
|  | Q4 | 43 | 44 | 45 | 46 | 47 | 48 |

- **Pane (across)**: This defines a boundary for index and causes index to increment across until it reaches the pane boundary, at which point the indexing restarts, as shown:

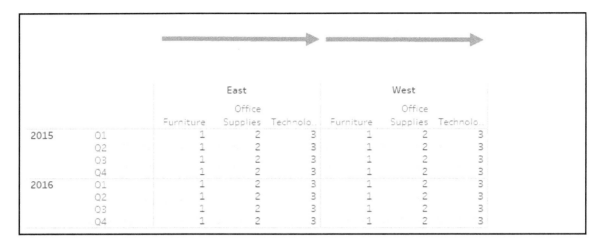

| | | East | | | West | | |
|---|---|---|---|---|---|---|---|
| | | Furniture | Office Supplies | Technolo.. | Furniture | Office Supplies | Technolo.. |
| 2015 | Q1 | 1 | 2 | 3 | 1 | 2 | 3 |
| | Q2 | 1 | 2 | 3 | 1 | 2 | 3 |
| | Q3 | 1 | 2 | 3 | 1 | 2 | 3 |
| | Q4 | 1 | 2 | 3 | 1 | 2 | 3 |
| 2016 | Q1 | 1 | 2 | 3 | 1 | 2 | 3 |
| | Q2 | 1 | 2 | 3 | 1 | 2 | 3 |
| | Q3 | 1 | 2 | 3 | 1 | 2 | 3 |
| | Q4 | 1 | 2 | 3 | 1 | 2 | 3 |

- **Pane (down)**: This defines a boundary for index and causes index to increment down until it reaches the pane boundary, at which point the indexing restarts, as shown:

| | | East | | | West | | |
|---|---|---|---|---|---|---|---|
| | | Furniture | Office Supplies | Technolo.. | Furniture | Office Supplies | Technolo.. |
| 2015 | Q1 | 1 | 1 | 1 | 1 | 1 | 1 |
| | Q2 | 2 | 2 | 2 | 2 | 2 | 2 |
| | Q3 | 3 | 3 | 3 | 3 | 3 | 3 |
| | Q4 | 4 | 4 | 4 | 4 | 4 | 4 |
| 2016 | Q1 | 1 | 1 | 1 | 1 | 1 | 1 |
| | Q2 | 2 | 2 | 2 | 2 | 2 | 2 |
| | Q3 | 3 | 3 | 3 | 3 | 3 | 3 |
| | Q4 | 4 | 4 | 4 | 4 | 4 | 4 |

- **Pane (across then down)**: This allows index to increment across the pane and continue by stepping down. The pane defines the boundary here, as shown:

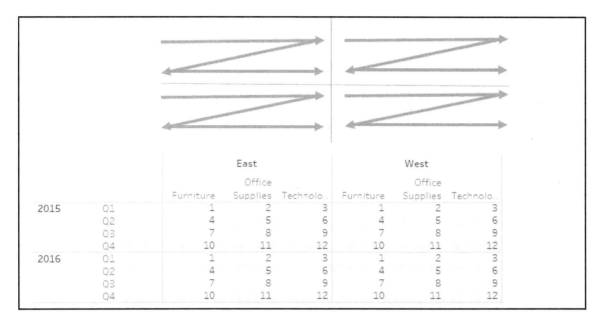

|      |    | East | | | West | | |
|------|----|------|------|------|------|------|------|
|      |    | Furniture | Office Supplies | Technolo.. | Furniture | Office Supplies | Technolo.. |
| 2015 | Q1 | 1 | 2 | 3 | 1 | 2 | 3 |
|      | Q2 | 4 | 5 | 6 | 4 | 5 | 6 |
|      | Q3 | 7 | 8 | 9 | 7 | 8 | 9 |
|      | Q4 | 10 | 11 | 12 | 10 | 11 | 12 |
| 2016 | Q1 | 1 | 2 | 3 | 1 | 2 | 3 |
|      | Q2 | 4 | 5 | 6 | 4 | 5 | 6 |
|      | Q3 | 7 | 8 | 9 | 7 | 8 | 9 |
|      | Q4 | 10 | 11 | 12 | 10 | 11 | 12 |

You can use scope and direction with any table calculation. Consider how a running total or percentage difference would be calculated using the same movement and boundaries that were shown previously. Keep experimenting with different options until you feel comfortable with how scope and direction work.

Scope and direction work relative to the table, so you can rearrange fields and the calculation will still continue to work in the same scope and direction. For example, you could swap **Year of Order Date** with **Department** and still see index calculated according to the scope and direction you defined.

# Addressing and partitioning

**Addressing** and partitioning are very similar to scope and direction, but they are most often used to describe how table calculations are computed with absolute reference to certain fields in the view. With addressing and partitioning, you define the dimensions in the view that define the addressing (direction), and all others define the partitioning (scope).

Using addressing and partitioning gives you a much finer control, because your table calculations are no longer relative to the table layout and you have many more options for fine-tuning the scope, direction, and order of the calculations.

To begin to understand how this works, let's consider a simple example; using the previous view, select **Edit Table Calculation** from the drop-down menu of the **Index** field on **Text**. In the resulting dialog box, check **Department** under **Specific Dimensions**.

Here is the result of selecting **Department**:

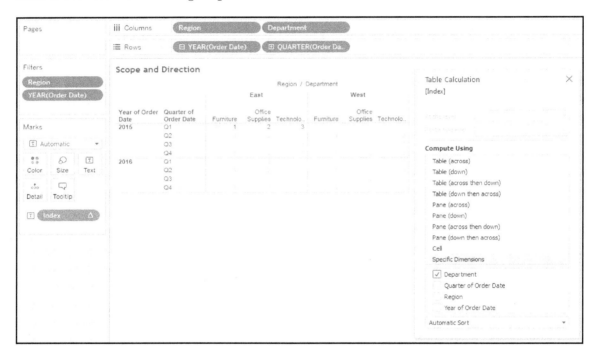

You'll notice that Tableau is computing **Index** along (in the direction of) the checked dimension, **Department**. In other words, you have used **Department** for addressing. All other unchecked dimensions in the view are implicitly used for partitioning, that is, they define the scope or boundaries at which the Index function must restart.

The preceding view looks identical to what you would see if you set **Index** to compute using **Pane (across)**. However, there is one major difference. When you use **Pane (across)**, index is always computed across the pane, even if you rearrange the dimensions in the view, remove some, or add others. But when you compute using a dimension for addressing, the table calculation will always compute using that dimension. Removing that dimension will break the table calculation (the field will turn red) and you'll need to edit the table calculation via the drop-down menu to adjust the settings. If you rearrange dimensions in the view, **Index** will continue to be computed along the **Department** dimension.

The following figure, for example, is the result of clicking the **Swap Rows and Columns button** in the toolbar:

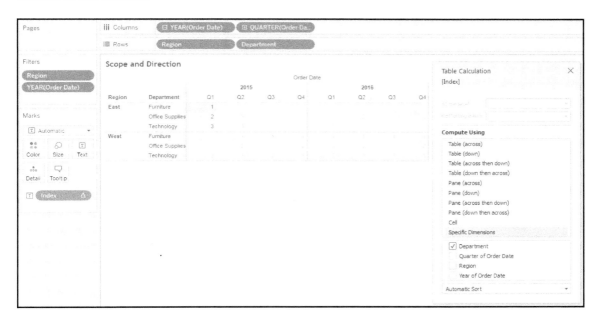

Note that index continues to be computed along **Department** even though the entire orientation of the table has changed. To complete the following examples, we'll undo the swap of **Rows** and **Columns** to return to the original orientation.

# Advanced addressing and partitioning

Take a look at a few other examples of what happens when you add additional dimensions. For example, if you check **Quarter of Order Date**, you'll see Tableau highlight a partition defined by **Region** and **Year of Order Date**, with index incrementing by the addressing fields of **Quarter of Order Date** and then **Department**:

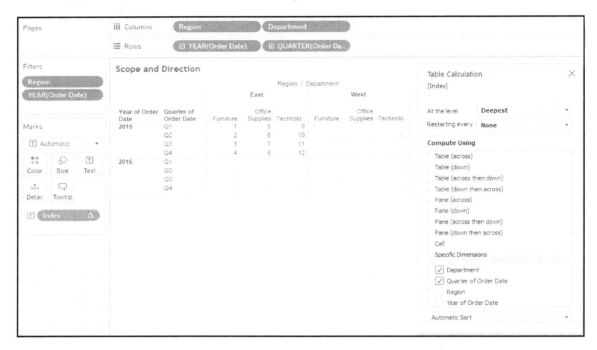

If you were to select **Department** and **Year of Order Date** as the addressing of index, you'd see a single partition defined by **Region** and **Quarter**, as shown:

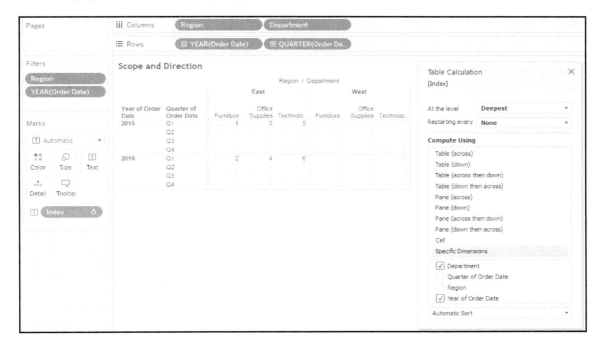

You'll notice in the preceding view that index increments for every combination of **Year** and **Department** within the partition of **Quarter** and **Region**.

There are a few other things to consider when working with addressing and partitioning, such as:

- You can specify the sort order. For example, if you want index to increment according to the value of the sum of **Sales**, you can use the dropdown at the bottom of the **Table Calculation** editor to define a **Custom Sort**.
- The **At the Level** option in the edit table calculation dialog box allows you to specify a level at which the table calculations are performed. Most of the time, you'll leave this set at **Deepest** (which is the same as setting it to the bottom-most dimension), but occasionally, you might want to set it at a different level, if you need to keep certain dimensions from defining the partition but need the table calculation to be applied at a higher level. You can also reorder the dimensions by dragging and dropping within the checkbox list of **Specific Dimensions**.

- The **Restarting Every** option effectively makes the field selected and all dimensions in the addressing above that field selected part of the partition, but allows you to maintain the fine tuning of the ordering.

- Dimensions are the only kinds of fields that can be used in addressing the field; however, a discrete (blue) measure can be used to partition table calculations. To enable this, use the drop-down menu on the field and uncheck **Ignore in Table Calculations**.

# Custom table calculations

Before we move on to some practical examples, let's briefly consider how you can write your own table calculations instead of using a quick table calculation. You can see a list of available table calculation functions by creating a new calculation and selecting **Table Calculation** from the dropdown under **Functions**.

You can think of table calculations broken down into several categories, shown here. In each of the examples, we'll set **Compute Using | Category**, which means **Department** is the partition. The following table calculations can be combined and even nested, similarly to other functions:

- **Meta Table Functions**: These are the functions that give you information about the partitioning and addressing. These functions also include `Index`, `First`, `Last`, and `Size`:

| Department | Category | Index | First | Last | Size |
|---|---|---|---|---|---|
| Furniture | Bookcases | 1 | 0 | 3 | 4 |
| | Chairs & Chairmats | 2 | -1 | 2 | 4 |
| | Office Furnishings | 3 | -2 | 1 | 4 |
| | Tables | 4 | -3 | 0 | 4 |
| Office Supplies | Appliances | 1 | 0 | 8 | 9 |
| | Binders and Binder Accessori.. | 2 | -1 | 7 | 9 |
| | Envelopes | 3 | -2 | 6 | 9 |
| | Labels | 4 | -3 | 5 | 9 |
| | Paper | 5 | -4 | 4 | 9 |
| | Pens & Art Supplies | 6 | -5 | 3 | 9 |
| | Rubber Bands | 7 | -6 | 2 | 9 |
| | Scissors, Rulers and Trimmers | 8 | -7 | 1 | 9 |
| | Storage & Organization | 9 | -8 | 0 | 9 |
| Technology | Computer Peripherals | 1 | 0 | 3 | 4 |
| | Copiers and Fax | 2 | -1 | 2 | 4 |
| | Office Machines | 3 | -2 | 1 | 4 |
| | Telephones and Communicati.. | 4 | -3 | 0 | 4 |

First gives the offset from the first row in the partition. So, the first row in each partition is 0. Last gives the offset to the last row in the partition. Size gives the size of the partition. Index, First, and Last are all affected by scope/partition and direction/addressing, while size will give the same result at each address of the partition no matter what direction is specified:

- **Lookup and Previous Value**: The first of these two functions gives you the ability to reference values in other rows, while the second gives you the ability to carry forward values. Note that the direction is very important for these two functions:

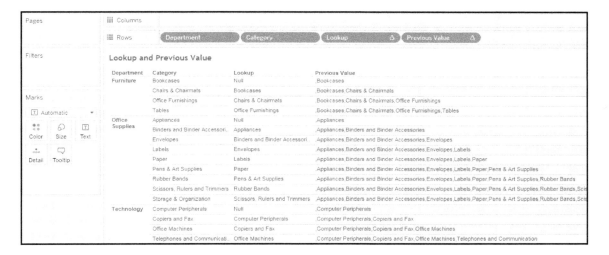

Both calculations are computed using an address of **Category** (so **Department** is the partition).

Here, we've used the code Lookup(ATTR([Category]), -1) that looks up the value of category in the row offset by -1 from the current value. The first row in each partition gets a null result from the lookup (because there isn't a row before it).

For the previous value, we used the following code:

```
Previous_Value("") +
"," +
ATTR([Category])
```

Note that in the first row of each partition, there is no previous value so `Previous_Value` simply returned what we specified as the default— an empty string. This was then concatenated together with a comma and the category in that row giving us the value, **Bookcases**.

In the second row, Bookcases is the previous value that gets concatenated with a comma, and the category in that row gives us the value; **Bookcases** and **Chairs & Chairmats** become the previous value in the next row. The pattern continues throughout the partition and then restarts in the partition defined by the **Office Supplies** department:

- **Running functions**: These functions run along the direction/addressing and include `Running_Avg`, `Running_Count`, `Running_Sum`, `Running_Min`, and `Running_Max`. Some examples are shown in the following figure:

| Department | Category | Sales | Running Sum of Sales | Running Minimum of Sales |
|---|---|---|---|---|
| Furniture | Bookcases | 507,496 | 507,496 | 507,496 |
| | Chairs & Chairmats | 1,164,586 | 1,672,082 | 507,496 |
| | Office Furnishings | 444,634 | 2,116,716 | 444,634 |
| | Tables | 1,061,922 | 3,178,638 | 444,634 |
| Office Supplies | Appliances | 456,736 | 456,736 | 456,736 |
| | Binders and Binder Accessori.. | 638,583 | 1,095,319 | 456,736 |
| | Envelopes | 147,915 | 1,243,234 | 147,915 |
| | Labels | 23,446 | 1,266,680 | 23,446 |
| | Paper | 253,620 | 1,520,300 | 23,446 |
| | Pens & Art Supplies | 103,265 | 1,623,565 | 23,446 |
| | Rubber Bands | 8,670 | 1,632,235 | 8,670 |
| | Scissors, Rulers and Trimmers | 40,432 | 1,672,667 | 8,670 |
| | Storage & Organization | 585,717 | 2,258,384 | 8,670 |
| Technology | Computer Peripherals | 490,851 | 490,851 | 490,851 |
| | Copiers and Fax | 661,215 | 1,152,066 | 490,851 |
| | Office Machines | 1,218,655 | 2,370,721 | 490,851 |
| | Telephones and Communicati.. | 1,144,284 | 3,515,005 | 490,851 |

Note that `Running_Sum(SUM[Sales]))` continues to add the sum of sales to a running total for every row in the partition. `Running_Min` keeps the value of the sum of sales, if it is the smallest value it has encountered so far, as it moves along the rows of the partition:

- **Window functions**: These functions operate across all rows in the partition at once and essentially aggregate the aggregates. They include `Window_Sum`, `Window_Avg`, `Window_Max`, `Window_Min`, and others:

| Department | Category | Sales | Window Sum | Window Max |
|---|---|---|---|---|
| Furniture | Bookcases | 507,496 | 3,178,638 | 1,164,586 |
| | Chairs & Chairmats | 1,164,586 | 3,178,638 | 1,164,586 |
| | Office Furnishings | 444,634 | 3,178,638 | 1,164,586 |
| | Tables | 1,061,922 | 3,178,638 | 1,164,586 |
| Office Supplies | Appliances | 456,736 | 2,258,384 | 638,583 |
| | Binders and Binder Accessori.. | 638,583 | 2,258,384 | 638,583 |
| | Envelopes | 147,915 | 2,258,384 | 638,583 |
| | Labels | 23,446 | 2,258,384 | 638,583 |
| | Paper | 253,620 | 2,258,384 | 638,583 |
| | Pens & Art Supplies | 103,265 | 2,258,384 | 638,583 |
| | Rubber Bands | 8,670 | 2,258,384 | 638,583 |
| | Scissors, Rulers and Trimmers | 40,432 | 2,258,384 | 638,583 |
| | Storage & Organization | 585,717 | 2,258,384 | 638,583 |
| Technology | Computer Peripherals | 490,851 | 3,515,005 | 1,218,655 |
| | Copiers and Fax | 661,215 | 3,515,005 | 1,218,655 |
| | Office Machines | 1,218,655 | 3,515,005 | 1,218,655 |
| | Telephones and Communicati.. | 1,144,284 | 3,515,005 | 1,218,655 |

- **Rank functions**: These functions provide various ways to rank based on aggregate values:

| Department | Category | Sales | Rank of Sales |
|---|---|---|---|
| Furniture | Bookcases | 507,496 | 3 |
| | Chairs & Chairmats | 1,164,586 | 1 |
| | Office Furnishings | 444,634 | 4 |
| | Tables | 1,061,922 | 2 |
| Office Supplies | Appliances | 456,736 | 3 |
| | Binders and Binder Accessori.. | 638,583 | 1 |
| | Envelopes | 147,915 | 5 |
| | Labels | 23,446 | 8 |
| | Paper | 253,620 | 4 |
| | Pens & Art Supplies | 103,265 | 6 |
| | Rubber Bands | 8,670 | 9 |
| | Scissors, Rulers and Trimmers | 40,432 | 7 |
| | Storage & Organization | 585,717 | 2 |
| Technology | Computer Peripherals | 490,851 | 4 |
| | Copiers and Fax | 661,215 | 3 |
| | Office Machines | 1,218,655 | 1 |
| | Telephones and Communicati.. | 1,144,284 | 2 |

- **R Script Functions**: These functions allow for integration with R, an analytics platform that can be used for complex scripting.
- **Total**: The `Total` function deserves its own category because it functions a little differently from the others. Unlike the other functions that work on the aggregate table in the cache, `Total` will re-query the underlying source for all the source data rows that make up a given partition. In many cases, this will yield the same result as a window function.

For example, `Total(SUM([Sales]))` gives the same result as `Window_Sum(SUM([Sales]))`, but `Total(AVG([Sales]))` will possibly give a different result from `Window_AVG(SUM([Sales]))` because TOTAL is giving you the actual average of underlying rows, while the window function is averaging the sums.

# Practical examples

Having looked at some of the foundational concepts of table calculations, let's consider some practical examples. We'll start with some simple ones and move toward complexity.

# Year – over – Year growth

Often, businesses want to compare year over year values, meaning they want to see how quarters (or months or weeks) in one year compared with the same quarters (or months or weeks) in the previous year.

Tableau exposes **Year over Year Growth** as one option in the **Quick Table Calculations**. Here, for example, is a view that demonstrates **Sales by Quarter** along with the percent difference in sales for a quarter compared with the same quarter in the previous year, as shown:

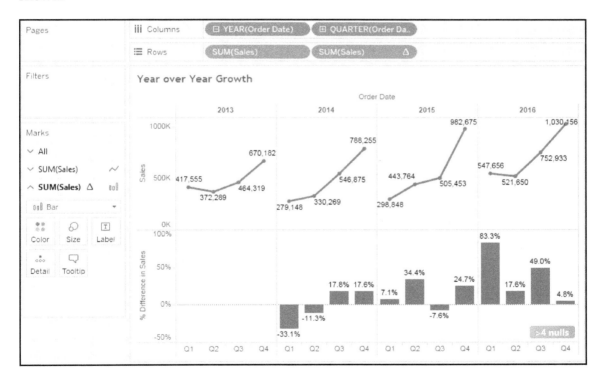

The second **Sum(Sales)** field has had the **Year over Year Growth** quick table calculation applied (and the mark type changed to bar). You'll notice the **>4 nulls** indicator in the lower-right corner alerting you to the fact that there are at least four null values (which makes sense as there is no 2012 to compare quarters in **2013**). If you filtered out **2013**, the nulls would appear in **2014**, as table calculations can only operate on values present in the aggregated data in the cache (and that data exists post filter).

As easy as it is to build a view similar to the previous one , take care, because Tableau assumes each year in the view has the same number of quarters. For example, if the data for **Q1** in **2013** was not present or filtered out, then the resulting view would not represent what you want:

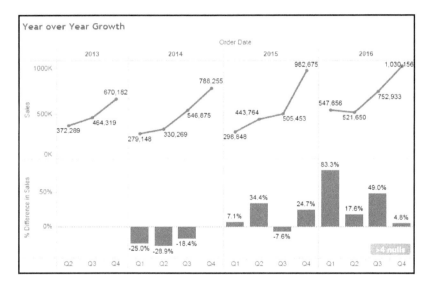

The problem here is that Tableau is calculating the quick table calculation using an addressing of **Year** and **Quarter,** and an **At the Level** of value of **Year of Order Date**. This works, assuming all quarters are present. However, here the first quarter in **2014** is matched with the first quarter present in **2013**, which is really **Q2**. To solve this, you would need to edit the table calculation to only use year for addressing. Quarter then becomes the partition and, for example, **Q2** is compared to previous values in the Q2 partition along the years.

You can hide the null indicator by right-clicking it and selecting **Hide Indicator**. Clicking on the indicator will reveal options to filter the data or display it as a default value (typically 0).

# Ranking within higher levels

When attempting to sort lower levels of headers, you may run into an issue such as the one shown here:

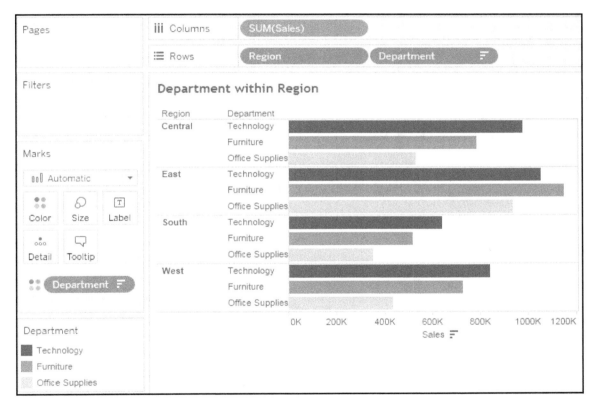

In this case, **Department** has been sorted in descending order by the sum of **Sales**. Note that **Technology** is listed first for every **Region**, even though there are regions where other departments have higher sales (for example, **Furniture** is the top selling **Department** in the **East** region). The reason this happens is that Tableau applies the sort at an overall level. Technology is the highest in terms of overall sales.

If you wanted to see a different sort order for each department, you might consider an approach similar to the following:

1. First, we'll create an ad hoc calculation by double-clicking on a blank area on the **Rows** shelf and typing the code RANK(SUM(Sales), 'desc'). It will look like this:

2. When you press *Enter* or click outside the ad hoc calculation space, Tableau will generate a field in the view. By default, Tableau makes the field continuous (green), which creates an axis and gives us a scatter plot. The continuous field must always appear to the right of the discrete fields on **Rows**.

3. Use the dropdown on the field to change it to discrete (blue). Now you will be able to move it to the left of **Department**. Tableau always sorts header levels left to right, so the **Rank** forces a different sort within each region:

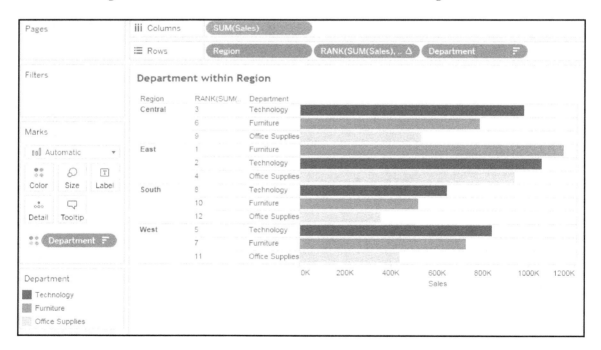

In this example, the row headers for the `Rank` function don't add anything useful other than the sort. You can hide the headers using the drop-down field on the **Rank** field to uncheck **Show Row Headers**.

# Late filtering

Let's say you've built a view that allows you to see the percentage of total sales for each department. You have already used a quick table calculation on the **Sales** field to give you a percentage of the total. You've also used **Department** as a quick filter. But this presents a problem.

Since table calculations are performed after the aggregate data is returned to the cache, the filter on **Department** has already been evaluated at the data source and the aggregate rows don't include any departments excluded by the filter. Thus, the percentage of total will always add up to 100%; that is, it is the percentage of the filtered total:

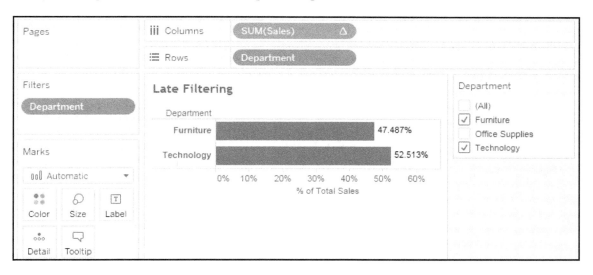

What if you wanted to see the percentage of total sales for all departments, even if you want to exclude some from the display? One option is to use a table calculation as a filter.

If you create a calculated field called `Department (late filter)` with the code `LOOKUP(ATTR([Department]), 0)`, and place that on the **Filters** shelf instead of the **Department** dimension, then the filter is not applied at the source, the aggregate data is visible to other table calculations and the table calculation filter merely hides departments from the final view:

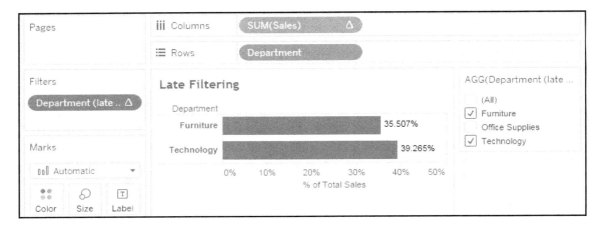

 You might have noticed the ATTR function used previously. Remember that table calculations require aggregate arguments. ATTR (which is short for attribute) is a special aggregation that returns the value of a field, if there is only a single value of that field present for a given level of detail, or a * if there is more than one value. To understand this, experiment with a view having both **Department** and **Category** on **Rows**. Using the drop-down menu on the active field in the view, change **Category** to **Attribute**. It will display as * because there is more than one **Category** for each **Department**. Then, undo and change **Department** to **Attribute**. It will display the department name because there is only one department per category.

# Data densification

**Data densification** is a broad term which indicates that missing values or records are filled in. Sometimes, specific terms, such as **domain padding** (filling in missing dates or bin values) or **domain completion** (filling in missing intersections of dimensional values), are used to specify the type of densification, but here we'll simply use the term data densification.

Data with missing values (such as data that doesn't have a record for every single date or only contains records for products that have been ordered as opposed to all products in the inventory) is referred to as **sparse data**.

Understanding when Tableau uses data densification and how you can turn it on or turn it off is important as you move toward mastering Tableau. There will be times when Tableau will engage data densification and you don't want it; you'll need to recognize it and understand the options to turn it off. At other times, you'll want to leverage data densification to solve certain types of problems or perform certain kinds of analysis.

# When and where data densification occurs

Data densification can take place in the source if you choose to fill in missing data with certain joins, unions, or custom queries. But here, we are focused on data densification that takes place in Tableau after aggregate data is returned from the source. Specifically, under certain circumstances that we'll consider, Tableau fills in missing values in the aggregate data in the cache, as seen in the following figure:

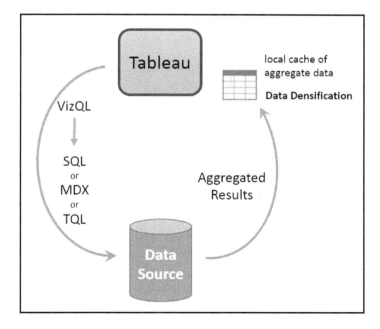

You'll recognize that the preceding figure is very similar to the figure we examined when we started the discussion of table calculations. In fact, data densification happens at relatively the same time as table calculations, and sometimes, can even be triggered by table calculations. Here are some examples of times when data densification is enabled:

- When the **Show Missing Values** option is enabled for dates or bins used as headers on **Rows** or **Columns**. Here, Tableau will show headers for dates or bin values (between the minimum or maximum dates/bin values), even if they don't occur in the data (or are eliminated by a filter). You can easily turn this densification on or off by selecting the desired option.
- With **Show Missing Values** enabled, certain table calculations used in the view will additionally add marks in the view for the missing headers. We'll take a look at an example later in this section.
- Enabling the **Show Empty Rows/Columns** option (from the top menu, navigate to **Analysis** | **Table Layout** | **Show Empty Rows/Columns**) causes Tableau to show all the row / column headers, even if particular values wouldn't normally be shown based on filter selections. This option is context-specific, so the domain of values shown is either for the entire dataset or for the context defined by context filters. Observe the difference between the **Categories** shown with and without the option checked:

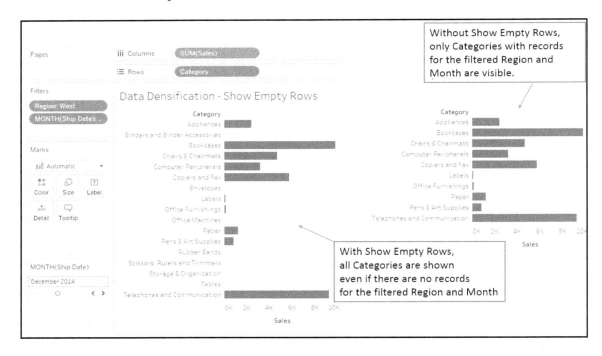

- Using certain table calculations with discrete dimensions on **Rows** and/or **Columns** will cause Tableau to turn on data densification. Let's take a look at an example and how to optionally turn off the resulting densification.

Observe the difference between the following two views:

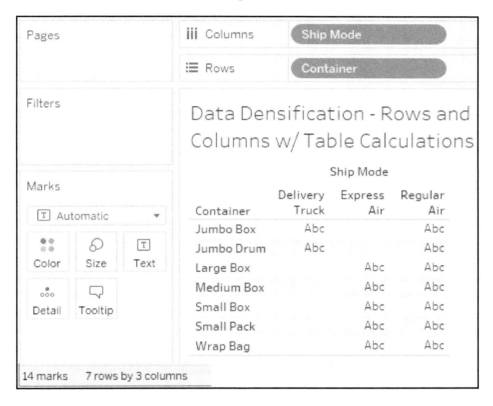

This view has **14 marks** (you can see the count in the status bar), indicating that there are fourteen valid intersections of **Containers** and **Ship Modes**. Some combinations simply don't occur in the data (for example, a **Jumbo Drum** is never sent by **Express Air**).

But adding a table calculation such as Index() to **Detail** causes Tableau to fill in the missing intersections, as shown:

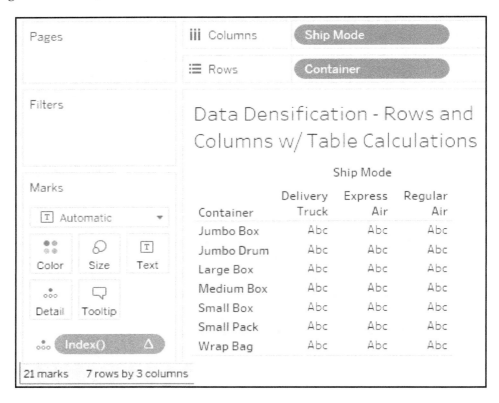

Tableau has filled in the combinations of **Containers** and **Ship Modes,** and there are now **21 marks**. Sometimes, this behavior might be useful (we'll see an example), but many times you may want to avoid the densification. How can you turn it off?

With an understanding that Tableau has enabled the densification because of the discrete dimensions on **Rows** and **Columns**, you can rearrange the view so that only one dimension remains on **Rows** or **Columns**. This view, for example, keeps **Ship Mode** on **Detail** to keep it as a part of the view level of detail, but uses the special aggregation **ATTR** on **Columns**:

The result is a view without data densification showing only **14 marks**.

Keep an eye on the status bar and the count of marks. This will help you identify possible cases of data densification. You will then be able to decide when you wish to leverage densification or when it is useful to turn it off.

# An example of leveraging data densification

Beyond simple examples of showing empty rows or missing dates, there are cases where you can use data densification to solve problems or get around limitations of the data, which would be very difficult otherwise.

Consider, for example, if you had a data that indicated dates when certain generators were turned **On** or **Off**:

| Generator | Date | Action |
|-----------|-----------|--------|
| A | 1//2017 | On |
| B | 1/22/2017 | On |
| C | 1/25/2017 | On |
| D | 1/25/2017 | On |
| B | 1/27/2017 | Off |
| E | 1/29/2017 | On |
| A | 1/30/2017 | Off |
| C | 1/30/2017 | Off |

What if you wanted a visualization that showed how many generators were **On** for any given date? The challenge is that the dataset is sparse. That is, there are only records for dates when an **On** or **Off** action occurred. It's easy to visualize the existing data in Tableau:

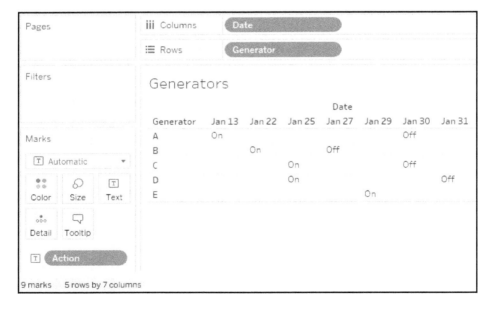

We only have **9 marks** to work with, but we've already seen that Tableau can fill in missing dates and additionally, we can further force data densification using certain table calculations to fill in a value for each generator for every date.

We'll start with a calculation that takes the human-friendly value of **On** or **Off** and changes it to a value we can easily add. The calculation is named Action Value, with the following code:

```
IF [Action] = "On" THEN 1 ELSE 0 END
```

This will give us 1 to count the generator when it is "On" and 0 otherwise.

An additional calculation combined with enabling the **Show Missing Values** of the **Date** field allows us to fill in every date with a value. The new calculated field is called Action Value for Date and has the following code:

```
IF NOT ISNULL(MIN([Action Value]))
THEN MIN([Action Value])
ELSE ZN(PREVIOUS_VALUE(MIN([Action Value])))
END
```

This implements a table calculation that we will set to calculate across the table. If MIN([Action Value]) is not null, then we have arrived at a date where the data gives an actual value, and we'll keep that. Otherwise, we'll carry forward the PREVIOUS_VALUE() (a 1 if the generator was turned on or a 0 if it was turned off). The ZN() function will turn any null values into 0s (we'll assume the generator is off until we encounter an "On"). We'll move across the table, carrying forward values until we come across a value present in the data. Then we'll carry that one forward.

The result is a table with all dates filled in with values, as shown:

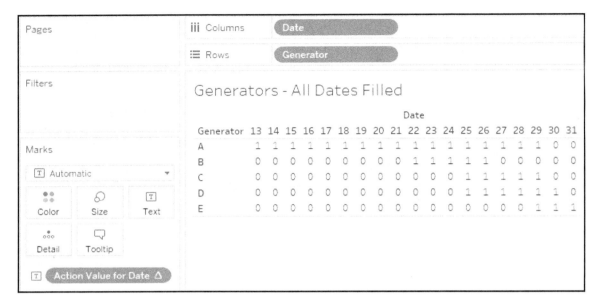

Note that every generator gets a **1** on the date it was turned on and that **1** is carried across the table until the generator is turned off, at which point we get the 0 and carry it across.

We're close, because all we have to do now is sum up the values for all generators for a given date to get the number of generators that were on. For example, on the 13th, there was only one. On the 25th, there were four.

We can accomplish this using one more calculation that nests our existing calculation. We'll name this calculated field `Generators Operating` and use the following code:

```
WINDOW_SUM([Action Value for Date])
```

The key here is that we want to sum all the values down the table, but we want those values to be calculated across the table. When you use nested table calculations (table calculations referenced within the code of other table calculations), you can specify the scope/direction or addressing/partitioning for each **Nested Calculation**.

Here, for example, we'll add the **Generators Operating** calculated field to **Rows** and use the drop-down menu to select the **Edit Table Calculation** option:

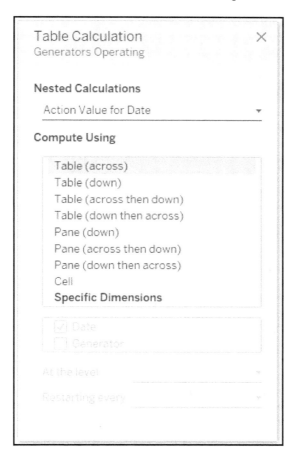

Observe that, under the **Nested Calculations** heading, there is a dropdown, where you can change the **Compute Using** options for each nested calculation. Here, we'll set **Generators Operating** to **Table (down)** and **Action Value for Date** to **Table (across)**.

Our final view, after a bit of cleanup, indicated here, will look similar to this:

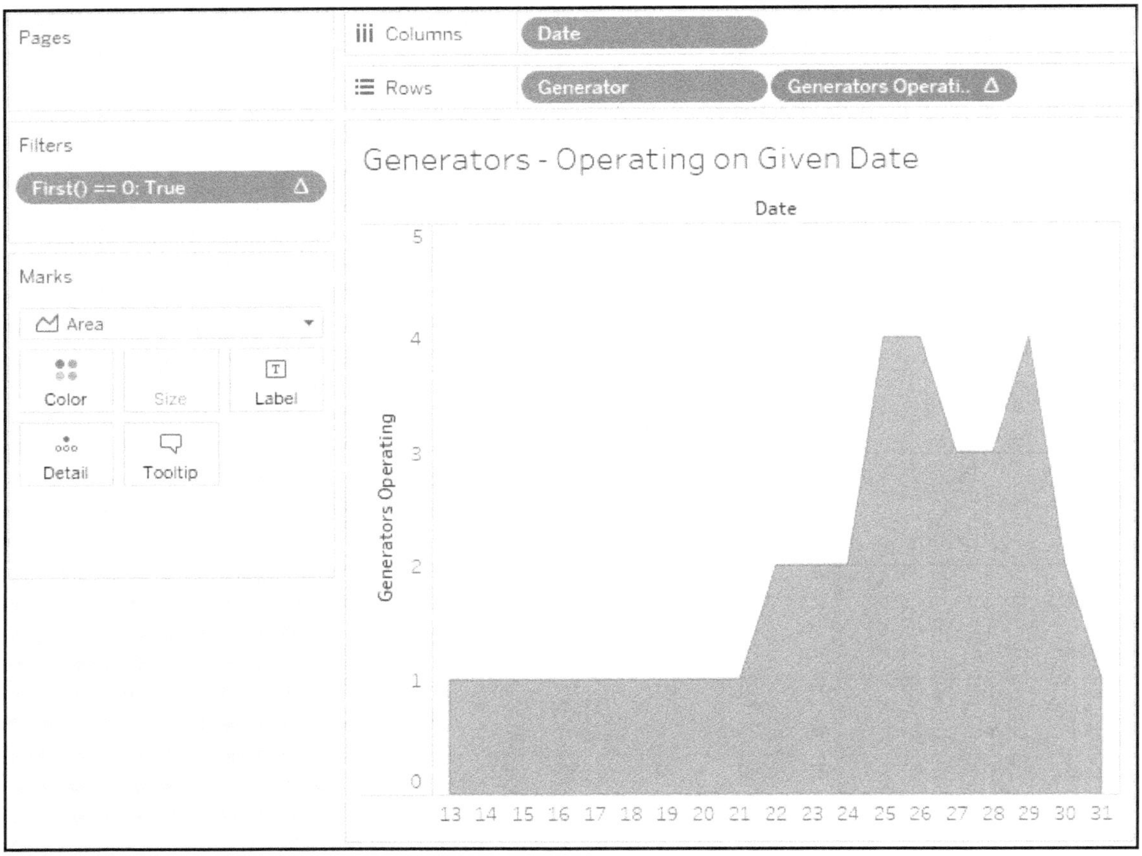

The final view gives us a clear indication of how many generators were on for any given date, even though many of those dates did not exist in the data, and we certainly didn't have a record for every generator for every date.

We've cleaned up the view a bit by doing the following:

- Added a `First()` `==` `0` filter, which is computed **Table (down),** because we're getting the total sum of `Action Values for Date` for each generator and we only need to show one set of totals
- Hidden the column headers for **Generator**, because the field needs to be in the view to define the view level of detail, but does not need to be shown
- Changed the **Marks** to **Area**

Would it have been easier or better to densify the data at the source by joining every generator with every date to get a record for each combination? Possibly. If it is possible, given your data source, to perform such a join (and Tableau 10 makes it even easier with the cross-database joins), you may end up with a dataset that is far easier to work within Tableau (without having to use data densification or complex table calculations). But you'll have to evaluate the feasibility of filling in missing data at the source based on volumes of data, underlying capabilities of the database, and how quickly such transformations can be accomplished. Having an understanding of data densification gives you some options to consider.

# Summary

We've covered a lot of concepts surrounding table calculations in this chapter. You now have a solid foundation for understanding everything from quick table calculations to advanced table calculations and data densification. The practical examples we covered barely scratch the surface of what is possible, but they should give you an idea of what can be achieved. The kinds of problems that can be solved and the diversity of questions that can be answered are almost limitless!

We'll turn our attention to some lighter topics in the next couple of chapters, with topics such as formatting and design, but we'll certainly see another table calculation or two before we're finished!

# 6
# Formatting a Visualization to Look Great and Work Well

Formatting is about more than just making a data visualization look good. Presentation can make a huge difference to the way it is received and understood. As you move beyond making great discoveries and doing great analysis, you'll want to consider how you will present the story of the data.

Tableau's formatting options give you quite a bit of flexibility. Fonts, titles, captions, colors, row and column banding, labels, shading, annotations, and much more can be customized to make your visualizations tell a story well.

This chapter will cover the following topics:

- Formatting considerations
- Understanding how formatting works in Tableau
- Adding value to visualizations

## Formatting considerations

Tableau employs good practices for formatting and visualization from the time you start dropping fields on shelves. Tableau 10 additionally introduces a variety of new fonts, colors, and defaults that emphasize aesthetic appeal. You'll find that the discrete palettes use colors that are easy to distinguish, fonts are pleasant, grid lines are faint where appropriate, and numbers and dates follow the default format settings defined in the metadata.

The default formatting is more than adequate for discovery and analysis. If your focus is analysis, you may not want to spend too much time fine-tuning the formatting until you have moved on in the cycle. However, when you start to consider how you will communicate the data to others, you will need to contemplate how adjustments to formatting can make a difference in how well the data story is told.

 Sometimes, you will have certain formatting preferences in mind when you start your design. In these cases, you might set formatting options in a blank workbook and save it as a template.

Here are some of the things you should consider:

- **Audience**: Who is the audience and what is the need?
- **Setting**: This is the environment in which the data story is communicated. Is it a formal business meeting where the format should reflect a high level of professionalism? Is it going to be shared on a blog to informally, or even playfully, tell a story?
- **Mode**: How will the visualizations be presented? You'll want to make sure rows, columns, fonts, and marks are large enough for a projector or compact enough for an iPad. If you are publishing to Tableau Server, Tableau Online, or Tableau Public, then did you select fonts that are safe for the web? Will you need to use the device designer to create different versions of a dashboard?
- **Mood**: Certain colors, fonts, and layouts elicit different emotional responses. Does the data tell a story that should invoke a certain response from your audience? The color red, for example, may connote danger, negative results, or indicate that an action is required. However, you'll need to be sensitive to your audience and the specific context. Colors have different meanings for different cultures and contexts. Red might not be a good choice to communicate negativity if it is also the color of the corporate logo.
- **Consistency**: Generally, use the same fonts, colors, shapes, line thickness, and row-banding throughout all visualizations. This is especially true when they will be seen together in a dashboard or even used in the same workbook. You can also consider how to remain consistent throughout the organization without being too rigid.

All of these considerations will inform your formatting decisions. As with everything else you do with Tableau, think of formatting as an iterative process. Look for feedback from your intended audience often and adjust as necessary to make sure your communication is as clear and effective as possible. The goal of formatting is to communicate the data more effectively.

# Understanding how formatting works in Tableau

Tableau uses default formatting that includes default fonts, colors, shading, and alignment. Additionally, there are several levels of formatting you can customize, as shown in the following diagram:

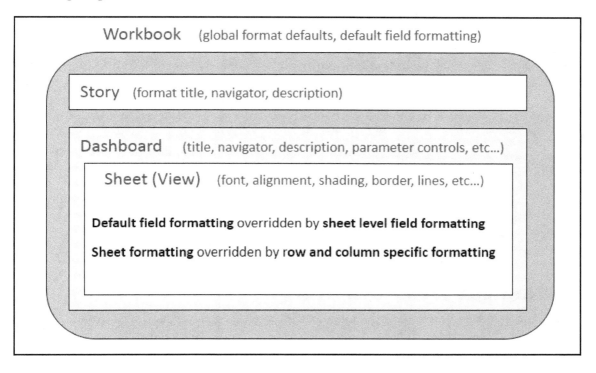

- **Workbook level**: The following type of formatting comes under this category:
  - **Workbook defaults**: from the menu, select **Format | Workbook**. The ability to set certain formatting as the default for the workbook is new to Tableau 10.
  - **Default field formatting**: Using the drop down menu on a field in the data pane, navigate to **Default Properties | Date Format** or **Default Properties | Number Format**. This sets the default format in Tableau's metadata and will be applied to any view where custom formatting has not been applied.

- **Story level**: Navigate to a story tab and navigate to **Format | Story** (or **Story | Format**) to edit formatting for story specific elements. These include options for customizing shading, title, navigator, and description.
- **Dashboard level**: Dashboard specific elements can be formatted. When viewing a dashboard, navigate to **Format | Dashboard** (or **Dashboard | Format**) to specify formatting for dashboard titles, subtitles, shading, and text objects.
- **Worksheet level**: We'll consider the various options in the following section. The following types of formatting are available for a worksheet:
    - **Sheet formatting**: This formatting includes font, alignment, shading, borders, and lines.
    - **Field level formatting**: This formatting includes fonts, alignment, shading, and number and date formats. This formatting is specific to how a field is displayed in the current view. The options you set at a field level override defaults set at a worksheet level. Number and date formats will also override the default field formatting.
    - **Additional formatting**: Additional formatting can be applied to titles, captions, tooltips, labels, annotations, reference lines, field labels, and more.
- **Rich text formatting**: Titles, captions, annotations, labels, and tooltips all contain text which can be formatted with varying fonts, colors, and alignment. This formatting is specific to the individual text element.

# Worksheet level formatting

You've already seen how to edit the metadata in previous chapters and we'll cover dashboards and stories in detail in future chapters. So let's start by considering worksheet level formatting.

Before we specifically look at how to adjust formatting, consider the following parts of a view as it relates to formatting:

Formatting: Parts of the View

| Department | Category | Consumer | Corporate | Home Office | Small Business | Grand Total |
|---|---|---|---|---|---|---|
| Furniture | Bookcases | 92,626 | 262,085 | 79,404 | 73,381 | 507,496 |
| | Chairs & Chairmats | 305,381 | 407,724 | 212,830 | 238,651 | 1,164,586 |
| | Office Furnishings | 69,528 | 115,506 | 197,188 | 62,412 | 444,634 |
| | Tables | 228,934 | 363,979 | 287,507 | 181,502 | 1,061,922 |
| | Total | 696,469 | 1,149,294 | 776,929 | 555,946 | 3,178,638 |
| Office Supplies | Appliances | 63,813 | 167,941 | 124,757 | 100,225 | 456,736 |
| | Binders and Binder Accessor.. | 103,625 | 225,160 | 148,472 | 161,326 | 638,583 |
| | Envelopes | 37,643 | 44,462 | 22,577 | 43,233 | 147,915 |
| | Labels | 3,713 | 7,929 | 5,411 | 6,393 | 23,446 |
| | Paper | 53,004 | 89,312 | 61,123 | 50,181 | 253,620 |
| | Pens & Art Supplies | 24,027 | 36,004 | 21,765 | 21,469 | 103,265 |
| | Rubber Bands | 1,710 | 2,197 | 2,294 | 2,469 | 8,670 |
| | Scissors, Rulers and Trimme.. | 14,628 | 9,625 | 12,947 | 3,232 | 40,432 |
| | Storage & Organization | 121,719 | 154,918 | 179,151 | 129,929 | 585,717 |
| | Total | 423,882 | 737,548 | 578,497 | 518,457 | 2,258,384 |
| Technology | Computer Peripherals | 80,805 | 224,142 | 110,840 | 75,064 | 490,851 |
| | Copiers and Fax | 148,504 | 205,639 | 174,718 | 132,354 | 661,215 |
| | Office Machines | 260,011 | 516,513 | 245,019 | 197,112 | 1,218,655 |
| | Telephones and Communicat.. | 225,571 | 436,295 | 282,962 | 199,456 | 1,144,284 |
| | Total | 714,891 | 1,382,589 | 813,539 | 603,986 | 3,515,005 |
| Grand Total | | 1,835,242 | 3,269,431 | 2,168,965 | 1,678,389 | 8,952,027 |

This view consists of the following parts which can be formatted:

1. **Field labels for rows**: Field labels can be formatted from the menu (**Format | FieldLabels...**) or by right-clicking on them in the view and selecting **Format...**) Additionally, you can hide field labels from the menu (**Analysis | Table Layout** and then uncheck the option for showing field labels) or by right-clicking on them in the view and selecting the option to hide. You can use the **Analysis | Table Layout** option on the top menu to show them again if desired.

2. **Field labels for columns**: These have the same options as above, but may be formatted or shown/hidden independently from the row field labels.

3. **Row headers**: These will follow formatting of headers in general, unless you specify different formatting for headers for Rows only. Notice that subtotals and grand totals have headers. The subtotal and grand totals headers marked **a** and **b**, in the preceding figure, are total row headers.

4. **Column headers**: These will follow formatting of headers in general, unless you specify different formatting for headers for columns only. Note that subtotals and grand totals have headers. The grand totals header marked **a** above is a column header.

5. **Pane**: Many formatting options include the ability to format the pane differently from the headers.

6. **Grand totals (column) pane**: This is the pane for grand totals that can be formatted at a sheet or column level.

7. **Grand totals (row) pane**: This is the pane for grand totals that can be formatted at a sheet or row level.

Worksheet level formatting is accomplished using the format window, which will appear on the left side, in place of the data pane.

To view the format window, select **Format** from the menu and then **Font...**, **Alignment...**, **Shading...**, **Border...**, or **Lines...**:

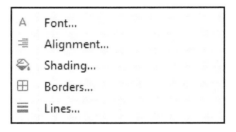

You can also right-click on nearly any element in the view and select **Format**. This will open the format window specific to the context of the element you selected. Just be certain to verify that the title of the format window pane matches what you expect. When you make a change, you should see the view update immediately reflect your formatting. If you don't, you are likely working in the wrong tab of the formatting window or you may have formatted something at a lower level (for example, **Rows**) which overrides changes made at a higher level (for example, **Sheet**).

You should now see the format window on the left. It will look similar to this:

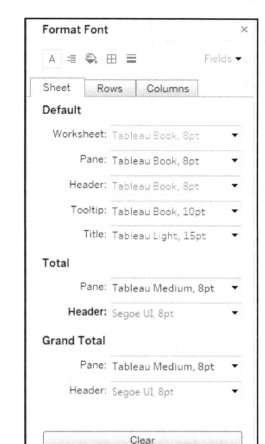

Note the following key aspects of the formatting window:

- The title of the window will give you the context for your formatting selections.
- The icons on the top match the selection options of the **Format** menu. This allows you to easily navigate through those options without returning to the menu each time.
- The three tabs, **Sheet**, **Rows**, and **Columns** allow you to specify options at a sheet level and then override those options and defaults at a row and column level. For example, you could make row grand totals have different pane and header fonts than column grand totals (though this specific choice would likely be jarring and is not recommended!).

- The **Fields** dropdown in the upper-right corner allows you to fine-tune formatting at a field level.
- Any changes that you make will be previewed and result in a bold label to indicate that the formatting option has been changed from the default. (Notice how the font for header under Total has been customized in the preceding figure, resulting in the label text of header being shown in bold.)

The three options for clearing formatting are as follows: **1) Clear single option** In the format window, right click the label or control of any single option you have changed and select **Clear** from the popup menu. **2) Clear all current options** At the bottom of the format window, click the **Clear** button to clear all visible changes. This applies only to what you are currently seeing in the format window. For example, if you are looking at **Shading** and the **Rows** tab, then click **Clear**, only the shading options you have changed on the **Rows** tab for will be cleared. **3) Clear sheet** From the menu navigate to **Worksheet | Clear | Formatting**. You can also use the drop down from the clear item on the toolbar. This clears all custom formatting on the current worksheet.

The other format options (alignment, shading, and so on) all work very similarly to the font option. There are only a few subtleties to mention:

- **Alignment**: This includes options for horizontal and vertical alignment, text direction, and text wrapping.
- **Shading**: This includes an option for **Row** and **Columns** banding. The banding allows for alternating patterns of shading that help to differentiate or group rows and columns. Light row banding is enabled by default for text tables, but can be useful in other visualization types such as horizontal bar charts as well. Row banding can be set to different levels which correspond to the number of discrete (blue) fields present on the **Rows** or **Columns** shelf.
- **Borders**: This refers to the borders drawn around cells, panes, and headers. It includes an option for **Row** and **Columns** dividers. You can see, the dividers between the departments in the view. By default, the level of the borders is set based on the next to last field on **Rows** or **Columns**.

- **Lines**: This refers to lines that are drawn on visualizations using an axis. This includes grid lines, reference lines, zero lines, and axis rulers. You can access a more complete set of options for reference lines and drop lines from the **Format** option on the menu.

# Field-level formatting

In the upper-right corner of the **Format SUM(Sales)** window is a little dropdown labeled **Fields**. Selecting this dropdown gives you a list of fields in the current view and selecting a field updates the format window with options appropriate for the field. Here, for example, is the window as it appears for the **SUM(Sales)** field:

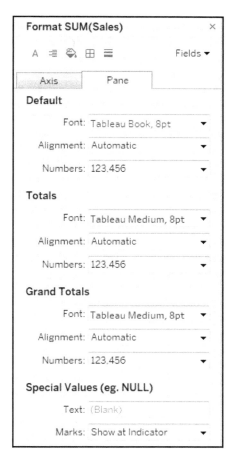

The title of the format window will alert you to the field you are formatting. Selecting an icon for **Font**, **Alignment**, and so on will switch back to the sheet level formatting. However, you can switch between the tabs: **Axis / Header** and **Pane**. The options for fields include font, alignment, shading, and number and date formats. The latter two options will over-ride any default metadata formats.

**Custom number formatting** When you alter the format of a number you can select from several standard formats as well as a custom format. The custom format allows you to enter a format string, which Tableau will use to format the number. The format string allows for up to three entries, separated by semi-colons to represent positive, negative, and zero formats. Here are some examples assuming the positive number **34,331.336000** and the negative number **-8,156.777700**:

| Format string | Resulting values | | |
|---|---|---|---|
| `#; -#` | 34331 | and | -8157 |
| `#,###.##; (#,###.##)` | 34,331.34 | and | (8156.78) |
| `#,###.000000; -#,###.000000` | 34,331.33600 | and | -8,156.777700 |
| `"up "#,###; "down "#,###; "same "` | up 34,331 | and | down 8,157 |

Notice how Tableau rounds the display of the number based on the format string. Always be aware that numbers you see as text, labels, or headers may have been rounded due to the format. Also observe how you can mix format characters such as the pound sign, commas, and decimal points with strings. The final example above would give a label of `"same"` where a value of 0 would normally have been displayed. Instead of using `"up"` or `"down"` as shown above, you could use a Unicode character, such as ▲ or ▼. Selecting a predefined format that is close to what you want and then switching to custom, will allow you to start with a custom format string that is close.

An additional aspect of formatting a field is specially formatting NULL values. When formatting a field, select the **Pane** tab and locate the **Special Values** section, as shown in the following figure:

Enter any text you would like to display in the pane (in the **Text** field) when the value of the field is null. You can also choose where marks should be displayed. The **Marks** drop down gives multiple options that define where and how the marks for null values should be drawn when an axis is being used. You have the following options:

- **Show at Indicator**: This results in a small indicator with the number of nulls in the lower right of the view. You can click the indicator for options to filter the nulls or show them at the default value. You can right-click the indicator to hide it.
- **Show at Default Value**: This option displays a mark at the default location (usually 0).
- **Hide (Connect Lines)**: This option makes sure that it does not place a mark for null values, but it does connect lines between all non-null values.
- **Hide (Break Lines)**: This causes the line to break where there are gaps created by not showing the null values.

You can see these options in the following screenshot, with the location of two null values indicated by a gray band:

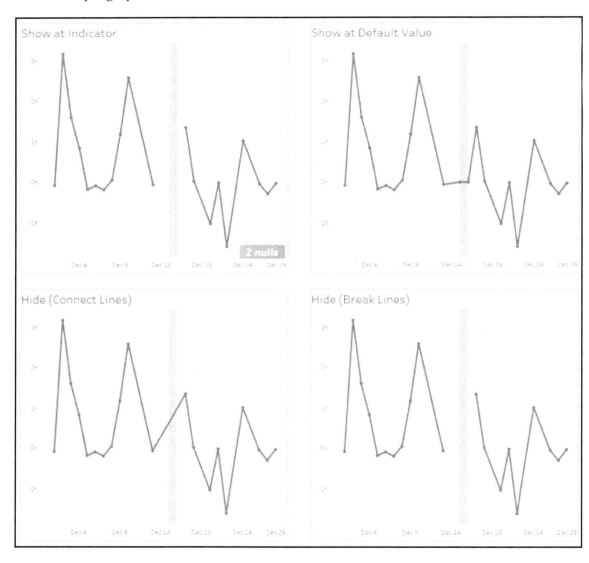

You'll notice that the preceding line charts have little circle markers at the location of each mark drawn in the view. When the mark type is a line, clicking on the **Color** shelf opens a menu that gives options for the markers. All mark types have standard options, such as color and transparency. Some mark types support additional options, such as border and/or halo as shown here:

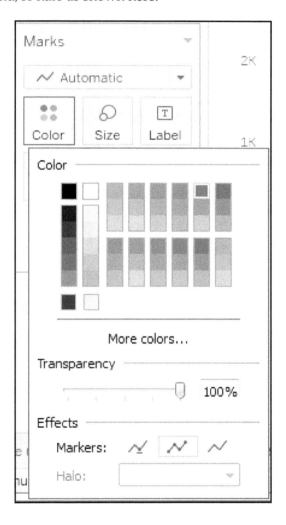

The **Hide (Break Lines)** and the **Show at Indicator** options works well in the preceding view because these two options do not obscure the null values. However, the formatting only helps with actual null values. These are the records which exist in the data, but have null, indicating no value. However, there are no records for some dates in December. In that case, the value isn't null, there isn't even a record of data. Tableau still connects the lines across those missing days, potentially making it difficult to tell that there are gaps. In that case, consider enabling data densification (you can accomplish this by ensuring the **Show Missing Dates** option is selected from the drop down of the **DAY(Order Date)** field on **Columns** and then adding certain table calculations such as **Index()** to the **Detail** of the view). This causes Tableau to generate records of data for the missing dates and treat the values as null:

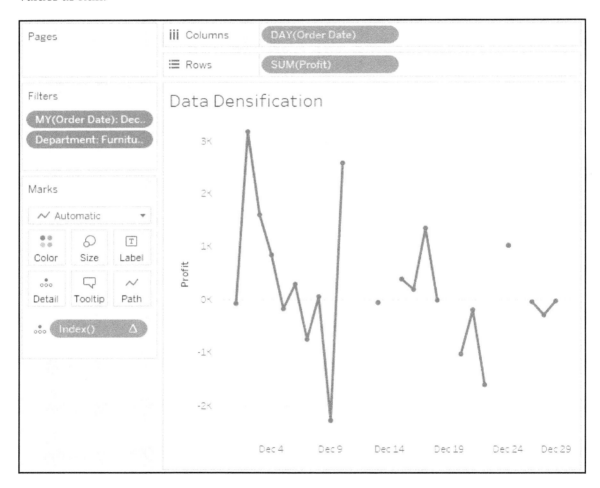

Or, as an alternative, use another visualization type, such as a bar chart, that more clearly indicates the missing days:

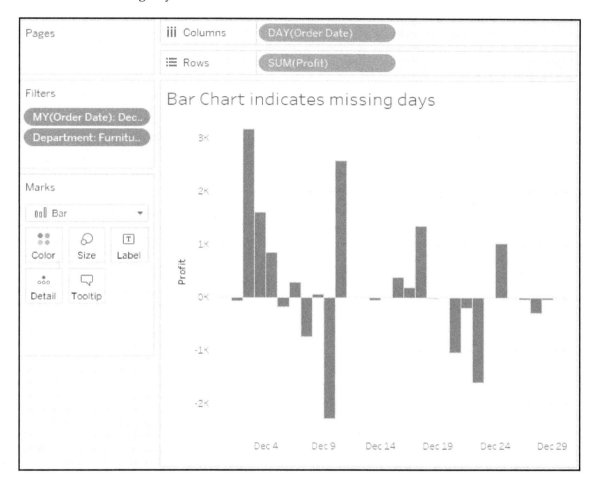

# Additional formatting options

Additional formatting options can also be accessed from the formatting window. These options include:

- A myriad of options for **Reference Lines**
- Line and text options for **Drop Lines**
- Shading and border options for **Titles and Captions**

- Text, box, and line options for **Annotations**
- Font, shading, alignment, and separator options for **Field Labels**
- Title and body options for **Legends, Quick Filters,** and **Parameters**
- **Cell Size** and **Workbook Theme** options

You'll find most of these fairly straightforward. A few options might not be as obvious:

- **Drop Lines**: They appear as lines drawn from the mark to the axis and can be enabled by right-clicking on any blank area in the pane of the view with an axis and selecting **Drop Lines | Show Drop Lines**. Additional options can be accessed using the same right-click menu and selecting **Edit Drop Lines**. Drop lines are only displayed in Tableau Desktop and Reader but are not available when a view is published to the Tableau Server, Online, or Public.
- **Titles** and **Captions** can be shown or hidden for any view by selecting **Worksheet** from the menu and then selecting the desired options. In addition to standard formatting, which can be applied to titles and captions, the text of a title or caption can be edited and specifically formatted by double clicking the title or caption, right-clicking on the title or caption and selecting **Edit**, or by using the drop-down menu of the title or caption (or the drop-down menu of the view on a dashboard). The text of titles and captions can dynamically include the values of parameters, values of any field in the view, and certain other data and worksheet specific values.
- **Annotations** can be created by right-clicking on a mark or space in the view and selecting **Annotate** and then selecting one of the following three types of annotations:

  - **Mark** annotations are associated with a specific mark in the view. If that mark does not show (due to a filter or axis range), then neither will the annotation. Mark annotations can include a display of the values of any fields that define the mark or its location.
  - **Point** annotations are anchored to a specific point in the view. If the point is not visible in the view, the annotation will disappear. Point annotations can include a display of any field values that define the location of the point (for example, the coordinates of the axis).

- **Area** annotations are contained within a rectangular area. The text of all annotations can dynamically include the values of parameters and certain other data and worksheet specific values.

You can copy formatting from one worksheet to another (within the same workbook or across workbooks) by selecting **Copy Formatting** from the **Format** menu while viewing the source worksheet (or select the **Copy Formatting** option from the right-click menu on the source worksheet tab). Then select **Paste Formatting** on the **Format** menu while viewing the target worksheet (or select the option from the right-click menu on the target worksheet tab). This option will apply any custom formatting present on the source sheet to the target. However, specific formatting applied during the editing of the text of titles, captions, labels, and tooltips is not copied to the target sheet.

# Adding value to visualizations

Now that we've considered how formatting works in Tableau, let's take a look at some ways in which formatting can add value to a visualization.

When you apply custom formatting, always ask yourself what the formatting adds to the understanding of the data. Is it making the visualization clearer and easier to understand? Or is it just adding clutter and noise?

In general, go for a minimalistic approach. Remove everything from the visualization that isn't necessary. Emphasize important values, text, and marks while de-emphasizing those which are only providing support or context.

Consider the following visualization using all default formatting:

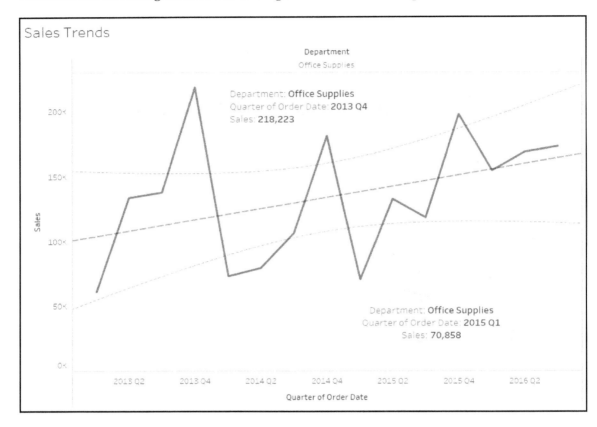

The default format works very well. But compare that with this visualization:

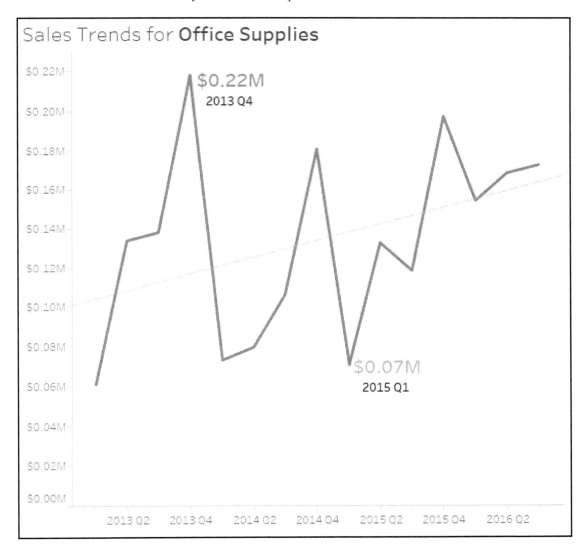

Both the preceding charts are showing sales by quarter, filtered to the office supplies department. With the exception that the top view has the department field on **Columns** in an attempt to make it clear that only office supplies sales are being shown, the field arrangement for the two views is exactly the same. The first view uses default formatting.

Consider some of the customizations in the second view:

- The **Title** has been adjusted to include the department name.
- The **Sales** field has been formatted to be shown using a custom currency with two decimal places and units of millions. This is true for the axis and the annotations. Often a high-level of precision can clutter visualization. The initial view of the data gives the trend and enough detail to understand the order of magnitude. Tooltips or additional views can be used to reveal detail and precision.
- The axis labels have been removed by right-clicking on the axis, selecting **Edit Axis** and then clearing the text. The title of the view clearly indicates that one is looking at **Sales**. The values alone reveal the second axis to be by quarter. If there are multiple dates in the data, you might need to specify which one is in use. Depending on your goals, you might consider hiding the axes completely.
- The gridlines on **Rows** have been removed. Gridlines can add a value to a view, especially in views where being able to determine values is of high importance. However, they can also clutter and distract. You'll need to decide, based on the view itself and the story you are trying to tell, whether gridlines are helpful or not.
- The trend line has been formatted to match the color of the line. Additionally, the confidence bands have been removed. You'll have to decide whether they add context or clutter based on your needs and audience.
- The **lines, shading,** and **boxes** have been removed from the annotations to reduce clutter.
- The **Size** and **Color** of the annotations has been altered to make them stand out. If the goal had been to simply highlight the minimum and maximum values on the line, labels might have been a better choice as they can be set to display at only **Min/Max**. In this case, however, the lower number is actually the second lowest point in the view.
- Axis rulers and ticks have been emphasized and colored to match the marks and reference line. (Axis rulers are available under the lines option on the format window). Alternately, we might have decided to hide the axes completely.

Formatting can also be used to dramatically alter the appearance of visualization. Consider the following chart:

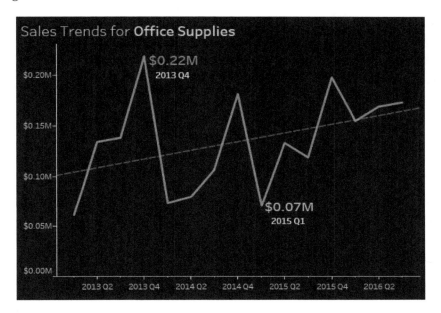

This visualization is nearly identical to the previous view. However, shading has been applied to the worksheet and the title. Additionally, fonts were lighted or darkened as needed to show up well on a black background. Some find this format more pleasing, especially on mobile devices. If the view is to be embedded in a website with a dark theme, this formatting may be very desirable. However, you may find some text more difficult to read on dark background. You'll want to consider your audience, the setting, and mode of delivery as you consider whether such a format is the best for your situation.

**Sequential color palettes** (a single color gradient based on a continuous field) should be reversed when using a black background. This is because the default of lighter (lower) to darker (higher) works well on a white background where darker colors stand out and lighter colors fade into white. On a black background, lighter colors stand out more and darker colors fade into black. You'll find the reverse option when you edit a color palette using the drop-down menu on the legend, double clicking the legend or right-clicking the legend and selecting **Edit Colors...** and then check **Reversed**.

# Tooltips

As they are not always visible, tooltips are an easily overlooked aspect of visualizations. However, when formatted well, they add a subtle professionalism. Consider the following default tooltip that displays when the end user hovers over one of the marks in the preceding view:

Compare it to this tooltip:

The tool-tip was edited using the menu option **Worksheet** | **Tooltip**, which brought up an editor allowing for the rich editing of text in the tooltip:

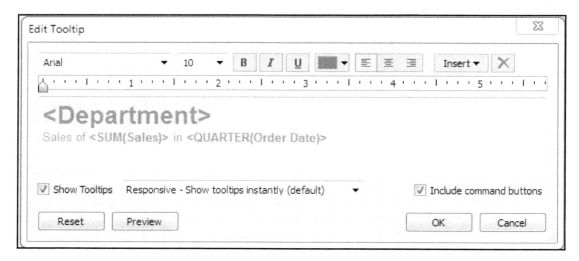

This editor is similar to those used for editing the text of labels, titles, captions, and annotations. Observe the **Insert** drop down in the upper right corner which allows you to insert fields, parameters, and other dynamic values. In the text, these are enclosed as a tag. You'll notice that the first tooltip above included command buttons (keep and exclude filters, creating sets, groups, and viewing the data). You'll need to decide if the command buttons add easy functionality or are distracting or confusing for your intended audience. The functionality is always available to the end-user via right-click.

 You can keep a tooltip from showing at all by unchecking the option in the editor. Also, keep in mind that tool-tips are not easily accessible by mobile users.

# Summary

The goal of formatting is to increase the effective communication of the data. Always consider the audience, setting, mode, mood, and consistency as you work through the iterative process of formatting. Look for formatting that adds value to your visualization and avoid useless clutter. With an understanding of how formatting works in Tableau, you'll have the ability to refine the visualizations you created in discovery and analysis into incredibly effective communication of your data story. Next, we'll look at how it all comes together in dashboards.

# Telling a Data Story with Dashboards

7

As you engage in data discovery and analysis, you will create numerous data visualizations. Each of these visualizations gives a snapshot of a story within the data. Each view into the data answers one, or maybe a couple of questions. At times, the discovery and analysis are enough to make a key decision and the cycle is complete. Many times, however, you will need to bring these visualizations together so that they communicate a comprehensive story to your intended audience.

Tableau allows you to bring together related data visualizations into a single dashboard. This dashboard could be a static view of various aspects of the data or a fully interactive environment, allowing users to dynamically filter, drill-down, and interact with the data visualizations.

This chapter will cover the following topics:

- Dashboard objectives
- Example - is least profitable always unprofitable?
- Designing for different displays and devices
- How actions work
- Example - regional scorecard
- Stories

We'll take a look at most of these concepts in the context of several in-depth examples where we'll walk through the dashboard design process. Along the way, you'll see some step-by-step instructions. As has been the case before, don't worry about memorizing lists of instructions. Instead, focus on understanding why and how components and aspects of dashboards work.

For the examples, we'll use the Superstore Sales sample data we've used in previous chapters. Go ahead and create a new workbook with a connection to that data set.

# Dashboard objectives

Every dashboard seeks to tell a story by giving a clear picture of a certain set of information. Before designing a dashboard, you should understand what story the data tells. How you tell the story will depend on numerous factors such as your audience, the way the audience will access the dashboard, and what response you want to elicit from your audience.

Stephen Few defines a dashboard as a *visual display of the most important information needed to achieve one or more objectives; consolidated and arranged on a single screen so the information can be monitored at a glance*. This definition is helpful to consider because it places some key boundaries around the data story and the way we will seek to tell it in Tableau. In general, your data story should follow these guidelines:

- The story should focus on the most important information. Anything that does not communicate or support the main story should be excluded. You may wish to include that information in other dashboards.
- The story that you tell must meet your key objectives. Your objectives may range from giving information, to providing an interface for further exploration, to prompting your audience to take action or make key decisions. Anything that doesn't support your objectives should be reserved for other dashboards.
- The main data story should be easily accessible and the primary idea should be obvious.

From a Tableau perspective, a **dashboard** is a set of worksheets along with other various components (such as legends, filters, parameters, text, containers, images, and web objects) arranged on a single canvas. Ideally, the visualizations and components should work together to tell a complete and compelling data story. Dashboards are usually interactive.

When you set out to build a dashboard, you'll want to carefully consider your objectives. Your discovery and analysis should have uncovered various insights into the data and its story. Now, it's your responsibility to package that discovery and analysis into a meaningful communication of the story to your particular audience in a way that meets your objectives and their needs.

Here are some possible approaches to building dashboards based on your objectives. It is by no means a comprehensive list:

- **Guided analysis**: You've done the analysis, made the discoveries, and thus have a deep understanding of the implications of the data story. Often it can be helpful to design a dashboard that guides your audience through a similar process of making the discoveries for themselves so the need to act is clear. For example, you may have discovered wasteful spending in the Manufacturing department but the Finance team may not be ready to accept your results unless they can see how the data led you to that conclusion.

- **Exploratory**: Many times, you do not know what story the data will tell when the data is refreshed in the next hour, next week, or next year. What may not be a significant aspect of the story today, might be a major decision point in the future. In these cases, your goal is to provide your audience with an analytical tool that gives them the ability to explore and interact with various aspects of the data on their own. For example, today customer satisfaction is high across all products, but your dashboard needs to give the marketing team the ability to continually track satisfaction over time, dynamically filter by region and price, and observe any correlations with quality.

- **Scorecard/Status snapshot**: There may be wide agreement on **Key Performance Indicators** (**KPI**s) or metrics that indicate good versus poor performance. You don't need to guide the audience through discovery or force them to explore. They just need a top-level summary and enough detail and to be able to drill down to quickly find and fix problems and reward success. For example, you may have a dashboard that simply shows how many support tickets are still unresolved. The manager can pull up the dashboard on a mobile device and immediately take action if necessary.

- **Narrative**: This type of dashboard tells a clear story. There may be aspects of exploration, guided analysis, or performance indication, but primarily you are showing what is necessary to communicate the meaning of the data. For example, you may desire to tell the story of the outbreak of a disease including where, when, and how it spread. Your dashboard tells the story, using the data in a visual way.

We'll take a look at several in-depth examples to better understand a few of these different approaches. Along the way, we'll incorporate many of the skills we've covered in previous chapters and we'll introduce key aspects of designing dashboards in Tableau.

# Example - is least profitable always unprofitable?

Let's say you've been tasked with helping Management for the superstore chain find which items are the least profitable. Management feels that the least profitable items should be eliminated from the inventory. However, as you've done your analysis, you've discovered that certain items, while not profitable overall, have made profit at times in various locations. Your primary objective is to give management the ability to quickly see an analysis of the least profitable items to identify whether an item has always been unprofitable. This example will combine aspects of a guided analytics dashboard and an exploratory tool.

## Building the views

Let's start by creating the individual views that will comprise your dashboard:

1. Create a bar chart showing profit by category. Sort the categories in descending order by the sum of profit.
2. Add the **Department** field to **Filters** and show a filter. To accomplish this, use the drop-down menu of the **Department** field in the data pane to select **Show Filter**.
3. Name the sheet **Overall Profit by Category**:

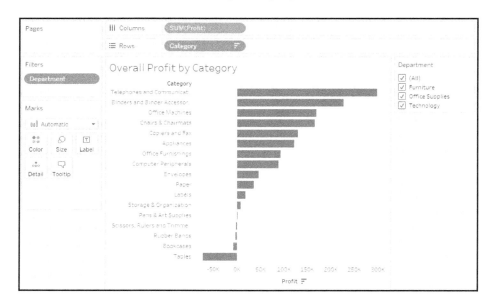

4. Create another, similar view showing profit by item. Sort the items in descending order by the **Sum** of **Profit**.

5. You'll notice that there are too many items to see at one time. For your objectives on this dashboard, you can limit the items to only the top **10** least profitable. Add the **Item** field to the filters shelf, select the **Top** tab and adjust the settings to filter **By field**. Specify the **Bottom 10** by **Sum (Profit)**:

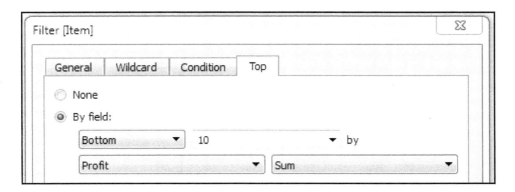

6. Rename the sheet **Top 10 Least Profitable Items**:

7. Create another sheet that displays a filled map of profit by state. You can accomplish this rather quickly by double-clicking the **State** field in the data window and then dropping **Profit** on the **Color** shelf.
8. Rename the sheet to **Profit by State**:

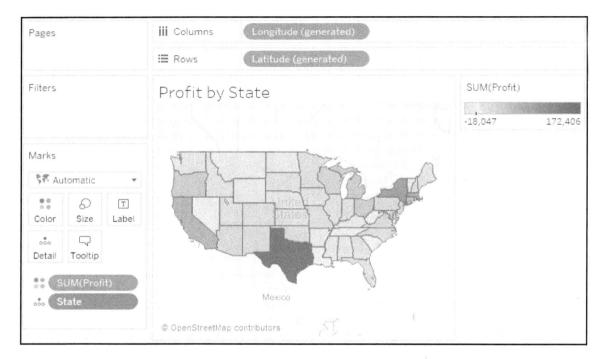

9. Create one final sheet to show when profits were made or lost. Ensure that the **Order Date** field has been added as the quarter date value and that it is continuous (green).
10. Add a linear trend line. To do this, switch to the **Analytics** tab on the left sidebar and drag **Trend Line** from **Model** to the view. Alternatively, right-click a blank area of the canvas of the view and navigate to **Trend Lines** | **Show Trend Lines**.

11. Rename the sheet **Profit Trend**:

# Creating the dashboard framework

At this point, you have all the views necessary to achieve the objectives for your dashboard. Now all that remains is to arrange them and enable the interactivity required to effectively tell the story:

1. Create a new dashboard by clicking the **New Dashboard** tab to the right of all existing worksheet tabs or by navigating to **Dashboard | New Dashboard** from the menu.
2. Rename the new dashboard **Is Least Profitable Always Unprofitable?**
3. At the bottom of the left sidebar, check **Show dashboard title**.

4. Add the views to the dashboard by dragging them from the **Dashboard** pane of the left sidebar and dropping them into the dashboard canvas. Arrange as shown:

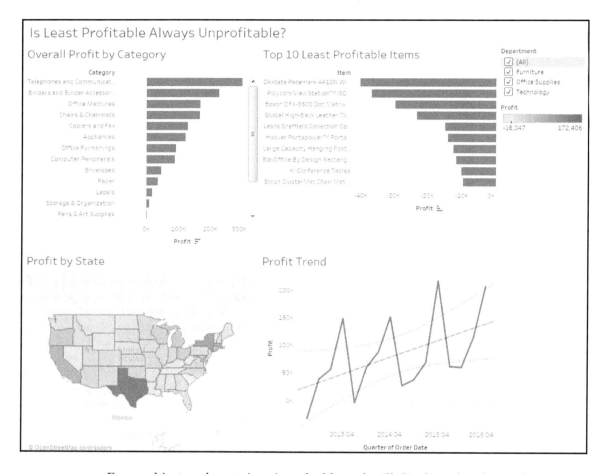

 Every object and container in a dashboard will display a border and several key controls when selected. The grip, in the middle of the top border, allows you to drag and drop the object to another location on the dashboard. The down caret opens a drop-down menu that gives you various options. For example, you can change the appearance and behavior of a filter, format an object, or hide titles and captions for a view. The X control will remove the object from the dashboard.

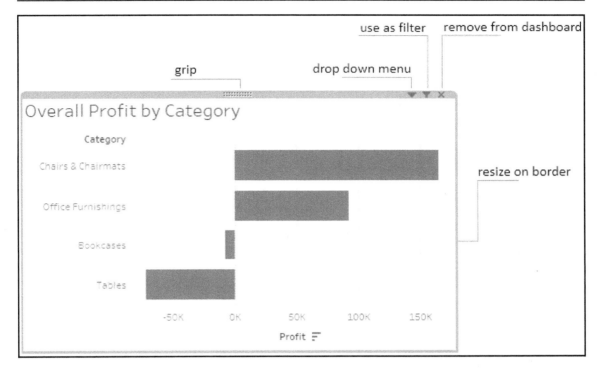

Notice how adding a view to the dashboard automatically adds any legends, filters, or parameters that are visible when editing the sheet. Here the **Department** filter was added along with **Profit by Category** and the color legend for **Profit** was added with **Profit by State**. By default, these items are added to the right.

 Many times you will need to include a legend, parameter, or filter that was not originally shown on a view in the dashboard. To add these after a view has been added, simply use the drop-down caret menu to select the object you wish to add.

After adding views to the dashboard, you'll want to take some time to reposition and resize various elements and views. So, for example, you might want to:

1. Use the drop-down menu on the **Department** filter and change the control to a **Single Value (dropdown)**.
2. You'll notice that changing the value of the filter only changes the **Overall Profit by Category** view. You can adjust which views the filter applies to using the drop-down menu. Using the drop-down menu, navigate to **Apply to Worksheets | All Using This Data Source**.

Options for applying filters may be set using the drop-down menu on the filter control or on the field on the **Filters** shelf in the view. The options include: **All using related data sources** The filter will be applied to all data sources where that field has been related between data sources. The relationships are the same as are used for data blending and may be edited from **Data | Edit Relationships** on the main menu. **All using this data source** The filter will be applied to any view using the data source as the primary data source. **Selected worksheets...** The filter will be applied to worksheets you select. **Only this worksheet** The filter will be applied only to the current worksheet.

3. Using the grip, move the **Department** filter immediately above the **Overall Profit by Category** view.

4. From the left sidebar, drag and drop a **Text** object above the **Top 10 Least Profitable Items** and enter the following instructions:

```
1. Select a Department from the dropdown.
2. Select a category below.
3. Select an Item below.
```

5. Size the text object to align the **Top 10** view with the **Overall** view.

6. Move the Profit color legend below the **Profit by State** view.

7. Using the drop-down menu of **Overall Profit by Category**, navigate to **Fit | Entire View**. This will ensure all categories are visible without the need for a scrollbar.

8. Additionally, fit the **Top 10 Least Profitable Items** to **Entire View**.

At this point, your dashboard should look similar to the following:

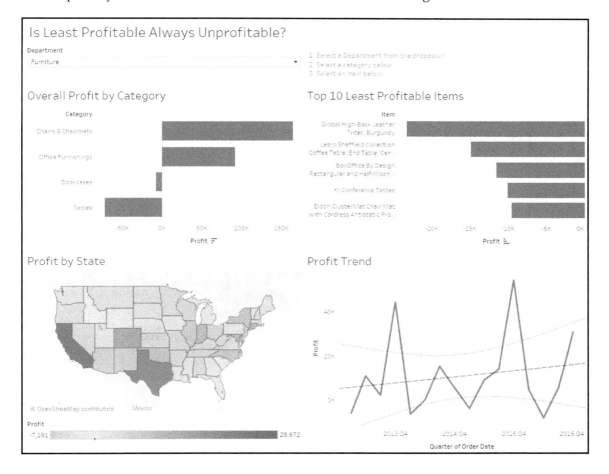

# Implementing actions to tell the story

You now have a framework that will support the telling of the data story. Your audience will be able to locate the least profitable items within the context of a selected category. Then, the selection of an item will answer the question as to whether it has always been unprofitable in every location. To enable this flow and meet your objectives, you'll often need to enable interactivity. In this case, we'll use actions. We'll conclude this example with some specific steps and then unpack the intricacies of actions:

1. Click the **Use as Filter** button on the **Overall Profit by Category** view. This will cause the view to be used as an interactive filter for the entire dashboard. That is, when the user selects a bar, all other views will be filtered based on the selection:

2. From the main menu, navigate to **Dashboard | Actions**. You'll see a list containing one action named **Filter 1 (generated)**. This is the action that was created when you selected **Use as Filter**, previously:

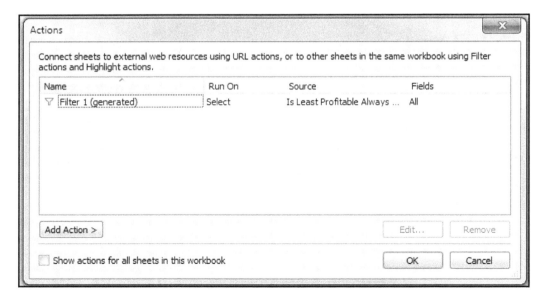

3. Click the **Add Action >** button and select **Filter**. The resulting dialog gives you options for selecting the source, target, and additional options for the action.

4. Here we want an action that filters everything except the **Overall Profit by Category** view when the user selects an item. So, in the **Add Filter Action** dialog set **Source Sheets** to **Top 10 Least Profitable Items** and **Target Sheets** to **Profit by State** and **Profit Trend**. Make sure the action is set to run on **Select**. Name the filter **Filter by Item** and then click **OK** on this dialog and again on the **Actions** dialog:

What you now have is an action that is run whenever you select an item. The action results in a filter being set in the two target views. When the selection is cleared, all values will be shown in the two target views.

Notice now that clicking a bar in the **Overall Profit by Category** view results in a filtered view of the top 10 items. When you click the same bar or a blank area in the view, the bar is de-selected and the top 10 items view has all values excluded, resulting in a blank view.

You may have noticed that, when you use the drop-down filter to select a single **Department** or select a single category, you have fewer than 10 items in the top 10 view. For example, selecting **Furniture** from the **Department** filter and clicking on the bar for **Tables** results in only three items being shown. This is because the top item filter is evaluated at the same time as the action filter. There are only three items with the category of **Tables** that are also in the top 10.

What if you want to see the top 10 items within the category of **Tables**? You can accomplish this using context filters.

 **Context filters** are a special kind of filter in Tableau and are applied before other filters. Other filters are then applied within the context of the context filters. Conceptually, context filters result in Tableau applying additional filters to a subset of data based on the context filters. **Top Filters**, **Computed Sets**, and **Fixed Level of Detail** calculations are all computed within the context defined by context filters.

In this case, navigate to the **Top 10** sheet and add the **Department** filter and the newly added **Action (Category)** filter to the context using the drop-down menu of the fields on the **Filters** shelf. Once added to the context, those fields will be gray on the filters shelf. Now, you will see the top 10 items within the context of the selected **Department** and **Action (Category)**:

Notice that adding filters to the context causes the fields to be color-coded gray on the
**Filters** shelf.

If you edit the action on the dashboard, the filter might be automatically
updated and you may have to re-add it to the context.

Go ahead and step through the actions by selecting a couple of different categories and a couple of different items. Observe how the final dashboard meets your objectives by telling a story:

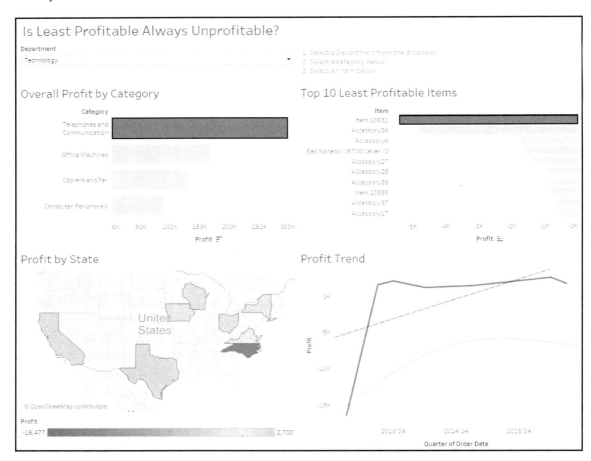

The user has selected **Technology** from the **Department** drop-down menu, **Telephones and Communications** from the category list, and then **Item 10631**, which is the least profitable item within the category. This reveals the states where the item was sold (color-coded by profit) and a time series of profit for the item.

Should management remove **Item 10631** from inventory? Not without first considering that the item only lost profit in one instance and the trend is positive toward greater profitability. Granted the original loss was a large loss, but it was also a long time ago and every subsequent sale of the item resulted in gain. The results of your findings may lead to further analysis to determine what factors play a part in profit and loss for the item and better decision-making by management.

When you look at the `Chapter 07 Completed` workbook, you'll only see a tab at the bottom for the dashboard and not the individual views that are in the dashboard. The individual views have been hidden. Hiding tabs for sheets used in dashboards or stories is a great way to keep your workbook clean and guide your audience away from looking at sheets meant to be seen in the context of a dashboard or story. To hide a sheet, right-click the tab and select **Hide Sheet**. To unhide a sheet, navigate to the dashboard or story using the sheet, right-click the sheet in the left side pane, and uncheck **Hide Sheet**. Additionally, you can hide or unhide all sheets used in a dashboard by right-clicking the dashboard tab and selecting the appropriate option.

# Designing for different displays and devices

When designing a dashboard, some of the first questions you'll often ask yourself are: How will my audience view this dashboard? What kind of device will they use? With the wide adoption of mobile devices, this question becomes very important because what looks great on a large flat screen monitor doesn't always look great on a tablet or phone.

Previous versions of Tableau have given you the ability to set sizes for dashboards, but Tableau 10 gives you even greater flexibility by allowing you to define layouts for different devices.

The top of the **Dashboard** tab on the left sidebar reveals a button to preview the dashboard on various devices as well as a drop-down menu for **Size** options.

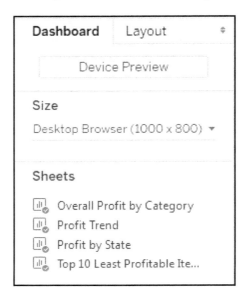

Clicking the **Device Preview** button not only allows you to see how your dashboard will look with various device types (and even specific models), but also allows you to add a layout for each device type that you can customize:

You can not only see how your dashboard will appear on various devices and models, but also how it will look based on the orientation of the device and whether the Tableau Mobile app is used (if available for the selected device).

Clicking the **Add Layout** button (for instance, the **Add Tablet Layout** button in the preceding screenshot), will add a layout under the **Dashboard** tab on the left sidebar:

Each layout can have its own size and fit options and the layout options allow you to switch from **Default** to **Custom**. This gives you the ability to rearrange the dashboard for any given layout. You can even remove views and objects for a certain layout. For example, you might simplify a dashboard to one or two views for a phone while leaving three or four in place for a desktop display.

The `Chapter 07 Completed` workbook contains an example of the profit analysis dashboard from the preceding section that has a couple of layout options. For example, here is that dashboard formatted for display on a phone in which the dashboard will fit according to the width of the phone and allow for scrolling up and down:

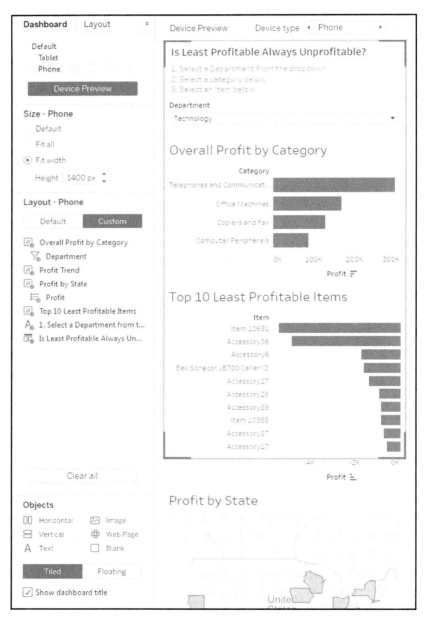

As you can see, the arrangement of the dashboard for the phone means that **Profit by State** and **Profit Trends** do not appear within the preview boundaries for a phone device. However, they are only a finger swipe away.

# How actions work

In Tableau, an **action** is a user-initiated event that triggers a response from Tableau. You've seen a few examples of actions used in dashboards. We'll now consider some details of how actions work in Tableau.

Tableau supports three kinds of action:

- **Filter actions**: The user's action causes one or more filters to be applied to one or more views
- **Highlight actions**: The user's action causes specific marks and headers to be highlighted in one or more views
- **URL actions**: The user's action causes a specific URL to be opened (either in a browser, a new tab, or in an embedded web object)

Certain actions are automatically generated by Tableau based on shortcuts. For example, you can select **Use as Filter** from the drop-down menu of a view on a dashboard, resulting in an automatically generated filter action. Enabling highlighting using the button on a discrete color legend or from the toolbar will automatically generate a highlight action:

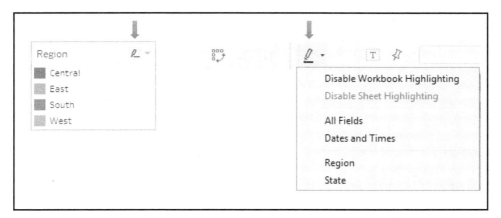

You can also create or edit dashboard actions by navigating to **Dashboard** | **Actions** from the menu. Let's consider the details of each type of action.

# Filter actions

Filter actions are defined by source sheet(s) that pass one or more dimensional values as filters to target sheets upon an action. Remember that every mark on a sheet is defined by a unique intersection of dimensional values. When an action occurs involving one or more of those marks, the dimensional values which comprise the mark(s) can be passed as filters to one or more target sheets.

When you create or edit a filter action, you will see options similar to these:

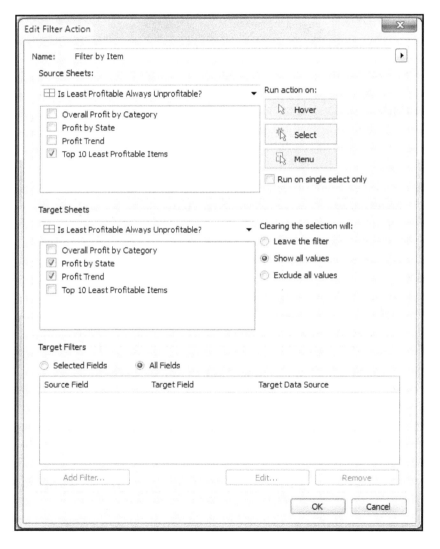

This screen allows you to:

- Name the filter.
- Choose source and target sheets. The source sheet is where the user will initiate the action (hover, selection, menu) and the target sheet is where the response will be applied (filtering in this example, but also highlighting).
- Set the action that triggers the filter and whether the selection of multiple marks or only a single mark initiates the action.
- Choose what happens when the selection is cleared.
- Specify which dimensions are used to pass filter values to the target sheet(s).

 Try to give your actions names that help you differentiate between multiple actions in the dashboard. Additionally, if your action is set to run on **Menu**, then the name you use will be shown as a link in the tooltip. Use the arrow to the right of the name to insert special field placeholders. These will be dynamically updated with the values of the fields for a mark when the user sees the menu option in a tooltip.

You may select as many source and target sheets as you desire. However, if you specify specific **Target filters** in the bottom section, the fields you select must be present in the source sheet (for example, on **Rows**, **Columns**, **Detail**, and so on). You will receive a warning if a field is not available for one or more source sheets and the action will not be triggered for those sheets. Most of the time your source and target will be the same dashboard. Optionally, you can specify a different target sheet or dashboard, which will cause the action to navigate to the target in addition to filtering.

 When filter actions are defined at a worksheet level (when viewing a worksheet, navigate to **Worksheet** | **Actions** from the menu) then a menu item for that action will appear as menu items for every mark on every sheet that uses the same data source. You can use this to quickly create navigation between worksheets and from dashboards to individual worksheets.

Filter actions can be set to occur on any one of three possible actions:

- **Hover**: The user moves the mouse cursor over a mark (or taps a mark on a mobile device).
- **Select**: The user clicks or taps a mark, rectangle/radial/lasso selects multiple marks by clicking and dragging a rectangle around them, clicks a header (in which case all marks for that header are selected.) A user may deselect by clicking/tapping the already selected mark, clicking/tapping an empty space in the view, or by clicking/tapping the already selected header.
- **Menu**: The user selects the menu option for the action on the tooltip.

Consider the following example of a filter action triggered when a bar is selected in the source:

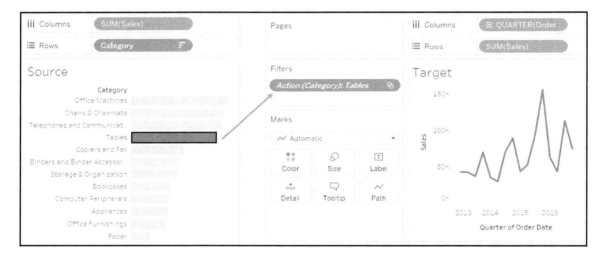

Each bar mark in the source is defined by the **Category** dimension. When the bar for **Tables** is selected, a single filter is set on the target.

If the mark is defined by more than one dimension (for example, **Category** and **Region**), then the **Target** sheet will still have a single filter with the combination of dimension values that were selected. In this example, the filter contains **Office Machines** and **West**, matching the dimensions that define the selected square:

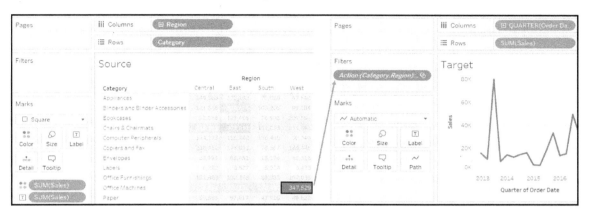

By default, all dimensions present in the source view are used in a filter action. Optionally, you can specify which fields should be used. You can use the **Selected Fields** option in the Edit Filter Actions dialog to accomplish the following:

- Filtering based on fewer dimensions. For example, if you only choose to use the **Region** field, then selecting the square shown previously would only pass the **West** region as a filter to the target.
- Filtering a target view using a different data source. The **Selected Fields** option allows you to map the source field to a target field (even if the target field has a different name, though the values must still match). For example, if the target used a data source where **East** was a possible value for a field named **Area**, you could map **Region** from the source to **Area** in the target.

# Highlight actions

This type of action does not filter target sheets. Instead, highlight actions cause marks that are defined, at least in part, by the selected dimensional value(s) to be highlighted in the target sheets. The options for highlight actions are very similar to filter actions, with the same options for source and target sheets and which event triggers the action.

Consider a dashboard with three views and a highlight action based on the **Region** field. When the action is triggered for the **East** region, all marks defined by **East** are highlighted. The dimension(s) used for highlighting must be present in all views where you want the highlighting to be applied. Both the map and scatter plot have **Region** on the **Detail** of the **Marks** card:

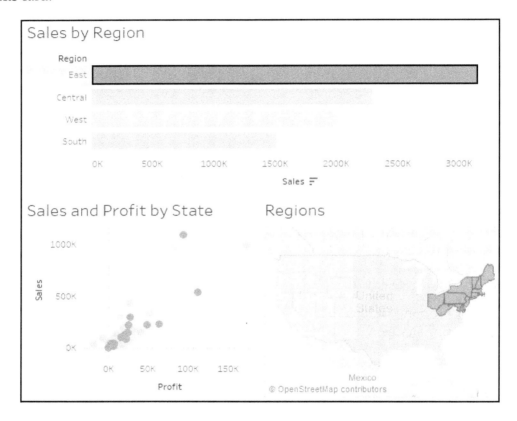

 Tableau 10 introduces data highlighters. **Highlighters** (also called **data highlighters**) are shown as user controls (similar to filters and parameters) that cause highlighting based on user interaction. They can be applied to one or more views and will highlight the marks of the views. They do not create an action. To add a highlighter, select any discrete (blue) field in the view and use the drop-down menu to **Show Highlighter** or use the menu and navigate to **Analysis | Highlighters**. On a dashboard you can add a highlighter by using a view's drop-down menu and selecting **Highlighters**.

# URL actions

URL actions allow you to dynamically generate a URL based on an action and open it within a web object in the dashboard or in a new browser window or tab. URL actions can be triggered by the same events as filter and highlight actions. The name of the URL action differentiates it and will appear as the link when used as a menu.

The URL includes any hardcoded values you enter as well as placeholders accessible via the arrow to the right of the URL text box. These placeholders include fields and parameters. The values will be dynamically inserted into the URL string when the action is triggered based on the values for the fields that make up the selected mark(s) and current values for parameters.

If you have included a web object in the dashboard, the URL action will automatically use that as the target. Otherwise, the action opens a new browser window (when the dashboard is viewed in Desktop or Reader) or a new tab (when the dashboard is viewed in a web browser).

Some web pages have different behaviors when viewed in iframes. The browser object does not use iframes in Tableau Desktop or Tableau Reader, but does when the dashboard is published to Tableau Server, Tableau Online, or Tableau Public. You will want to test URL actions based on how your dashboards will be viewed by your audience.

# Example - regional scorecard

We'll consider another example dashboard which demonstrates slightly different objectives. Let's say everyone in the organization has agreed upon a key performance indicator of **Profit Ratio KPI**. Furthermore, there is consensus that the cut-off between an acceptable and poor profit ratio is **15.00%** but management would like to have the option of adjusting the value dynamically to see if other targets might be better.

Consider the following dashboard:

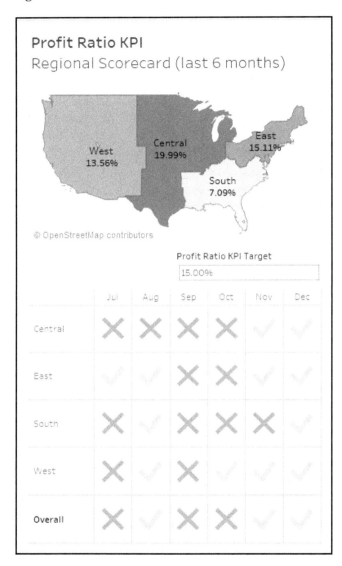

This dashboard allows your audience to very quickly evaluate the performance of each region over the **last 6 months**. Executive management could very quickly pull this dashboard up on their mobile device and take appropriate action as needed.

The dashboard provides interactivity with the KPI target parameter. Additional means of drilling down into other dashboards or views could be provided if desired. If this view were published on Tableau Server, it is not unreasonable to think that regional managers might subscribe to the view and receive a scheduled e-mail containing an up-to-date image of this dashboard.

Let's consider how to create a similar dashboard:

1. Create a float type parameter named `Profit Ratio KPI Target` set to an initial .15 and format it as a percentage.
2. Create a calculation named `Profit Ratio` with the code `SUM([Profit]) / SUM([Sales])`. This is an aggregate calculation that will divide the sum of profit by the sum of sales at the level of detail defined in the view.
3. Create a second calculation named `KPI - Profit Ratio` with the code:

```
IF [Profit Ratio] >= [Profit Ratio KPI Target]
THEN "Acceptable"
ELSE "Poor"
END
```

   This code will compare the profit ratio to the parameterized cut-off value. Anything equal to or above the cut-off will get the value of **Acceptable** and everything below will get the value of **Poor**.

4. Create a new sheet named **Region Scorecard**. The view consists of **Region** on **Rows**, **Order Date** as a discrete date part on **Columns**, and the **AGG (KPI - Profit Ratio)** field on both shape and color. You'll observe that the shapes have been edited to use checkmarks and Xs and the color palette is using color-blind-safe blue and orange.
5. Column Grand Totals have been added using the Analytics pane and custom-formatted with a custom label of **Overall**, bold font, and light gray shading.

6. **Order Date** has been added as a filter and is set to the Top 6 by field (Order Date as Min). This will dynamically filter the view to the last 6 months:

7. Create another sheet named **Profit Ratio by Region**.
8. Use the drop-down menu on **Region** to navigate to **Geographic Role | Create from... | State**. This tells Tableau to treat **Region** as a geographic field based on its relationship with the geographic field, **State**.
9. Double-click the **Region** field in the data pane. Tableau will automatically generate a geographic visualization based on **Region**. We'll examine the creation of custom geographies in more detail in `Chapter 10`, *Advanced Visualizations, Techniques, Tricks, and Trips*.
10. Place **Profit Ratio** on **Color** and also **Label**. You will also want to format **Profit Ratio** as a percentage. You may do so by formatting the field in this view specifically or by setting the default number format for the field in the data pane (the latter is probably preferred as you will almost always want it to display as a percentage).
11. Additionally, add **Region** to **Label**. Rearrange the fields in the marks card to reorder the label or click the **Label** shelf to edit the label text directly.

12. Apply the same filter to this view as you did to the **Region Scorecard** view. You may wish to navigate to the **Region Scorecard** sheet and use the drop-down on **Order Date** on the **Filters** shelf to apply the existing filter to multiple sheets.

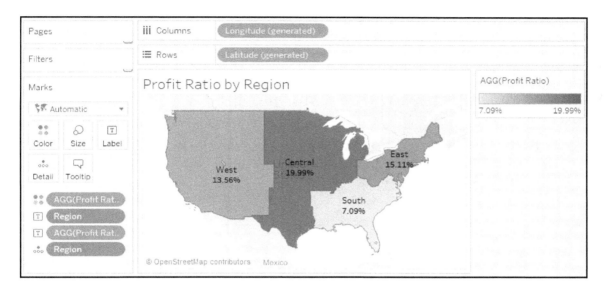

Once both views have been created, the dashboard can be constructed by arranging the two sheets, parameter control, and text appropriately. The example in the Chapter 07 Completed workbook has a phone layout applied.

By default, all objects added to the dashboard are tiled. Tiled objects snap in place and appear beneath floating objects. Any object can be added to the dashboard as a floating object by switching the toggle under **New Objects** in the left window or by holding the *Shift* key while dragging the objects to the dashboard. Existing objects can be switched between floating and tiled by holding the *Shift* key while moving the object or using the drop-down caret menu. The drop-down caret menu also gives options for adjusting the floating order of objects. Additionally, floating objects can be resized and positioned with pixel precision by selecting the floating object and using the positioning and sizing controls on the lower left. You can mix tiled and floating elements, but many designers prefer to build dashboards that are composed entirely of one or the other. This ensures consistency between different layouts and sizes of screens (especially if the dashboard is set to an **Automatic** or **Range** sizing option).

# Stories

The stories feature allows you to tell a story using interactive snapshots of dashboards and views. The snapshots become points in a story. This allows you to construct a guided narrative or even an entire presentation.

Let's consider an example in which **story points** might be useful. Executive managers are pleased with the regional scorecard dashboard you developed above. Now, they want you to make a presentation to the board and highlight some specific issues for the South region. With minimal effort, you can take your simple scorecard, add a few additional views, and tell an entire story:

1. First we'll build a couple of additional views. Create a simple geographic view named **Profit Ratio KPI by State**. Make this a filled map with the **AGG (KPI - Profit Ratio)** field defining the color.
2. Add **Profit Ratio** to the **Detail** of the **Marks** card so it is available for later use:

3. Create one additional view named **Profit Ratio by Quarter**. Use **Order Date** as a continuous date value on **Columns** and **Profit Ratio** on **Rows**.

4. Set the mark type to bars. Add a reference line for the **Profit Ratio KPI Target** parameter value (you can right-click the **Profit Ratio** axis to add a reference line).

5. Add **AGG (KPI - Profit Ratio)** to **Color**. You may also wish to click the **Color** shelf and add a border.

6. Go ahead and filter the view to the **South Region** and use the drop-down menu to apply that filter to the **Profit Ratio KPI by State** view as well:

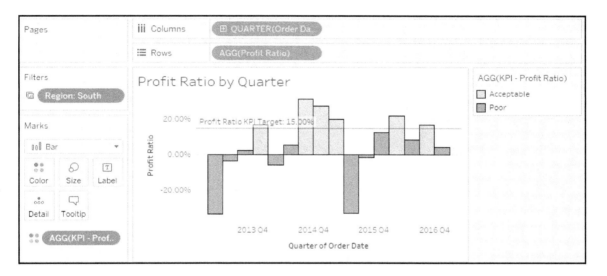

7. Create a new dashboard with the two new views arranged something like below. Add the **Profit Ratio KPI Target** parameter and **Region** filter if they do not show.

8. Use the drop-down menu on **Profit Ratio KPI by State** to use that view as a filter.

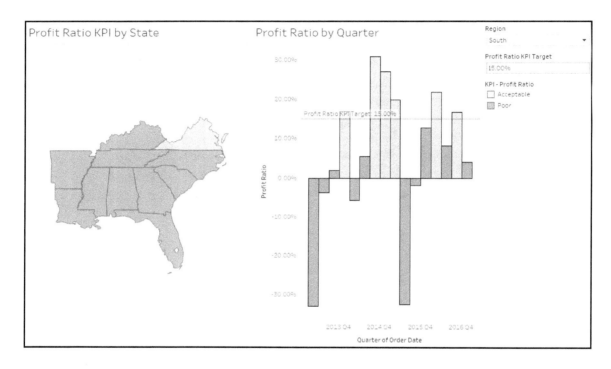

9. Create a new story by navigating to **Story** | **New Story** from the menu or using the new story tab at the bottom, next to the existing sheets.

The story interface consists of a sidebar with all visible dashboards and views. At the top, you'll see the **Story Title**, which can be edited. Each new point in the story will appear as a navigation box with text that can also be edited. Clicking on the box will give you access to the story point to which you can add a single dashboard or view.

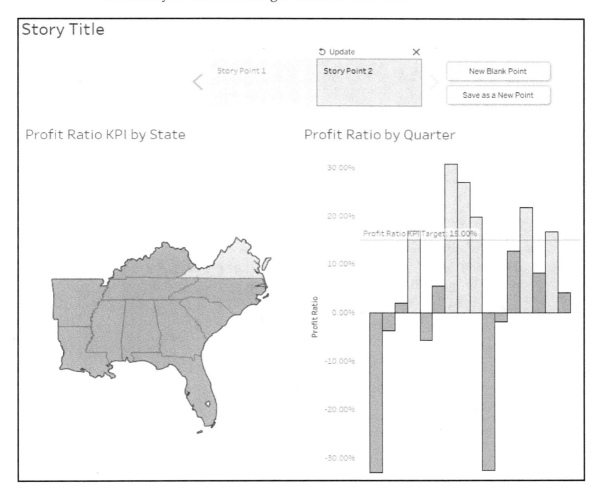

You can create a new story point using the **New Blank Point** button (for a new story point), the **Duplicate** button (which will create a duplicate snapshot of the currently selected story point), or the **Save as New Point** button (which will capture the current state of the dashboard as a new story point).

Clicking on a story point navigation box will bring up the snapshot of the view or dashboard for that story point. You may interact with the dashboard doing such things as making selections, changing filters, changing parameter values, and adding annotations. Changing any aspect of the dashboard will present you with an option to **Update** the existing story point to the current state of the dashboard. Alternately, you can use the revert button above the navigation box to return to the original state of the dashboard. Clicking the X will remove the story point.

Each story point contains an entirely independent snapshot of a dashboard. Filter selections, parameter values, selections, and annotations will be remembered for a particular story point, but will have no impact on other story points or any other sheet in the dashboard. You may rearrange story points by dragging and dropping the navigation boxes.

We'll build the story by completing the following steps:

1. Give the story the title **South Region Analysis**.
2. Add the **Regional Scorecard** dashboard as the first story point. Select the **South** region in the map. Give the story point the text: The South Region has not performed well the last 6 months:

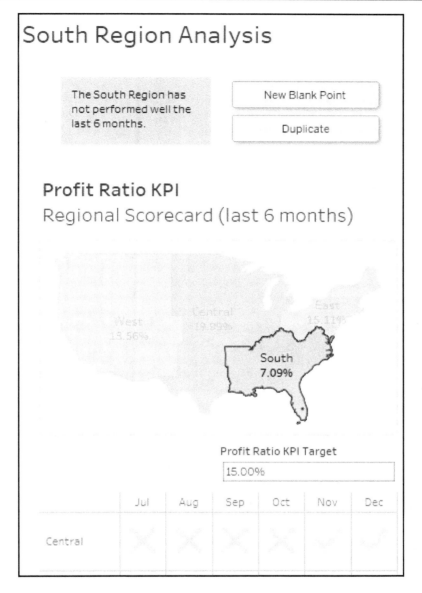

3. Click the **New Blank Point** button to create a new story point and add the **Profit Ratio Analysis** dashboard to the point.

4. Give this story point a caption of Only one state has met the 15% target overall.

5. Right click **Virginia** in the map and navigate to **Annotate** | **Mark**. Keep the state and profit ratio as part of the annotation:

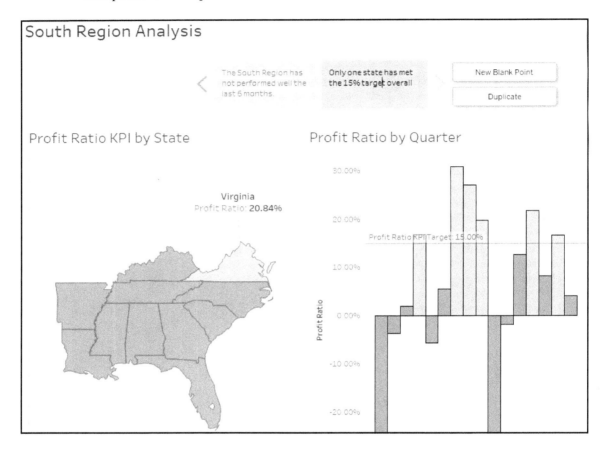

6. Click the **Duplicate** button to copy the current story point. Give this new story point the caption: `3 states would meet a goal of 10%`. Set the **Profit Ratio KPI Target** to **10.00%** and update the point.
7. Click the **Duplicate** button again and give the newly created point the caption: `Certain states have performed well historically.`
8. Right-click the annotation for **Virginia**, select **Remove** to delete it, then add a similar annotation for **Louisiana,** and then click **Louisiana** to select that state.
9. Make sure you click the **Update** button to capture the state of the dashboard:

In presentation mode, the buttons for adding, duplicating, updating, or removing story points are not shown. Your final story should look similar to this:

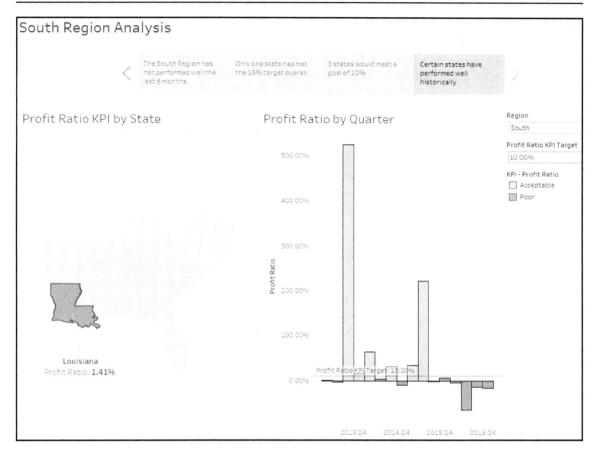

Take some time to walk through the presentation. Clicking navigation boxes will show the associated story point. You can fully interact with the dashboard in each story point. In this way, you can answer questions on the fly and dig into details, and then continue through the story.

A great way to learn dashboard techniques (and data visualization techniques in general) is to subscribe to Viz of the Day (http://www. tableau.com/public/community/viz-of-the-day). A new visualization, dashboard, or story is featured each day. When you see a design technique or visualization you want to understand, you can often download the workbook and explore the various techniques that were used.

# Summary

When you are ready to share your discovery and analysis you will likely use dashboards to relate the story to your audience. The way in which you tell the story will depend on your objectives as well as your audience and the mode of delivery. Using a combination of views, objects, parameters, filters, and legends, you can create an incredible framework for telling a data story. Tableau allows you to specifically design layouts for different devices to ensure your audience has the best experience. By introducing actions and interactivity, you can invite your audience to participate in the story. Story points will allow you to bring together many snapshots of dashboards and views to craft and present entire narratives.

Next we'll turn our attention to some deeper analysis with trends, distributions, forecasting, and clustering.

# 8
# Deeper Analysis - Trends, Clustering, Distributions, and Forecasting

Sometimes, quick data visualization needs a slightly deeper analysis. For example, a simple scatterplot can reveal outliers and correlation of values. But often you want to understand the distribution. A simple time series helps you see the rise and fall of a measure over time. But many times you want to see the trend or make predictions of future values.

Tableau enables you to quickly enhance your data visualizations with statistical analysis. Built-in features such as trending, clustering, distributions, and forecasting, allow you to quickly add value to your visual analysis. Additionally, Tableau integrates with R, an extensive statistical platform that opens up endless options for statistical analysis of your data. This chapter will cover the built-in statistical models and analysis.

This chapter will cover the following topics:

- Trending
- Clustering
- Distributions
- Forecasting

We'll take a look at these concepts in the context of a few examples using some sample data sets. You can follow and reproduce these examples using the Chapter 08 workbook.

# Trending

`World Population.xlsx` is included in the `Chapter 08` directory. It contains one record for each country for each year from **1960** to **2015**, measuring population. Using this data set, let's take a look at the historical trends of various countries. Create a view similar to the following, which shows the change in population over time for **Afghanistan** and **Australia**. You'll notice that **Country Name** has been filtered to include only **Afghanistan** and **Australia** and the field has additionally been added to the **Color** and **Label** shelves:

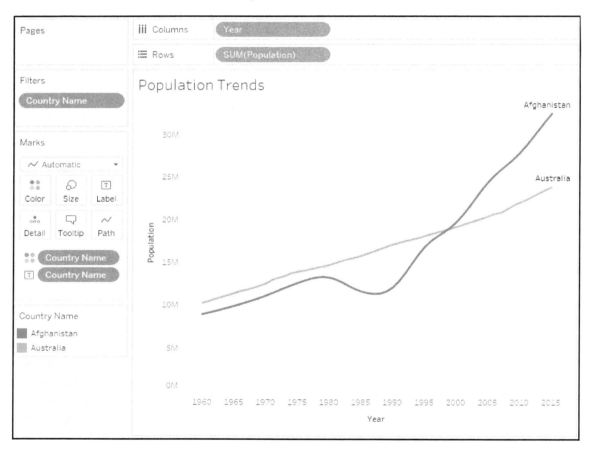

From this visualization alone you can make several interesting observations. The growth of the two countries' populations was fairly similar up to **1980**. At that point the population of **Afghanistan** went into decline until **1988** when the population of **Afghanistan** started to increase recover. At some point around **1996** the population of **Afghanistan** exceeded that of **Australia**. The gap has grown wider ever since.

While we have a sense of the two trends, they become even more obvious when we see them. Tableau offers several ways of adding trend lines:

- From the menu, navigate to **Analysis | Trend Lines | Show Trend Lines**
- Right-click an empty area in the pane of the view and select **Show Trend Lines**
- Switch to the **Analytics** pane in the left sidebar and drag and drop **Trend Line** on to the trend model of your choice (we'll use **Linear** for now and discuss the others later in this chapter)

The third option is indicated here:

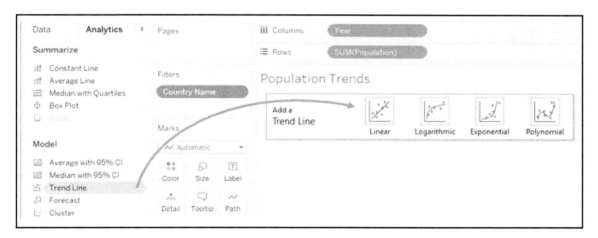

Once you have added the trend line to your views should contain two trend lines (one for each country) and lighter lines indicating confidence bands. We'll take a look at how we can customize the display shortly. For now, edit the trend lines and uncheck the option for confidence bands (right-click the trend line or blank space in the view and select **Trend Lines** | **Edit Trend Lines...** or select the option from the **Analytics** menu.) At this point, your view should look like this:

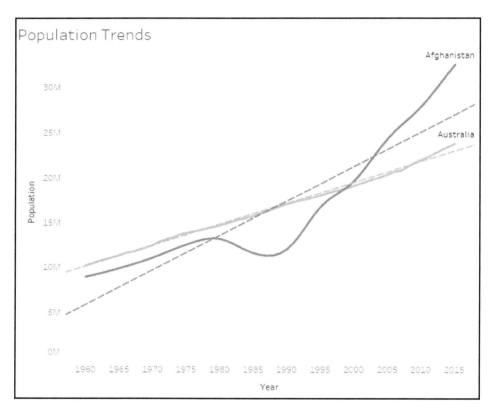

Trends are calculated by Tableau after querying the data source. Trend lines are drawn based on various elements in the view:

- **The two fields that define X and Y coordinates**: The fields on **Rows** and **Columns** that define the $x$ and $y$ axes describe coordinates allowing Tableau to calculate various trend models. In order to show trend lines, you must use a continuous (green) field or discrete (blue) date fields and have one such field on both **Rows** and **Columns**. If you use a discrete (blue) date field to define headers, the other field must be continuous (green).

- **Additional fields that create multiple, distinct trend lines**: Discrete (blue) fields on the **Rows**, **Columns**, or **Color** shelves can be used as factors to split a single trend line into multiple, distinct trend lines.
- **The trend model selected**: We'll examine the differences in models in the next section.

Observe in the preceding view that there are two trend lines. Since **Country Name** is a discrete (blue) field on **Color** it defines a trend line per color by default.

Earlier, we observed that the population for Afghanistan increased and decreased within various historical periods. Notice that the trend lines are calculated along the entire date range. What if we want to see different trend lines for those time periods?

One option is to simply select the marks in the view for the time period of interest. Tableau will, by default, calculate a trend line for the current selection. Here, for example, the points for Afghanistan from 1980 to 1988 have been selected and a new trend is displayed:

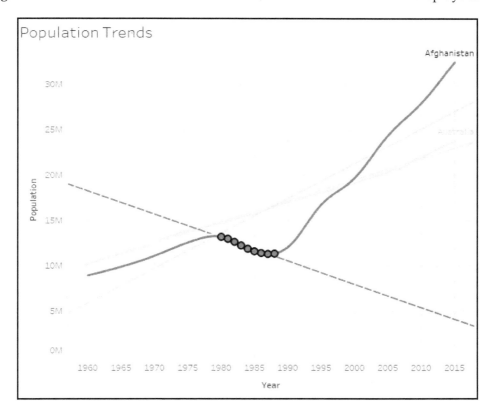

Another option is to instruct Tableau to draw distinct trend lines using a discrete field on **Rows**, **Columns**, or **Color**.

Go ahead and create a calculated field called **Period** that defines discrete values for the different historical periods using code like this:

```
IF [Year] <= 1979
    THEN "1960 to 1979"
ELSEIF [Year] <= 1988
    THEN "1980 to 1988"
ELSE "1988 to 2015"
END
```

When you place it on columns, you'll get a header for each time period, which breaks the lines and causes separate trends to be shown for each time period. You'll also observe that Tableau keeps the full date range in the axis for each period. You can set an independent range by right-clicking one of the date axes by selecting **Edit Axis**, and then checking the option for **Independent axis** range for each row or column.

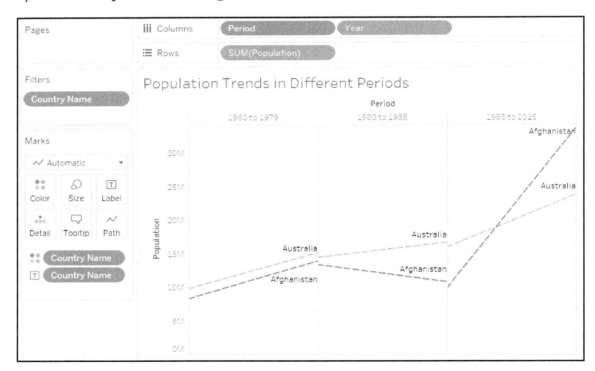

In this view, transparency has been applied to **Color** to help the trend lines stand out. Additionally, the axis for **Year** was hidden (by unchecking the **Show Header** option on the field). Now you can clearly see the difference in trends for different periods of time. Australia's trends only slightly change in each period. Afghanistan's trends were quite different.

# Customizing trend lines

Let's take a look at another example, which will allow us to consider various options for trend lines. Using the **Real Estate Listings** data source, create a view similar to this one:

Here we've created a scatterplot with the sum of **Size (Sq Ft)** on **Columns** to define the X-axis and the sum of **Price** on **Rows** to define the Y axis. **Address** has been added to the **Detail** of the **Marks** card to define the level of aggregation. So each mark on the scatterplot is a distinct address at a location defined by the size and price. **Type of Sale** has been placed on **Color**. Trend lines have been shown. Based on Tableau's default settings there are three: one trend line per color. The confidence bands have been hidden.

Assuming a good model, the trend lines demonstrate how much and how quickly **Price** is expected to rise with an increase in size for each type of sale.

In this data set we have two fields, **Address** and **ID**, either of which define a unique record. Adding one of those fields to the level of detail effectively dis-aggregates the data and allows us to plot a mark for each address. Sometimes you may not have a field in the data that defines uniqueness. In those cases, you can disaggregate the data by unchecking **Aggregate Measures** from the **Analysis** menu. Alternately, you can use the drop-down menu on each of the measure fields on **Rows** and **Columns** to change them from measures to dimensions while keeping them continuous. As dimensions, each individual value will define a mark. Keeping them continuous will retain the axes required for trend lines.

Let's consider some of the options available for trend lines. You can edit trend lines by using the menu and navigating to **Analysis | Trend Lines | Edit Trend Lines...** or by right-clicking on a trend line and then selecting **Edit Trend Lines...**. When you do, you'll see a dialog box similar to this:

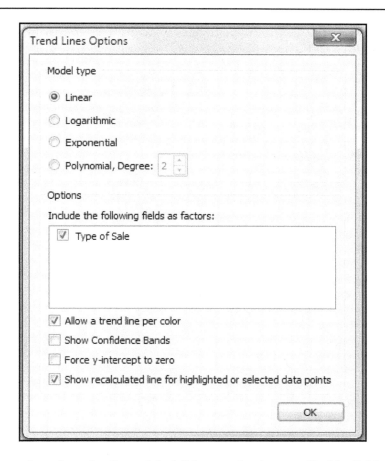

Here, you have options for selecting a **Model type**, selecting applicable fields as factors in the model, allowing discrete colors to define distinct trend lines, showing confidence bands, and forcing the y-intercept to zero. We'll examine these options in further detail. For now, experiment with the options for a bit. Notice how either removing the **Type of Sale** field as a factor or unchecking the **Allow a trend line per color** option results in a single trend line.

You can also see the result of excluding a field as a factor in the following view where **Type of Sale** has been added to **Rows**:

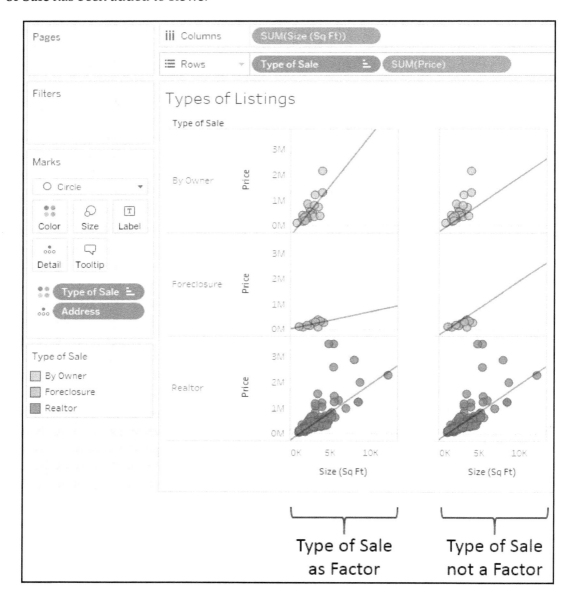

As represented in the left portion of the preceding screenshot, **Type of Sale** is included as a factor. This results in a distinct trend line for each type of sale. When **Type of Sale** is excluded as a factor of the same trend line, which is the overall trend for all types, it is drawn three times. This technique can be quite useful for comparing subsets of data to the overall trend.

# Trend models

We'll return to the original view and stick with a single trend line as we consider the trend models available. The following models can be selected from the **Trend Line Options** window:

- **Linear**: We'd use this model if we assumed that, as **Size** increases, the **Price** will increase at a constant rate. No matter how much **Size** increased, we'd expect **Price** to increase such that new data points fell close to the straight line:

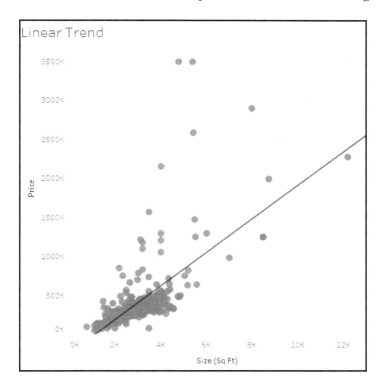

- **Logarithmic**: We'd use this model if we expect that there is a law of diminishing returns in effect. That is, size can only increase so much before buyers will stop paying much more:

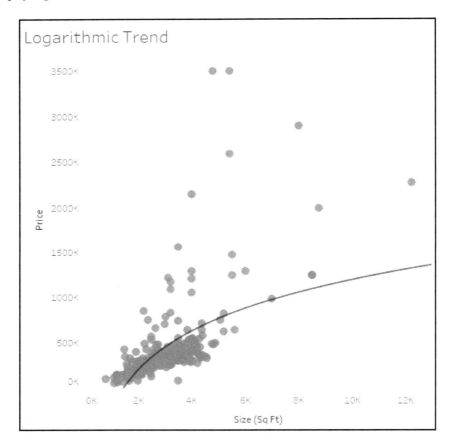

- **Exponential**: We'd use this model to test the idea that each additional increase in size results in a dramatic (exponential!) increase in price:

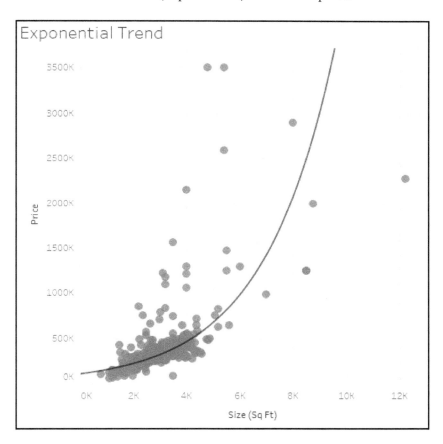

- **Polynomial**: We'd use this model if we felt the relationship between **Size** and **Price** was complex and followed more of an **S** shape curve where, initially, increasing the size dramatically increased the price but at some point price leveled. You can set the degree of the polynomial model anywhere from two to eight. The trend line shown here is a 3rd degree polynomial:

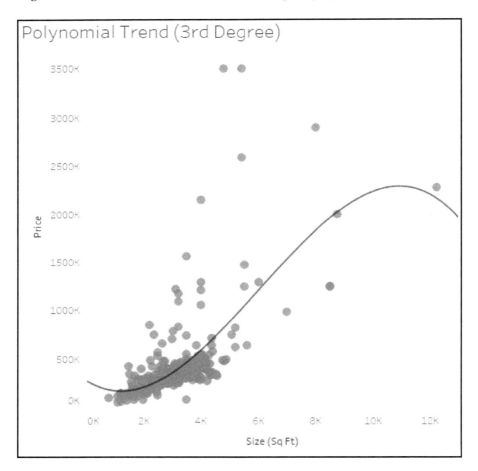

# Analyzing trend models

It can be useful to observe trend lines, but often we'll want to understand if the trend model we've selected is statistically meaningful. Fortunately, Tableau gives us some visibility into trend models and calculations.

Simply hovering over a single trend line will reveal the formula as well as the **R-Squared** and **P-Value** for that trend line:

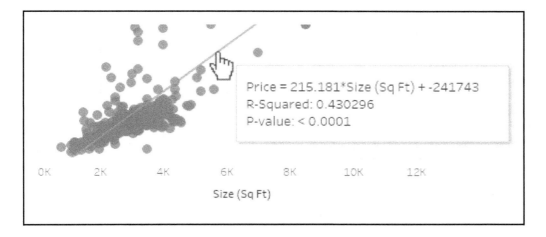

A **P-value** is a statistical concept that describes the probability that the results of assuming no relationship between values (random chance) are at least as close as results predicted by the trend model. A **P-value** of 5% (.05) would indicate a 5% chance of random chance describing the relationship between values at least as well as the trend model. This is why a **P-value** of 5% or less is considered to indicate a significant trend model. If your **P-value** is higher than 5% then you should not consider that trend to significantly describe any correlation.

Additionally, you can see a much more detailed description of the trend model by navigating to **Analysis | TrendLines | Describe Trend Model...** from the menu or by using the similar menu from a right-click on the view's pane. When you view the trend model, you will see the **Describe Trend Model** window:

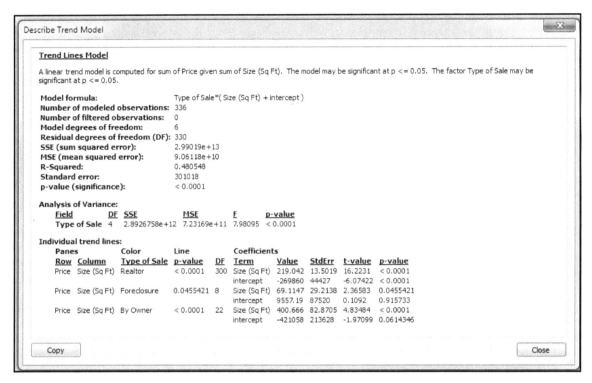

You can also get a trend model description in the worksheet description, which is available from the **Worksheet** menu, or by pressing *Ctrl + e*. The worksheet description includes quite a bit of other useful summary information about the current view.

The wealth of statistical information shown in the window includes a description of the trend model, the formula, number of observations, and P-value for the model as a whole as well as for each trend line. Notice that, in the window shown above, the **Type** field was included as a factor defining three trend lines. At times, you may observe that the model as a whole is statistically significant even though one or more trend lines may not be.

Additional summary statistical information can be displayed in Tableau Desktop for a given view by showing the **Summary**. From the menu, select **Worksheet | Show Summary**. The information displayed in the summary can be expanded using the drop-down menu on the **Summary** card.

| Summary | |
| --- | ---: |
| Count: | 336 |
| **SUM(Price)** | |
| Sum: | 134,239,384 |
| Average: | 399,521.98 |
| Minimum: | 50,000 |
| Maximum: | 3,500,000 |
| Median: | 300,000.00 |
| Standard deviation: | 414,528 |
| First quartile: | 211,500.00 |
| Third quartile: | 410,000.00 |
| Skewness: | 4.59 |
| Excess Kurtosis: | 25.74 |
| **SUM(Size (Sq Ft))** | |
| Sum: | 1,001,318 |
| Average: | 2,980.11 |
| Minimum: | 784 |
| Maximum: | 12,200 |
| Median: | 2,800.50 |
| Standard deviation: | 1,264 |
| First quartile: | 2,108.50 |
| Third quartile: | 3,627.00 |
| Skewness: | 2.27 |
| Excess Kurtosis: | 10.95 |

Tableau also gives you the ability to export data, including data related to trend models. This allows you to more deeply, and even visually, analyze the trend model itself. Let's analyze the 3rd degree polynomial trend line of the real estate price and size scatterplot without any factors. To export data related to the current view, use the menu and select **Worksheet | Export | Data**. The data will be exported as a **Microsoft Access Database** (`.mdb`) and you will be prompted where to save the file.

The ability to export data to Access is limited to a PC only. If you are using a Mac, you won't have the option. In this case, you may wish to read through this section for informational purpose.

On the **Export Data to Access** screen, specify an Access table name and select whether you wish to export data from the entire view or the current selection. You may also specify that Tableau should connect to the data. This will generate the data source and make it available with the specified name in the current workbook:

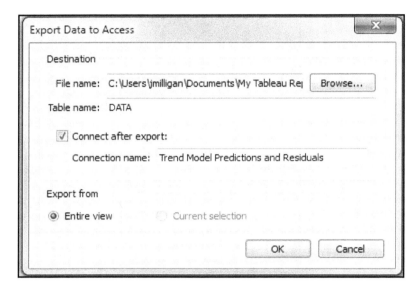

The new data source connection will contain all the fields that were in the original view as well as additional fields related to the trend model. This allows us to build a view such as the following using the residuals and predictions:

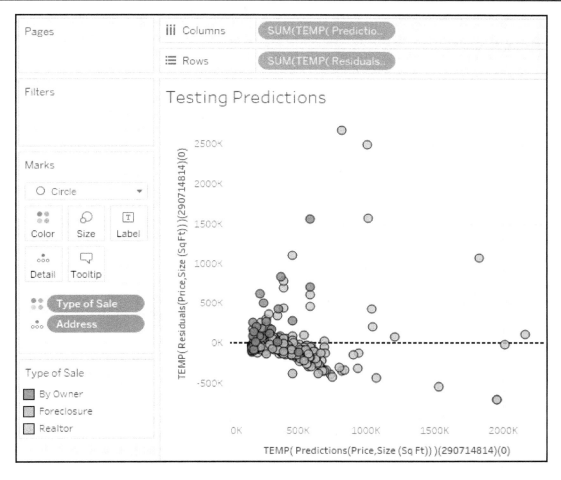

A scatterplot of predictions (*X* axis) and residuals (*Y* axis) allows you to visually see how far each mark was from the location predicted by the trend line. It also allows you to see if residuals are distributed evenly on either side of zero. An uneven distribution would likely indicate problems with the trend model.

You can include this new view along with the original in a dashboard to explore the trend model visually. Use the highlight button on the toolbar to highlight by the **Address** field:

With the highlight action defined, selecting marks in one view will allow you to see them in the other. You could extend this technique to export multiple trend models and dashboards to evaluate several trend models at the same time:

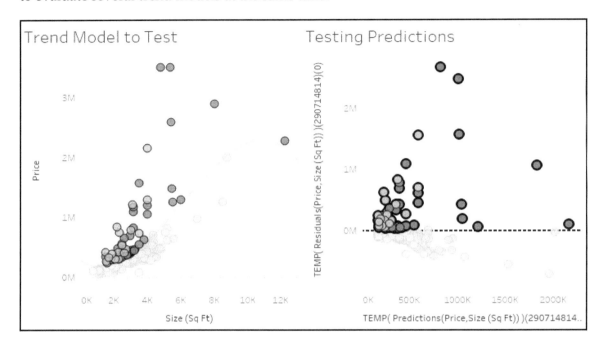

 You can achieve even more sophisticated statistical analysis by leveraging Tableau's ability to integrate with R. **R** is an open source statistical analysis platform and programming language with which you can define advanced statistical models. R functions can be called from Tableau using special table calculations (all of which start with `SCRIPT_`). These functions allow you to pass expressions and values to a running R server, which will evaluate the expressions using built-in libraries or custom-written R scripts and return results to Tableau. You can learn more about Tableau and R integration from this whitepaper (you will need to register a free account first): `http://www.tableau.com/learn/whitepapers/using-r-and-tableau`.

# Clustering

Tableau 10 introduces the ability to quickly perform clustering analysis in your visualizations. This allows you to find groups, or clusters, of individual data points that are similar based on any number of variables of your choosing. This can be useful in many different industries and fields of study, for example:

- Marketing may find it useful to determine groups of customers related to each other based on spending amounts, frequency of purchases, times and days of orders, and so on
- Patient care directors in hospitals may benefit from understanding groups of patients related to each other based on diagnoses, medication, length of stay, and number of read missions
- Immunologists may search for related strains of bacteria based on drug resistance or genetic markers
- Renewable energy professionals would like to pinpoint clusters of windmills based on energy production and then correlate that with geographic location

 Tableau uses a standard k-means clustering algorithm that will yield consistent results every time the view is rendered. Tableau will automatically assign the number of clusters (k), but you have the option of adjusting the value as well as assigning any number of variables.

As we consider clustering, we'll turn once again to the **Real Estate** data to see if we can find groupings of related houses on the market and then determine if there is any geographic pattern based on the clusters we find.

Although you can add clusters to any visualization, we'll start with a scatterplot because a scatterplot already allows us to see the relationship between two variables. That will give us some insight into how clustering works and then we can add additional variables to see how the clusters are redefined.

Beginning with a basic scatterplot of **Address** by **Size** and **Price**, switch to the **Analytics** pane, and drag **Cluster** to the view:

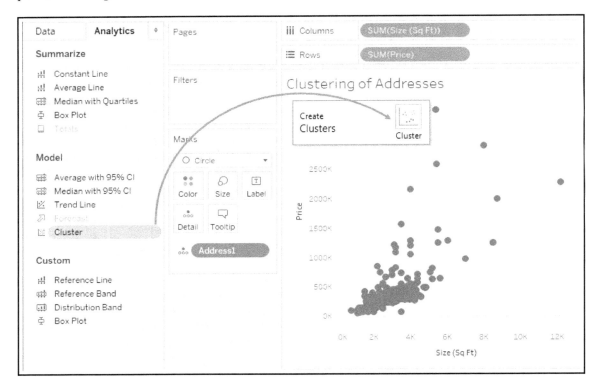

When you drop **Cluster** onto the view, Tableau will generate a new **Clusters** field (automatically placed on **Color** in this case) and will display a **Clusters** window containing the fields used as **Variables** and an option to change the **Number of Clusters**. The **Variables** will contain the measures already in the view by default:

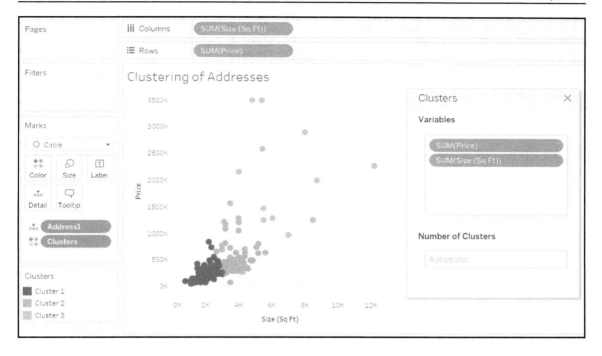

The **Variables** are all the factors that the clustering algorithm uses to determine related data points. The **Number of Clusters** determines into how many groups the data is partitioned. In the view above, you'll observe three clusters of houses:

- Those with low price and smaller size
- Those in the middle
- Those with high price and large size

Because the two variables used for the clusters are the same as those used for the scatterplot, it is relatively easy to see the boundaries of the clusters (you can imagine a couple of diagonal lines partitioning the data).

You can drag and drop nearly any field into and out of the **Variables** section (from the data pane or the view) to add or remove variables. The clusters will automatically update as you do so. Experiment by adding **Bedrooms** to the **Variables** list and observe that there is now some overlap between **Cluster 1** and **Cluster 2** because some larger homes only have two or three bedrooms while some smaller homes might have four or five. The number of bedrooms now helps define the clusters. Remove **Bedrooms** and notice that the clusters are immediately updated again.

Once you have meaningful clusters, you may materialize the clusters as groups in the data source by dragging them from the view and dropping them into the data pane:

The group will not be recalculated at render time as the clusters would, but there are some reasons you may wish to use groups:

- Groups can be used across multiple visualizations and can be used in actions in dashboards
- Groups can be edited and individual members moved between groups if desired
- Group names can be aliased, allowing more descriptive names than **Cluster 1**, **Cluster 2**, and so on
- Groups can be used in calculated fields (starting with Tableau 10), while clusters cannot

For example, the following is a map of the addresses that has been color-coded by the **Address (clusters)** group in the previous view to help us see if there is any geographic correlation to the clusters based on price and size. While, the clusters could have been created directly in this visualization, the group has some of the advantages mentioned:

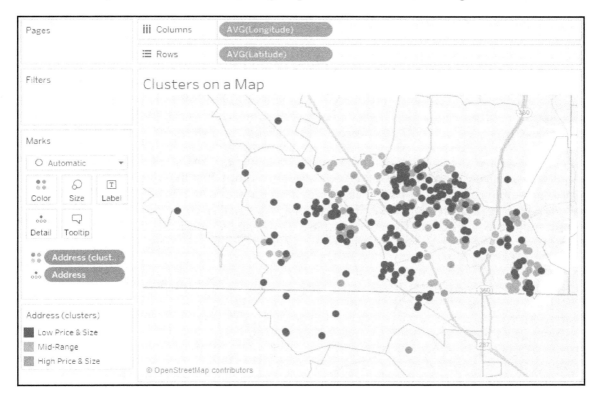

In the view here, each original cluster is now a group that has been aliased to give a better description of the cluster. You can use the drop-down for the group field in the data pane or alternately right click the item in the color legend to edit aliases.

There are a lot of options for editing how maps appear. You can adjust the layers that are shown on maps to help provide additional context for the data you are plotting. From the top menu, navigate to **Maps** | **Map Layers**. The layer options will show in the left side-bar. The map above has had streets, highways, county borders, and zip code borders enabled to give each address a more precise location context. The layers that are available for selection will depend on the zoom level of the map.

In looking at the previous view, you do indeed find neighborhoods that are almost exclusively the **Low Price & Size** (**Cluster 1**) and others that are almost exclusively **Mid-Range** (**Cluster 2**). Consider how a real estate investor might use such a visualization to look for a good buy of a low-priced house in a mid-range neighborhood.

# Distributions

Analyzing distributions can be quite useful. We've already seen that certain calculations are available for determining statistical information such as averages, percentiles, and standard deviations. Tableau also makes it easy to quickly visualize various distributions including confidence intervals, percentages, percentiles, quantiles, and standard deviations.

You may add any of these visual analytic features using the **Analytics** pane (alternately, you can right-click an axis and select **Add Reference Line**). Just like reference lines and bands, distribution analytics can be applied within the scope of a **Table**, **Pane**, or **Cell**. When you drag and drop the desired visual analytic, you'll have options for selecting the scope and the axis. In the following example we've dragged and dropped **Distribution Band** from the **Analytics** pane onto the scope of **Pane** for the axis defined by **Sum(Price)**:

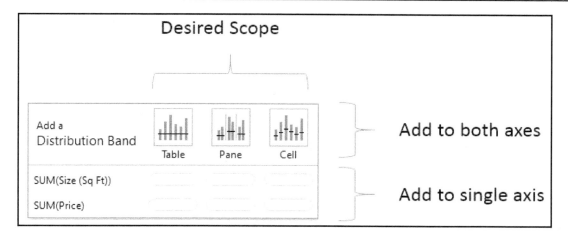

Once you have selected the scope and axis, you will be given options to change settings. You may also edit lines, bands, distributions and box plots by right-clicking the analytic feature in the view or by right-clicking the axis or the reference lines themselves.

As an example, let's take the scatterplot of addresses by price and size with **Type of Sale** on **Columns** in addition to color:

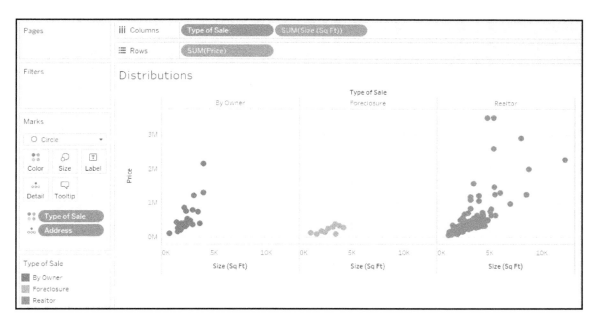

Next, we'll drag and drop **Distribution Band** from the **Analytics** pane onto **Pane** only for the axis defined by **Price**. When we do, we'll get a dialog box to set the options:

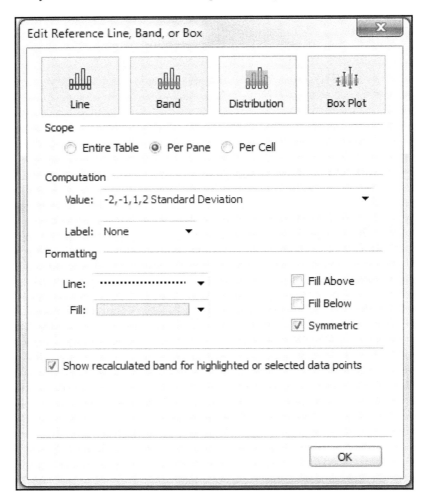

Each specific **Distribution** option specified in the **Value** drop-down menu under **Computation** has unique settings. **Confidence Interval** for example, allows you to specify a percent value for the interval. **Standard Deviation** allows you to enter a comma-delimited list of values that describes how many standard deviations there are, and at what intervals. The previous settings reflect specifying standard deviations of **-2, -1, 1, 2**. After adjusting the **Label** and **Formatting** as shown, you should see results like this:

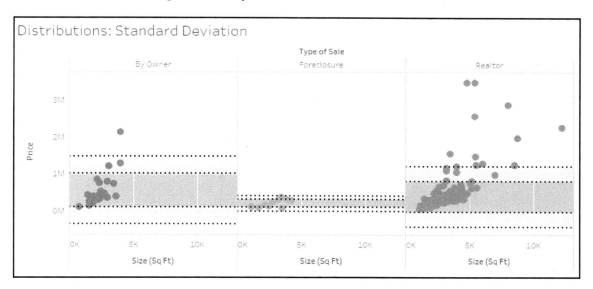

Since you applied the **Standard Deviations** for each Pane, you get different bands for each type of sale. Each axis can support multiple distributions, reference lines, and bands. You could, for example, add an average line in the view to help a viewer understand the center of the standard deviations.

On a scatterplot, using a distribution for each axis can yield a very useful way for analyzing outliers. Showing a single standard deviation for both Area and Price allows you to easily see properties that fall within norms for both, one, or neither. (You might consider purchasing a house that was on the high end of size, but within normal price limits!):

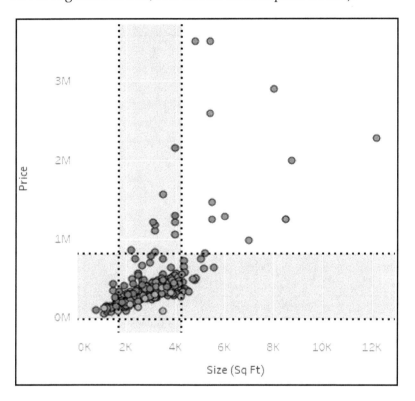

# Forecasting

As we've seen, trend models make predictions. Given a good model, you expect additional data to follow the trend. When the trend is over time, you can get some idea of where future values may fall. However, predicting future values often requires a different type of model. Factors such as seasonality can make a difference not predicted by a trend alone. Starting with version 8.0, Tableau includes built-in forecasting models that can be used to predict and visualize future values.

To use forecasting, you'll need a view that includes a date field or enough date parts for Tableau to reconstruct a date (for example, a Year and a Month field). Tableau 10 also allows for forecasting based on integers instead of dates. You may drag and drop a **Forecast** from the **Analytics** pane, navigate to **Analysis | Forecast | Show Forecast** from the menu, or right click the view's pane and select the option from the context menu.

Here, for example is the view of the population growth over time of **Afghanistan** and **Australia** with forecasts shown:

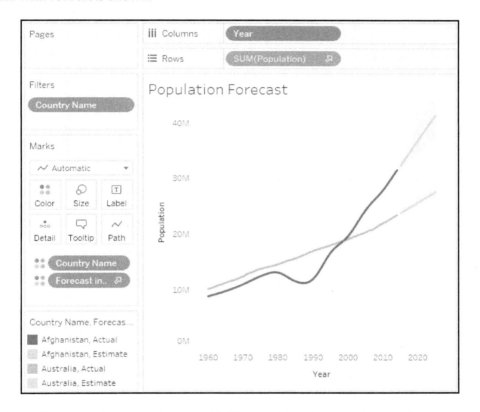

Notice that, when you show the forecast, Tableau adds a forecast icon to the **SUM(Population)** field on **Rows** to indicate that the measure is being forecast. Additionally, Tableau adds a new special **Forecast indicator** field to **Color** so that forecast values are differentiated from actual values in the view.

You can move the **Forecast indicator** field or even copy it (hold the *Ctrl* key while dragging and dropping) to other shelves to further customize your view.

When you edit the forecast by navigating to **Analysis** | **Forecast** | **Forecast Options...** from the menu, or using the right-click context menu on the view, you will be presented with various options for customizing the trend model, like this:

Here, you have options to set the length of the forecast, determine aggregations, customize the model, and set whether you wish to show prediction intervals. The forecast length is set to **Automatic** by default but you can extend the forecast by a custom value.

The options under source data allow you to optionally specify a different grain of data for the model. For example, your view might show a measure by year but you could allow Tableau to query the source data to retrieve values by month and use the finer grain to potentially achieve better results.

Tableau's ability to separately query the data source to obtain data at a finer grain for more precise results works well with relational data sources. However, OLAP data sources are not compatible with this approach which is one reason forecasting is not available when working with cubes.

By default, the last value is excluded from the model. This is useful when you are working with data where the most recent time period is incomplete. For example, when records are added daily, the last (current) month is not complete until the final records are added on the last day of the month. Prior to that last day, the incomplete time period might skew the model unless it is ignored.

The model itself can be set to **Automatic** with or without seasonality or can be customized to set options for seasonality and trend. To understand the options, consider the following view of **Sales** by month from the **Superstore** sample data:

The data displays a distinct cyclical or seasonal pattern. This is very typical for retail sales. Many other data sets will exhibit similar patterns. The results of selecting various custom options are as follows:

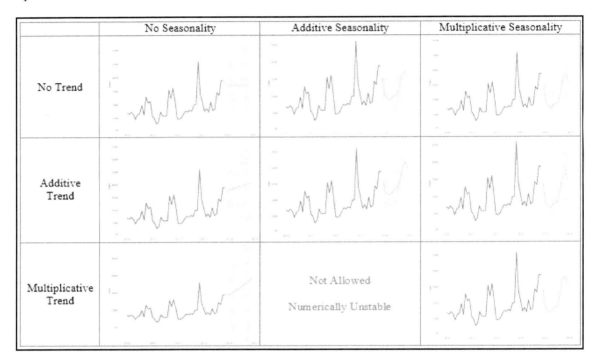

|  | No Seasonality | Additive Seasonality | Multiplicative Seasonality |
|---|---|---|---|
| No Trend | | | |
| Additive Trend | | | |
| Multiplicative Trend | | Not Allowed Numerically Unstable | |

Much like trends, forecast models and summary information can be accessed using the menu. Navigating to **Analysis** | **Forecast** | **Describe Forecast** will display a window with tabs for both the summary and details concerning the model:

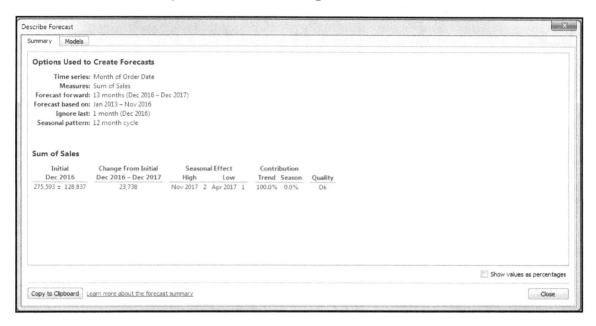

Clicking the link at the bottom of the window will give you much more information on the forecast models used in Tableau.

Forecast models are only enabled given a certain set of conditions. If the option is disabled, ensure that you are connected to a relational database and not OLAP, you're not using table calculations, and you have at least five data points.

# Summary

Tableau provides an extensive set of features for adding value to your analysis. Trend lines allow you to more precisely identify outliers, determine which values fall within the predictions of certain models, and even make predictions of where measurements are expected. Tableau gives extensive visibility into trend models and even allows you to export data containing trend model predictions and residuals. Clusters enable you to find groups of related data points based on various factors. Distributions are useful for understanding a spread of values across a set of data. Forecasting allows for a complex model of trends and seasonality to predict future results. Having a good understanding of these tools will give you the ability to clarify and validate your initial visual analyses.

Next, we'll turn our attention back to the data. We considered very early on how to connect to data and we've been working with data ever since. However, we've spent most of our time working with clean, well-structured data. In the next chapter, we'll consider how to deal with messy data.

# Making Data Work for You

**9**

Up to this point, most of the examples we've looked at in this book assume that data is well structured and fairly clean. Data in the real world isn't so pretty at times. Maybe it's messy or it doesn't have a good structure. It may be missing values or have duplicate values. It might be at the wrong level of detail.

How can you deal with this messy data? Tableau offers quite a bit of flexibility for addressing data issues within the tool. We'll take a look at some of the features and techniques that will enable you to overcome data structure obstacles. Having a good understanding of what data structures work well with Tableau is the key to understanding how you will be able to resolve certain issues.

In this chapter, we'll focus on some principles for structuring data to work well with Tableau, as well as some specific examples of how to address common data issues. This chapter will cover the following topics:

- Structuring data for Tableau
- Techniques for dealing with data structure issues
- Overview of advanced fixes for data problems

## Structuring data for Tableau

We've already seen that Tableau can connect to nearly any data source. Whether it's a built-in direct connection, ODBC, or using the **Tableau Data Extract API** to generate an extract, no data is off limits. However, there are certain structures that make data easier to work within Tableau.

There are two keys to ensuring a good data structure that works well with Tableau:

- Every record of a source data connection should be at a meaningful level of detail
- Every measure contained in the source should match the level of detail or possibly be at a higher level of detail, but should never be at a lower level of detail

For example, let's say you have a table of test scores with one record per classroom in a school. Within the record, you may have three measures: the average GPA for the classroom, the number of students in the class, and the number of students in the school:

| School | Classroom | Average GPA | Number of Students | Number of Students (School) |
|--------|-----------|-------------|--------------------|-----------------------------|
| Pickaway Elementary | 4th Grade | .78 | 153 | 1038 |
| Pickaway Elementary | 5th Grade | .73 | 227 | 1038 |
| Pickaway Elementary | 6th Grade | .84 | 227 | 1038 |
| McCord Elementary | 4th Grade | .82 | 94 | 915 |
| McCord Elementary | 5th Grade | .77 | 89 | 915 |
| McCord Elementary | 6th Grade | .84 | 122 | 915 |

The first two measures are at the same level of detail as the individual record of data (per classroom in the school). Number of Students (School) is at a higher level of detail (per school). As long as you are aware of this, you can do careful analysis. However, you would have a data structure issue if you tried to store each student's GPA in the class record. If the data were structured in such a way (maybe with a column for each student, or a field containing a comma-separated list of student scores), we'd need to do some work to make the data more usable in Tableau.

Understanding the level of detail of the source (often referred to as **granularity**) is vital. Every time you connect to a data source, the very first question you should ask and answer is: what does a single record represent? If, for example, you were to drag and drop the **Number of Records** field into the view and observed 1,000 records, then you should be able to complete the statement, *I have 1,000 _____*. It could be 1,000 students or 1,000 test scores, or 1,000 schools. Having a good grasp of the granularity of the data will help you avoid poor analysis and allow you to determine whether you even have the data necessary for your analysis.

A quick way to find the level of detail of your data is to put the **Number of Records** on the **Text** shelf, and then try different dimensions on the **Rows** shelf. When all the rows display a **1** and the total displayed in the lower-left status bar equals your known number of records, then that dimension (or combination of dimensions) is at the lowest level of detail of your data.

Under the key principle of the granularity of the data, there are certain data structures that allow you to work seamlessly and efficiently in Tableau. Tableau continues to make data integration and shaping easier and more efficient from within Tableau. However, sometimes it is preferable to restructure the data at the source using tools specifically designed for **Extract, Transform, and Load** (ETL). Sometimes, restructuring the source data isn't possible or is not feasible. We'll take a look at some options in Tableau for those cases. For now, let's consider what kinds of data structures work well with Tableau.

# Good structure - tall and narrow instead of short and wide

The two keys to the good structure mentioned above should result in a data structure where a single measure is contained in a single column. You may have multiple different measures, but any single measure should not be divided into multiple columns. Often, the difference is described as wide data versus tall data.

## Wide data

**Wide data** describes a structure in which a measure in a single row is spread over multiple columns. This data is often more *human-readable*. Wide data often results in fewer rows with more columns.

Here is an example of what wide data looks like in this table of population numbers:

| Country name | 1960 | 1961 | 1962 | 1963 | 1964 |
|---|---|---|---|---|---|
| Afghanistan | 8774440 | 8953544 | 9141783 | 9339507 | 9547131 |
| Australia | 10276477 | 10483000 | 10742000 | 10950000 | 11167000 |

Notice that the table contains a row for every country. However, the measure (population) is not stored in a single column for each country. Instead, the measure is stored per country per year. This data is wide because it has a single measure (population) that is being divided into multiple columns (a column for each year). The wide table violates the second key to good structure, in that the measure is at a lower level of detail than the individual record.

# Tall data

**Tall data** describes a structure in which each distinct measure in a row is contained in a single column. Tall data often results in more rows and fewer columns.

Consider the following table, which represents the same data as above, but in a tall structure:

| Country name | Year | Population |
|---|---|---|
| Afghanistan | 1960 | 8774440 |
| Afghanistan | 1961 | 8953544 |
| Afghanistan | 1962 | 9141783 |
| Afghanistan | 1963 | 9339507 |
| Afghanistan | 1964 | 9547131 |
| Australia | 1960 | 10276477 |
| Australia | 1961 | 10483000 |
| Australia | 1962 | 10742000 |
| Australia | 1963 | 10950000 |
| Australia | 1964 | 11167000 |

Now we have more rows (a row for each year for each country). Individual years are no longer separate columns and population measurements are no longer spread across those columns. Instead, one single column represents Year and another single column represents Population. The number of rows has increased while the number of columns has decreased. Now the measure of population is at the same level of detail as the individual row.

# Wide and tall in Tableau

You can easily see the difference between wide and tall data in Tableau. Here is what the wide table of data looks like in the left data window:

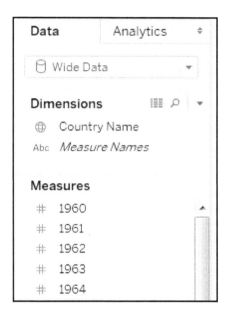

As we'd expect, Tableau treats each column in the table as a separate field. The wide structure of the data works against us. We end up with a separate measure for each year. If you wanted to plot a line graph of population per year, you would likely struggle. What dimension represents the date? What single measure can you use for population?

This isn't to say that you can't use wide data in Tableau. For example, you might use **Measure Names** / **Measure Values** to plot all the **Year** measures in a single view, like this:

You'll notice that every **Year** field has been placed in the **Measure Values** shelf. The good news is that you can create visualizations from poorly structured data. The bad news is that views are often more difficult to create and certain advanced features may not be available. In the preceding view, for example:

- Because Tableau doesn't have a single date or integer dimension, you cannot use forecasting
- Because Tableau doesn't have a date or continuous field on **Columns**, you cannot enable trend lines

- Because each measure is a separate field, you cannot use quick table calculations (such as running total, percent difference, and so on)
- Determining things such as average population across years will require a tedious custom calculation instead of simply changing the aggregation of a measure
- You don't have an axis for the date (just a bunch of headers for the measure names), so you won't be able to add reference lines

In contrast, the tall data looks like this in the data pane:

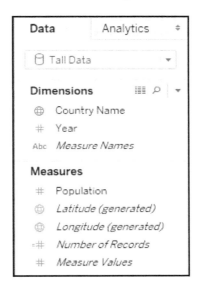

This data source is much easier to work with. There's only one measure (**Population**) and a **Year** dimension to slice the measure. If you want a line chart of the population by year, you can simply drag and drop the **Population** and **Year** fields to **Columns** and **Rows**. Forecasting, trend lines, clustering, averages, standard deviations, and other advanced features will all work as you have come to expect.

# Good structure - star schemas

Assuming they are well designed, star schema data models (such as those used in data warehouses and data marts) work very well with Tableau because they have well-defined granularity, measures, and dimensions. Additionally, if they are implemented well, they can be extremely efficient to query. This allows for a good experience when using live connections in Tableau.

**Star schemas** are so named because they consist of a single fact table surrounded by related dimension tables forming a star pattern. **Fact tables** contain measures at a meaningful granularity and **dimension tables** contain attributes for various related entities. The following diagram illustrates a simple star schema with a single fact table (**Hospital Visit**) and three dimensions (**Patient**, **PrimaryPhysician**, and **Discharge Details**):

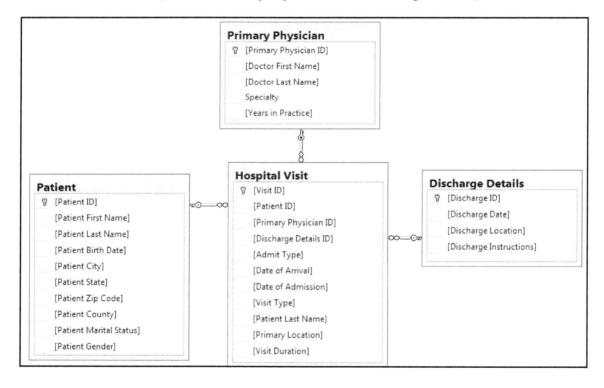

Fact tables are joined to the related dimension using what is often called a **surrogate key** or **foreign key** that references a single dimension record. The fact table defines the level of granularity and contains measures. In this case, **Hospital Visit** has a granularity of one record for each visit. Each visit, in this simple example, is for one patient who saw one primary physician and was discharged. The **Hospital Visit** table explicitly stores a measure of **Visit Duration** and implicitly defines another measure of **Number of Visits** (in other words, **Number of Records**).

Data modeling purists would point out that date values have been stored in the fact table (and even some of the dimensions) above and would instead recommend having a date dimension table, with extensive attributes for each date, and only a surrogate (foreign) key stored in the fact table. A date dimension can be very beneficial. However, Tableau's built-in date hierarchy and extensive date options make storing a date in the fact table a viable option. Consider using a date dimension if you need specific attributes of dates not available in Tableau (for example, which days are corporate holidays), have complex fiscal years, or if you need to support legacy BI reporting tools.

A well-designed star schema allows for the use of inner joins, as every surrogate key should reference a single dimension record. In cases where dimension values are not known or not applicable, special dimension records are used. For example, a **Hospital Visit** that is not yet complete (the patient is still in the hospital) may reference a special record in the **Discharge Details** table marked *Not yet discharged*. When connecting to a star schema in Tableau, start with the fact table and then add the dimension tables, as shown here:

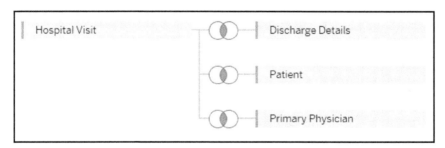

The resulting data connection (shown as an example, but not included in the `Chapter 09` workbook) allows you to see the dimensional attributes by table. The measures come from the single fact table:

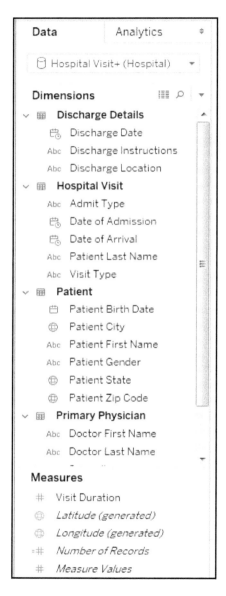

Well-implemented star schemas are particularly attractive for use in live connections because Tableau can gain performance by implementing join culling. **Join culling** is Tableau's elimination of unnecessary joins in queries it sends to the data source engine. For example, if you were to place the **Physician Name** on **Rows** and the average of **Visit Duration** on **Columns** to get a bar chart of average visit duration per physician, then joins to the Treatment and Patient tables may not be needed. Tableau will eliminate unnecessary joins as long as you are using a simple star schema with only joins from the central fact table and have referential integrity enabled in the source or allow Tableau to assume referential integrity (select the data source connection from the **Data** menu or use the context menu from the data source connection and choose **Assume Referential Integrity**).

# Techniques for dealing with data structure issues

In some cases, restructuring data at the source is not an option. The source may be secured and read-only. Or you might not even have access to the original data and instead receive periodic dumps of data in a specific format. In such cases, there are techniques for dealing with structural issues once you have connected to the data in Tableau.

We'll consider some examples of data structure issues to demonstrate some techniques for handling those issues in Tableau. None of the solutions is the *only right way* to resolve the given issue. Often, there are several approaches that might work. Additionally, these are only examples of issues you might encounter. Take time to understand how the proposed solutions build on the foundational principles we've considered in previous chapters and how you can use similar techniques to solve your data issues.

# Restructuring data in Tableau connections

The Excel workbook `World Population Data.xlsx`, included in the `Chapter 09` directory of the resources included with this book, is typical of many Excel documents. Here is what it looks like:

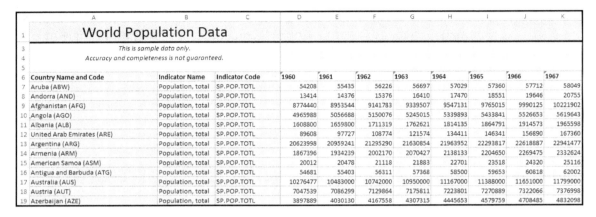

Excel documents like this are often more human-readable but contain multiple issues for data analysis in Tableau. The issues in this particular document include:

- Excessive headers (titles, notes, and formatting) that are not part of the data
- Merged cells
- Country name and code in a single column
- Columns that are likely unnecessary (**Indicator Name** and **Indicator Code**)
- The data is wide: there is a column for each year and the population measure is spread across these columns within a single record

When we initially connect to the Excel document in Tableau, the connection screen will look similar to this:

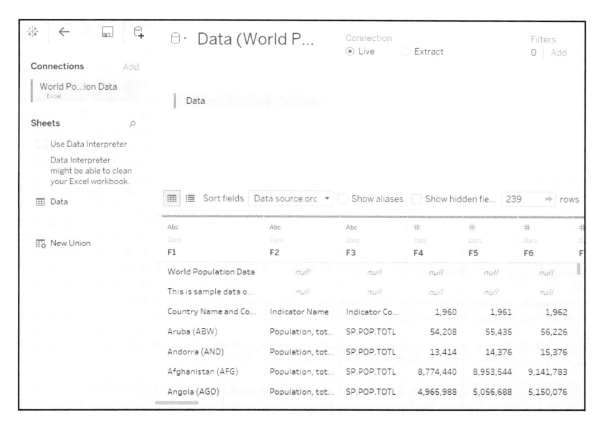

The data preview reveals some of the issues resulting from the poor structure:

- Since the column headers were not in the first Excel row, Tableau gave the defaults of **F1**, **F2**, and so on to each column
- The title **World Population Data** and note about sample data were interpreted as values in column **F1**
- The actual column headers are treated as a row of data (the third row)

Fortunately, these issues can be addressed in the connection window. First, we can correct many of the excessive header issues by turning on the **Tableau Data Interpreter**, a component which specifically identifies and resolves common structural issues in Excel or Google Sheets documents. When you check the **Use Data Interpreter** option, the data preview reveals much better results:

| Country Name and ... | Indicator Name | Indicator Code | 1960 | 1961 | 1962 | 1963 | 1964 | 1965 |
|---|---|---|---|---|---|---|---|---|
| Aruba (ABW) | Population, total | SP.POP.TOTL | 54,208 | 55,435 | 56,226 | 56,697 | 57,029 | 57,360 |
| Andorra (AND) | Population, total | SP.POP.TOTL | 13,414 | 14,376 | 15,376 | 16,410 | 17,470 | 18,551 |
| Afghanistan (AFG) | Population, total | SP.POP.TOTL | 8,774,440 | 8,953,544 | 9,141,783 | 9,339,507 | 9,547,131 | 9,765,015 |
| Angola (AGO) | Population, total | SP.POP.TOTL | 4,965,988 | 5,056,688 | 5,150,076 | 5,245,015 | 5,339,893 | 5,433,841 |
| Albania (ALB) | Population, total | SP.POP.TOTL | 1,608,800 | 1,659,800 | 1,711,319 | 1,762,621 | 1,814,135 | 1,864,791 |
| United Arab Emirates (... | Population, total | SP.POP.TOTL | 89,608 | 97,727 | 108,774 | 121,574 | 134,411 | 146,341 |

Clicking the **Review the results...** link that appears under the checkbox will cause Tableau to generate a new Excel document that is color-coded to indicate how the data interpreter parsed the Excel document. Use this feature to verify that Tableau has correctly interpreted the Excel document and retained the data you expect.

Observe the elimination of the excess headers and the correct names of columns. A few additional issues still need to be corrected.

First, we can hide the **Indicator Name** and **Indicator Code** columns if we feel they are not useful for our analysis. Clicking the drop-down arrow on a column header reveals a menu of options. **Hide** will keep the field from showing in the data pane and even prevent it from being stored in extracts:

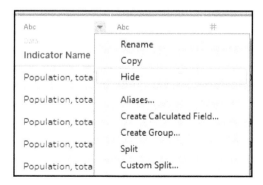

Second, we can use the option on the same menu to split the **Country Name** and **Country Code** column into two columns so we can work with the name and code separately. In this case, the **Split** option on the menu works well and Tableau perfectly splits the data, even removing the parentheses from around the code. In cases where the split option does not initially work, try the **Custom Split...** option. We'll also use the **Rename...** option to rename the split fields from `Country Name and Code - Split 1` and `Country Name and Code - Split 2` to `Country Name` and `Country Code` respectively. Then we'll Hide the original **Country Name** and **Country Code** field.

At this point, most of the data structure issues have been remedied. However, you'll recognize that the data is in a **wide** format and we previously saw the issues we'll run into:

| Country Name | Country Code | 1961 | 1962 | 1963 | 1964 | 1965 | 1966 |
| --- | --- | --- | --- | --- | --- | --- | --- |
| Aruba | ABW | 55,435 | 56,226 | 56,697 | 57,029 | 57,360 | 57,712 |
| Andorra | AND | 14,376 | 15,376 | 16,410 | 17,470 | 18,551 | 19,646 |
| Afghanistan | AFG | 8,953,544 | 9,141,783 | 9,339,507 | 9,547,131 | 9,765,015 | 9,990,125 |
| Angola | AGO | 5,056,688 | 5,150,076 | 5,245,015 | 5,339,893 | 5,433,841 | 5,526,653 |
| Albania | ALB | 1,659,800 | 1,711,319 | 1,762,621 | 1,814,135 | 1,864,791 | 1,914,573 |
| United Arab Emirates | ARE | 97,727 | 108,774 | 121,574 | 134,411 | 146,341 | 156,890 |

Our final step is to **pivot** the **Year** columns. This means that we'll reshape the data in such a way that every country will have a row for every year. Select all the **Year** columns by clicking the **1960** column, scroll to the far right, and hold *Shift* key while clicking the **2013** column. Finally, use the drop-down menu on any one of the year fields and select the **Pivot** option.

The result is two columns (**Pivot field names** and **Pivot field values**) in place of all the year columns. Rename the two new columns **Year** and **Population**. Your dataset is now narrow and tall instead of wide and short.

Finally, notice from the icon on the **Year** column that it is recognized by Tableau as a text field. Clicking the icon will allow you to change the data type directly. In this case, selecting **Date** will result in NULL values, but changing the data type to a **Number (whole)** will give you integer values that will work well in most cases:

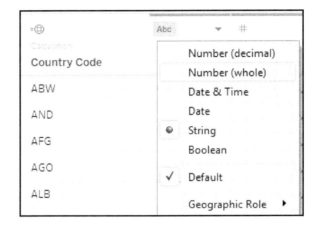

Alternatively, you could use the first drop-down menu on the **Year** field and select **Create Calculated Field...** This would allow you to create a calculated field named **Year (date)** which parses the year string as a date with code like this:

`DATE(DATEPARSE("yyyy", [Year]))` This code will parse the string and then convert it to a simple date without time. You can then hide the original **Year** field. You can hide any field, even if it is used in calculations, so long as it isn't used in a view. This leaves you with a very clean data set.

The final data set is far easier to work with in Tableau than the original:

| Country Name | Country Code | Year | Population |
|---|---|---|---|
| Aruba | ABW | 1961 | 55,435 |
| Andorra | AND | 1961 | 14,376 |
| Afghanistan | AFG | 1961 | 8,953,544 |
| Angola | AGO | 1961 | 5,056,688 |
| Albania | ALB | 1961 | 1,659,800 |
| United Arab Emirates | ARE | 1961 | 97,727 |
| Argentina | ARG | 1961 | 20,959,241 |
| Armenia | ARM | 1961 | 1,934,239 |
| American Samoa | ASM | 1961 | 20,478 |
| Antigua and Barbuda | ATG | 1961 | 55,403 |
| Australia | AUS | 1961 | 10,483,000 |

# Union files together

Often, you may have multiple individual files or tables that, together, represent the entire set of data. For example, you might have a process that creates a new monthly data dump as a new text file in a certain directory. Or you might have an Excel file where data for each department is contained in a separate sheet.

The ability to union file-based data sources together was introduced in Tableau 9 and the capabilities are expanded in Tableau 10. A **union** is a concatenation of data tables that brings together rows of each table into a single data source. For example, consider the following three tables of data:

# Originals

| Name | Occupation | Bank account balance |
|------|-----------|----------------------|
| Luke | Farmer | $2,000 |
| Leia | Princess | $50,000 |
| Han | Smuggler | -$20,000 |

# Prequels

| Name | Occupation | Bank account balance |
|------|-----------|----------------------|
| Watto | Junk Dealer | $9,000 |
| Darth Maul | Face Painter | $10,000 |
| Jar Jar | Sith Lord | -$100,000 |

# Sequels

| Name | Occupation | Bank account balance |
|------|-----------|----------------------|
| Rey | Scavenger | $600 |
| Poe | Pilot | $30,000 |
| Kylo | Unemployed | $0 |

A union of these tables would give a single table containing the rows of each individual table:

| Name | Occupation | Bank account balance |
|------|-----------|----------------------|
| Luke | Farmer | $2,000 |
| Leia | Princess | $50,000 |
| Han | Smuggler | -$20,000 |
| Watto | Junk Dealer | $9,000 |
| Darth Maul | Face Painter | $10,000 |
| Jar Jar | Sith Lord | -$100,000 |
| Rey | Scavenger | $600 |
| Poe | Pilot | $30,000 |
| Kylo | Unemployed | $0 |

Tableau allows you to union together tables from file-based data sources, including the following:

- Text files (`.csv`, `.txt`, and so on)
- Sheets (tabs) within Excel documents
- Subtables within an Excel sheet
- Multiple Excel documents (Tableau 10)
- Google Sheets (Tableau 10)

 Use the **Data Interpreter** feature to find subtables in Excel or Google Sheets. They will show as additional tables of data in the left sidebar.

To create a union in Tableau, create a new data source from the menu, toolbar, or **Data Source** screen, starting with one of the files you wish to be part of the union. Then drag additional files into the **Drag table to union** drop zone just beneath the existing table in the designer:

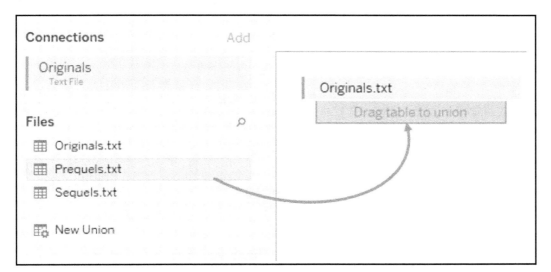

Once you've created a union, you can use the drop-down menu on the table in the designer to configure options for the union. Alternatively, you can drag the **New Union** object from the left sidebar into the designer to replace the existing table. This will reveal options for creating and configuring the union:

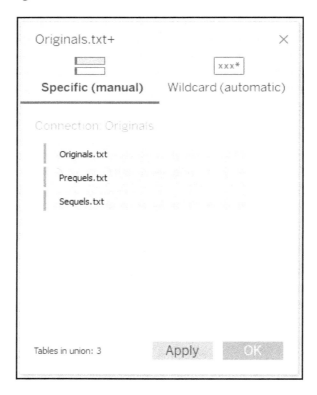

The **Specific (manual)** tab allows you to drag tables into and out of the union. The **Wildcard (automatic)** tab allows you to specify wildcards for filenames and sheets (for Excel and Google Sheets) that will automatically include files and sheets in the union based on a wildcard match.

 Use the **Wildcard (automatic)** feature if you anticipate additional files being added in the future. For example, if you have a specific directory where data files are dumped on a periodic basis, the wildcard feature will ensure you don't have to manually edit the connection. As of this writing, the union wildcard feature is slated for release in Tableau 10.1.

Once you have defined the union, you can use the resulting data source to visualize the data. Additionally, a union table may be joined with other tables in the designer window, giving you a lot of flexibility in working with data!

In a union, Tableau will match columns between tables by name. Columns that exist in one file/table but not in others will appear as part of the union table but values will be NULL in files/tables where the column did not exist. For example, if one of the files above contained a column named **Job** instead of **Occupation**, the final union table would contain a column named **Job** and another named **Occupation**, with NULL values where the column did not exist. You can merge the mismatched columns by selecting the columns and using the drop-down menu. This will **coalesce** (keep the first non-null of) the values per row of data in a single new column:

| Abc Name | Abc Occupation | Abc Job | Abc | Abc |
| --- | --- | --- | --- | --- |
| Luke | Farmer | *null* | Rename | |
| Leia | Princess | *null* | Copy | |
| Han | Smuggler | *null* | Hide | |
| Watto | *null* | Junk Dealer | Create Calculated Field... | |
| Darth Maul | *null* | Face Painter | Prequels | Prequels |
| Jar Jar | *null* | Sith Lord | Pivot | |
| Rey | Scavenger | *null* | Merge Mismatched Fields | |
| Poe | Pilot | *null* | Sequels | Sequels |
| Kylo | Unemployed | *null* | Sequels | Sequels |

When you create a union, Tableau will include one or more new fields in your data source that help you identify the file, sheet, and table where the data originated. **Path** will contain the file path (including filename), **Sheet** will contain the sheet name (for Excel or Google Sheets), and **Table Name** will contain the subtable or text file name.

You can use these fields to help you identify data issues and also to extend your data set as needed. For example, if you had a directory of monthly data dump files named `2016-01.txt`, `2016-02.txt`, `2016-03.txt`, and so on but no actual date field in the files, you could obtain the date using a calculated field with code like this:

```
DATEPARSE('yyyy-MM', [Table Name] )
```

# Cross-database joins

Tableau 10 introduces the ability to join data across data connections. This means you can join tables of data from completely different database and file formats. For example, you could join a table in SQL Server with a union table of text files with a Google Sheets document.

You'll recall that the concept of joins and the specifics of cross-database joins were introduced in `Chapter 2`, *Working with Data in Tableau*. While cross-database joins are quite useful in bringing together **disparate data** sources (data contained in different systems and formats), they can be used to solve other data issues too, such as reshaping data to make it easier to meet your objectives in Tableau.

 You can work through the following example in the `Chapter 9` workbook; however, the server database data source is simulated with a text file (`Patient Visits.txt`) and you will not need to generate any custom SQL mentioned in the following section.

Let's say you have a table in a server database (such as SQL Server or Oracle) that contains one row per hospital patient and includes the **Admit Date** and **Discharge Date** as separate columns for each patient:

| Patient ID | Patient Name | Admit Date | Discharge Date |
|---|---|---|---|
| 1 | David | 12/1/2016 | 12/20/2016 |
| 2 | Solomon | 12/3/2016 | 12/7/2016 |
| 3 | Asa | 12/5/2016 | 12/22/2016 |
| 4 | Jehoshaphat | 12/5/2016 | 12/6/2016 |
| 5 | Joash | 12/9/2016 | 12/16/2016 |
| 6 | Amaziah | 12/10/2016 | 12/14/2016 |
| 7 | Uzziah | 12/12/2016 | 12/24/2016 |
| 8 | Jotham | 12/16/2016 | 12/29/2016 |
| 9 | Hezekiah | 12/18/2016 | 12/22/2016 |
| 10 | Josiah | 12/22/2016 | 12/23/2016 |

While there is nothing wrong with the way this data set is structured, you would find it difficult if you wanted to visualize the number of patients in the hospital day by day for the month of December.

For one thing, which date field do you use for the axis? Even if you pivoted the table, so that you had all dates in one field, you would find that you had gaps in the data. **Sparse data**, data in which records do not exist for certain values, is quite common. Specifically, in this case, you have a single record for each admit or discharge date but no records for the days in between.

Sometimes, it might be an option to restructure the data at the source, but if the database is locked down, you may not have that option. You could also use Tableau's ability to fill in gaps in the data (**data densification**) to solve the problem. However, that solution could be intricate and potentially brittle or difficult to maintain.

An alternative is to use a cross database join to create the rows for all dates. So, you might quickly create an Excel sheet with a list of dates you want to see, like this:

|  | A | B |
|---|---|---|
| 1 | Date | Join |
| 2 | 12/1/2016 | 1 |
| 3 | 12/2/2016 | 1 |
| 4 | 12/3/2016 | 1 |
| 5 | 12/4/2016 | 1 |
| 6 | 12/5/2016 | 1 |
| 7 | 12/6/2016 | 1 |
| 8 | 12/7/2016 | 1 |
| 9 | 12/8/2016 | 1 |
| 10 | 12/9/2016 | 1 |
| 26 | 12/25/2016 | 1 |
| 27 | 12/26/2016 | 1 |
| 28 | 12/27/2016 | 1 |
| 29 | 12/28/2016 | 1 |
| 30 | 12/29/2016 | 1 |
| 31 | 12/30/2016 | 1 |
| 32 | 12/31/2016 | 1 |

The Excel file includes a record for each date and also a column named **Join** which has the value 1 for each row. This will be used to **cross-join** (join every row from one table with every row in another) the data between the database table and the Excel table. With this accomplished, you will have a row for every patient for every date.

Joining every record in one dataset with every record in another data set creates what is called a **Cartesian product**. The resulting data set will have N1 * N2 rows (where N1 is the number of rows in the first data set and N2 is the number of rows in the second). Take care when using this approach. It works well with smaller datasets. As you work with ever larger data sets, the Cartesian product may quickly grow so large as to be untenable.

You might have noticed that the original database table does not contain a **Join** field, and we already established that modifying the data structure in the database is not an option in this case. So what field will you use for the join?

With many server-based data sources, you can use **Custom SQL** as a data source. On the **Data Source** screen, with the **Patient Visits** table in the designer, one could use the top menu to select **Data | Convert to Custom SQL** to edit the SQL script Tableau uses for the source. Alternatively, you can write your own custom SQL using the **New Custom SQL** object on the left sidebar:

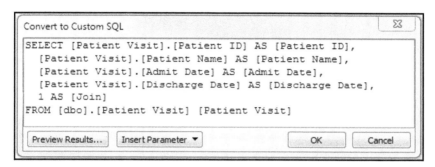

The preceding script has been modified to include `1 AS [Join]` to create a field called **Join** with a value of `1` for every row. At this point, we can **Add** a new connection and join the Excel file we created above on the **Join** field:

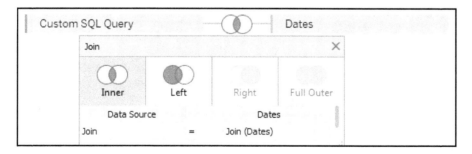

This new data set contains a record for every patient for every date and we can create a quick calculation to see whether a patient should be counted as part of the hospital population on any given date. The calculated field, named `Patients in Hospital`, has the following code:

```
IF [Admit Date] <= [Date] AND [Discharge Date] >= [Date]
THEN 1
ELSE 0
END
```

This allows us to easily visualize the flow of patients, and even potentially perform advanced analytics based on averages, trends, and even forecasting:

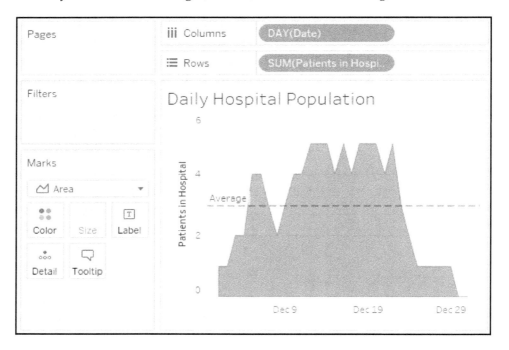

Ultimately, for a long-term solution, you might want to speak to IT about developing a server-based data source that gives the structure needed for the desired analysis. But cross database joins allowed us to achieve the analysis without waiting on a long development cycle.

# Working with different Level of Detail

Remember that the two keys to good structure are having a level of detail that is meaningful and having measures that match the level of detail or that are possibly at higher levels of detail. Measures at lower levels tend to result in wide data, and can make some analysis difficult or even impossible. Measures at higher levels of detail can, at times, be useful. As long as we are aware of how to handle them correctly, we can avoid some pitfalls.

Consider, for example, this data (included as `Apartment Rent.xlsx` in the `Chapter 9` directory), which gives us a single record each month per apartment:

| Apartment | Month | Rent Collected | Square Feet |
|---|---|---|---|
| A | Jan | $0 | 900 |
|  | Feb | $0 | 900 |
|  | Mar | $0 | 900 |
|  | Apr | $0 | 900 |
|  | May | $0 | 900 |
|  | Jun | $1,500 | 900 |
|  | Jul | $1,500 | 900 |
|  | Aug | $1,500 | 900 |
|  | Sep | $1,500 | 900 |
|  | Oct | $1,500 | 900 |
|  | Nov | $1,500 | 900 |
|  | Dec | $1,500 | 900 |
| B | Jan | $1,200 | 750 |
|  | Feb | $1,200 | 750 |
|  | Mar | $1,200 | 750 |
|  | Apr | $1,200 | 750 |
|  | May | $1,200 | 750 |
|  | Jun | $1,200 | 750 |
|  | Jul | $0 | 750 |
|  | Aug | $0 | 750 |
|  | Sep | $0 | 750 |
|  | Oct | $0 | 750 |
|  | Nov | $0 | 750 |
|  | Dec | $0 | 750 |

The two measures are really at different Levels of Detail:

- **Rent Collected** matches the level of detail of the data, as there is a record of how much rent was collected for each apartment for each month
- **Square Feet**, on the other hand, does not change month to month. Rather, it is at the higher level of apartment only

This can be observed when we remove the date from the view and look at everything at the apartment level:

Notice that the **Sum** of **Rent Collected** makes perfect sense. You can add up rent collected per month and get a meaningful result per apartment. However, you cannot **Sum** up **Square Feet** and get a meaningful result per apartment. Other aggregations such as average, minimum, and maximum do give the right results per apartment.

However, imagine that you were asked to come up with the ratio of total rent collected to square feet per apartment. You know it will be an aggregate calculation because you have to sum the rent collected prior to dividing. But which of these is the correct calculation?

- SUM([Rent Collected]) / SUM([Square Feet])
- SUM([Rent Collected]) / AVG([Square Feet])
- SUM([Rent Collected]) / MIN([Square Feet])
- SUM([Rent Collected]) / MAX([Square Feet])

The first one is obviously wrong. We've already seen square feet should not be added each month. Any of the final three would be correct if we ensure **Apartment** continues to define the level of detail of the view.

However, once we look at a view that has a different Level of Detail (for example, the total for all apartments or monthly for multiple apartments), the calculations don't work. To understand why, consider what happens when we turn on column grand totals (from the menu, navigate to **Analysis | Totals | Show Column Grand Totals** or drag and drop **Totals** from the **Analytics** tab):

| Apartment | Rent Collected | Sum of Square Feet | Avg. Square Feet | Min. Square Feet | Max. Square Feet |
|---|---|---|---|---|---|
| A | $10,500 | 10,800 | 900 | 900 | 900 |
| B | $7,200 | 9,000 | 750 | 750 | 750 |
| Grand Total | $17,700 | 19,800 | 825 | 750 | 900 |

The problem here is that the Grand Total line is at the Level of Detail of *all apartments (for all months)*. What we really want as the **Grand Total** of square feet is **900 + 750 = 1,650**. But here, the sum of square feet is the addition of square feet for all apartments for all months. The average won't work. The minimum finds the value **750** as the smallest measure for all apartments in the data. The maximum likewise picks **900** as the single largest value. So none of the proposed calculations above would work at any Level of Detail that does not include the individual apartment.

You can adjust how subtotals and grand totals are computed by clicking the individual value and using the drop-down menu to select how the total is computed. Alternatively, right-click the active measure field and select **Total Using**. You can change how all measures are totaled at once from the menu by navigating to **Analysis | Totals | Total All Using**. Using this **two pass total** technique could result in correct results in the view above, but would not universally solve the problem. For example, if you wanted to show price per square foot for each month (by removing Apartment from the view completely), you'd have the same issue.

Fortunately, Tableau gives us the ability to work with different levels of detail in a view. Using **Level of Detail (LoD)** calculations, which we encountered briefly in Chapter 4, *Using Row-Level, Aggregate, and Level of Detail Calculations*, we can calculate the square feet per apartment.

Here, we'll use a fixed LoD calculation to keep the level of detail fixed at apartment. We'll create a calculated field named Square Feet perApartment with the code:

```
{ INCLUDE [Apartment] : MIN([Square Feet]) }
```

The curly braces surround an LoD calculation and the keyword INCLUDE indicates that we want to include **Apartment** as part of the level of detail for the calculation, even if it is not included in the view level of detail. MIN is used in the preceding code, but MAX or AVG could have been used as well because all give the same result per apartment.

As you can see, the calculation returns the correct result in the view at the apartment level and at the grand total level, where Tableau includes apartment to find **900** (the minimum for A) and **750** (the minimum for B) and sum them to get **1,650**:

| Apartment | Rent Collected | Square Feet per Apartment |
|---|---|---|
| A | $10,500 | 900 |
| B | $7,200 | 750 |
| Grand Total | $17,700 | 1,650 |

Now we can use the LoD calculated field in another calculation to determine the desired results. We'll create a calculated field named Rent Collected per Square Foot with the code:

```
SUM([Rent Collected]) / SUM([Square Feet per Apartment])
```

When that field is added to the view and formatted to show decimals, the final outcome is correct:

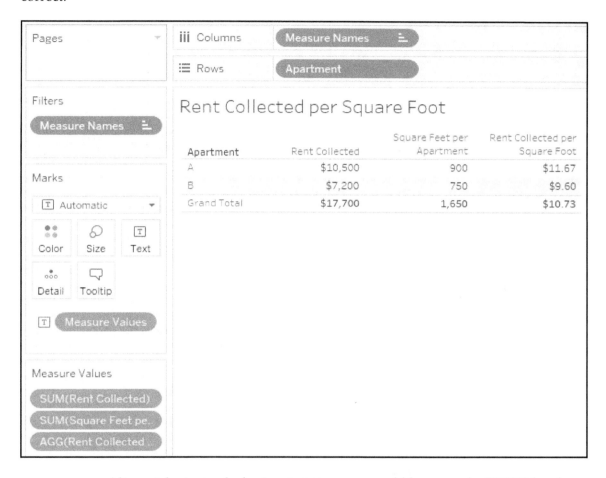

| | Columns | Measure Names | |
| Pages | Rows | Apartment | |

**Rent Collected per Square Foot**

| Apartment | Rent Collected | Square Feet per Apartment | Rent Collected per Square Foot |
|---|---|---|---|
| A | $10,500 | 900 | $11.67 |
| B | $7,200 | 750 | $9.60 |
| Grand Total | $17,700 | 1,650 | $10.73 |

**TIP**

Alternately, instead of using INCLUDE, we could have used a **FIXED** level of detail which is always performed at the Level of Detail of the dimension(s) following the FIXED keywords, regardless of what level of detail is defined in the view. This would have told Tableau to always calculate the minimum square feet per apartment, regardless of what dimensions define the view level of detail. While very useful, be aware that FIXED level of detail calculations are calculated for the entire context (either the entire data set or the subset defined by **context filters**). Using them without understanding this can yield unexpected results.

# Overview of advanced fixes for data problems

In addition to the techniques previously mentioned in this chapter, there are some additional possibilities for dealing with data structure issues. It is outside the scope of this book to develop these concepts fully. However, if you have some familiarity with these approaches, you broaden your ability to deal with challenges as they arise.

1. **Custom SQL**: This can be used in the data connection to resolve some data problems. Beyond giving a field for a cross database join, as we saw previously, custom SQL can be used to radically reshape the data retrieved from the source. Custom SQL is not an option for all data sources but is for many relational databases and for the legacy JET driver connections for Excel and text files. Consider a custom SQL script that takes the wide table of country populations mentioned earlier in this chapter and restructures it into a tall table:

```
SELECT [Country Name],[1960] AS Population, 1960 AS Year
FROM Countries

UNION ALL

SELECT [Country Name],[1961] AS Population, 1961 AS Year
FROM Countries

UNION ALL

SELECT [Country Name],[1962] AS Population, 1962 AS Year
FROM Countries
...
...
```

And so on; it might be a little tedious to set up but will make the data much easier to work with in Tableau! However, most data sources using complex custom SQL will need to be extracted for performance reasons.

2. **Unions**: Tableau's ability to union data sources such as Excel, text files, and Google Sheets can be used in a manner similar to the Custom SQL example to reshape data into tall data sets. You can even union the same file or sheet to itself. This can be useful in cases where you need multiple records for certain visualizations. For example, visualizing a path from a source to destination is difficult (or impossible) with a single record having a source column and destination column. But unioning the data set to itself yields two rows, one of which can be visualized as the source and the other as a destination.

3. **Table calculations**: Table calculations can be used to solve a number of data challenges, from finding and eliminating duplicate records to working with multiple levels of detail. Since table calculations can work within partitions at higher levels of detail, you can use multiple table calculations and aggregate calculations together to mix levels of detail in a single view. A simple example of this is the `Percentage of Total` table calculation, which compares an Aggregate calculation at the level of detail in the view with a total at a higher level of detail.

4. **Data blending**: Data blending can be used to solve numerous data structure issues. Because you can define the linking fields used, you control the level of detail of the blend. For example, the apartment rental data problem above could be solved with a secondary source that had a single record per apartment with the square feet. Blending at the apartment level would allow you to achieve the desired results.

5. **Data scaffolding**: Data scaffolding extends the concept of data blending. With this approach you construct a scaffold of various dimensional values to use as a primary source and then blend to one or more secondary sources. In this way, you can control the structure and granularity of the primary source while still being able to leverage data contained in secondary sources.

# Summary

Up until this chapter, we'd looked at data which was, for the most part, well-structured and easy to use. In this chapter, we considered what constitutes good structure and ways to deal with poor data structure. Good structure consists of data that has a meaningful level of detail and which has measures that match that level of detail. When measures are spread across multiple columns, we get data that is **wide** instead of **tall**.

You've got some experience now in applying various techniques to deal with data that has the wrong shape or has measures at the wrong level of detail. Tableau gives us the power and flexibility to deal with some of these structural issues, but it is often preferable to fix data structure at the source.

In the next chapter, we'll continue looking at some advanced and powerful techniques. These will be exciting and fun. Instead of looking at how to fix problems, we'll look at some tips and tricks to expand your creativity and take Tableau to the next level!

# 10
# Advanced Visualizations, Techniques, Tips, and Tricks

With a solid understanding of the foundational principles, it is possible to push the limits with Tableau. In addition to exploring, discovering, analyzing, and communicating data, members of the Tableau community have used the software to create and do amazing things like simulate an enigma machine, play tic-tac-toe or other games, generate fractals with only two records of data, and much more! Unlike traditional BI packages that force you to create a chart based on a predefined template, Tableau really is a blank canvas and the only limits are your creativity and imagination.

In this chapter, we'll take a look at some advanced techniques in a practical context. You'll learn things like creating advanced visualizations, dynamically swapping views on a dashboard, using custom images, and advanced geographic visualizations. The goal of this chapter is not to provide a comprehensive list of every possible technique. Instead, we'll look at a few varied examples that demonstrate some possibilities. Many of the examples are designed to stretch your knowledge and challenge you.

We'll take a look at the following advanced techniques in this chapter:

- Advanced visualizations
- Sheet swapping and dynamic dashboards
- Advanced mapping techniques
- Using background images
- Animation

# Advanced visualizations

In `Chapter 3`, *Moving from Foundational to More Advanced Visualizations*, we took a look at variations of some foundational visualizations, such as bar charts, time series, distributions, and scatterplots. Now, we'll consider some non-standard visualization types. These are merely examples of Tableau's amazing flexibility and are meant to inspire you to think through new ways of seeing, understanding, and communicating your data.

Each of the following visualizations is created using the supplied Superstore data. Instead of providing step-by-step instructions, we'll point out specific advanced techniques used to create each chart type. The goal is not to memorize steps, but to understand how to leverage Tableau's features to build whatever you want.

You can find completed examples in the `Chapter 10 Complete` workbook or test your growing Tableau skills by building everything from scratch using `Chapter 10 Starter`.

# Slope chart

A **slope chart** shows a change of values from one period or status to another. For example, here is a slope chart demonstrating the change in sales rank for each state in the **West Region** from **2015** to **2016**:

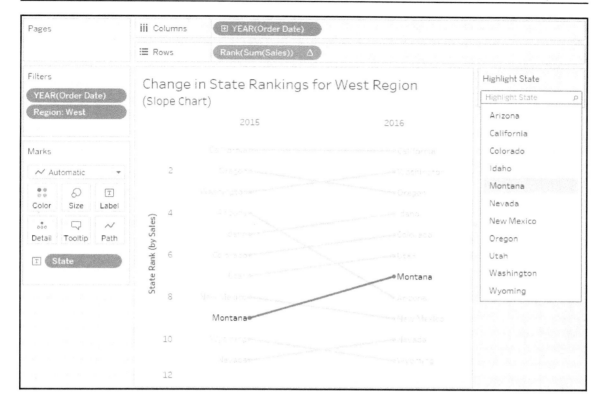

Here are some features and techniques used to create the preceding slope chart:

- The `Rank(Sum(Sales))` table calculation is computed along (addressed by) **State**. This means that each state is ranked within the partition of a single **Year**.
- **Grid Lines** for **Rows** have been set to `None`.
- The axis has been reversed (right-click on the axis and select **Edit**; then check the option to reverse).
- The label has been edited (by clicking on **Label**) to show on both ends of the line and to center vertically.
- The **Year** column headers have been moved from the bottom of the view to the top (from the top menu, go to **Analysis | TableLayout | Advanced** and uncheck the option to show the innermost level at the bottom).
- A **data highlighter** has been added (using the dropdown on the State field in the view, select **Show Highlighter**) to give the end user the ability to highlight one or more states.

Data highlighters are new in Tableau 10, and give the user the ability to highlight marks in a view by selecting values from the drop-down list or by typing (any match on any part of a value will highlight the mark, so for example, typing *ne* would highlight Nevada and New Mexico in the preceding view). Data highlighters can be shown for any field you use as discrete (blue) in the view and will function across multiple views in a dashboard as long as that same field is used in those views.

Slope charts can use absolute values (for example, the actual values of **Sales**) or relative values (for example, the rank of **Sales** as shown in this example). If you were to show more than two years to observe the change in rankings over multiple periods of time, the resulting visualization might be called a **bump chart**, like this:

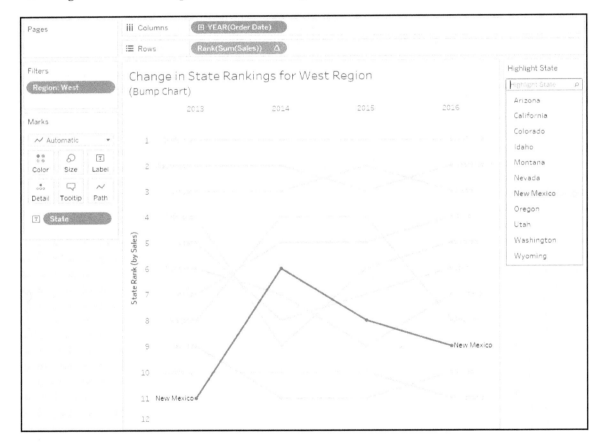

# Lollipop chart

A **lollipop chart** is very similar to a bar chart, but typically uses thinner lines ending in a circle. This allows for some stylistic interest as well as a place to show values or other labels. Here, for example, is a lollipop chart for sales of categories in the **Technology** department:

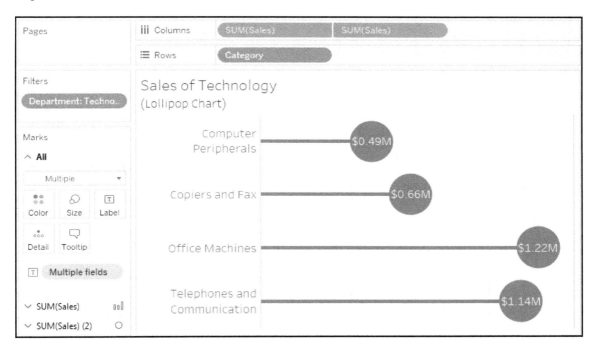

Features and techniques used to create this chart include:

- A *synchronized* **dual axis** for **SUM(Sales)**, with one mark type set to bar and sized to be very thin and the other mark type set to circle and sized to be large enough for a label
- **Sales** added to the label of the circle and formatted using a custom currency
- Axes have been hidden (right-click and uncheck **Show Header**)

Additional variations of this chart type might include flipping of orientation to be vertical, sorting of values, and using color or highlighting to call out certain values.

# Waterfall chart

A **waterfall chart** is useful when you want to show how parts successively build up to a whole. Here, for example is a waterfall chart showing how profit builds up to a grand total across **Departments** and **Categories** of products. Sometimes profit is negative, so the waterfall chart takes a dip, while positive values build up toward the total:

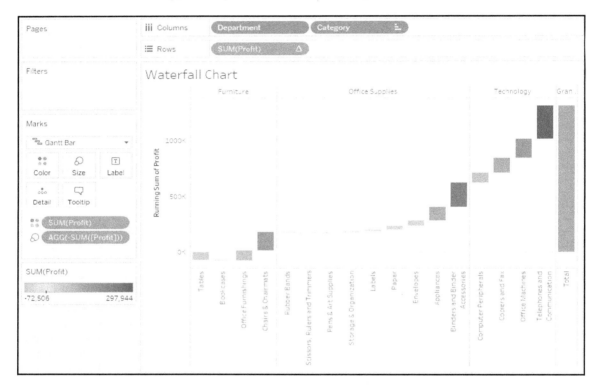

Here are the features and techniques used to build the chart:

- **Row Grand Totals** have been added to the view (dragged and dropped via the **Analytics** pane).
- The **SUM(Profit)** field on **Rows** is a running total table calculation (added using a quick table calculation) and is computed across the table.
- The mark type is set to **Gantt Bar** and an ad-hoc calculation is used with code:

  -SUM(Profit). This allows the Gantt bars to be drawn back down (or up for negative profit) toward the end of the previous mark.

# Sparklines

**Sparklines** refers to a visualization that uses multiple small line graphs that are designed to be read and compared quickly. The goal of sparklines is to render a visualization that can be understood at a glance. You aren't trying to communicate exact values but rather give the audience the ability to quickly understand trends, movements, and patterns.

Among various uses of this type of visualization, you may have seen sparklines used in financial publications to compare the movement of stock prices. Recall that in `Chapter 1,` *Creating Your First Visualizations and Dashboard,* we considered the initial start of a sparklines visualization as we looked at iterations of line charts. Here is a far more developed example:

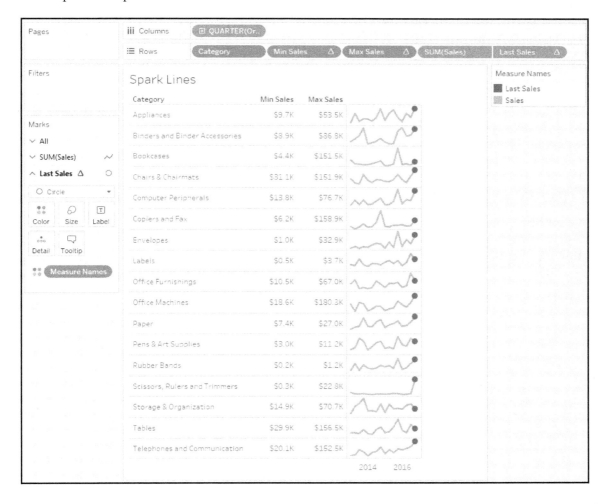

This chart was built using the following features and techniques:

- Start with a simple view of the **Sum(Sales)** by **Quarter** of **Order Date** (as a *date value*) with **Category** on **Rows**.
- Two calculated fields have been created to show the minimum and maximum quarterly sales values for each category. **Min Sales** has the code WINDOW_MIN(SUM(Sales)) and **Max Sales** has the code WINDOW_MAX(SUM(Sales)). Both have been added to **Rows** as *discrete* (blue) fields.
- The **Last Sales** calculation with the code IF LAST() = 0 THEN SUM([Sales]) END has been placed on **Rows** and uses a *synchronized* dual axis with a circle mark type to emphasize the final value of sales for each timeline.
- The axis for **SUM(Sales)** has been edited to have **Independent axis ranges for each row or column**. And the axes have been hidden. This allows the line movement to be emphasized. Remember, the goal is not to show the exact values but rather allow your audience to see the patterns and movement.
- **Grid Lines** have been hidden for **Rows**.
- The view has been resized (horizontally compressed and set to **Fit Height**). This allows the sparklines to fit into a small space, facilitating quick understanding of patterns and movement.

# Dumbbell chart

A **dumbbell chart** is a variation of the circle plot; it compares two values for each slice of data, emphasizing the distance between the two values. Here, for example, is a chart showing the difference in profit between **East** and **West** regions for each category of products:

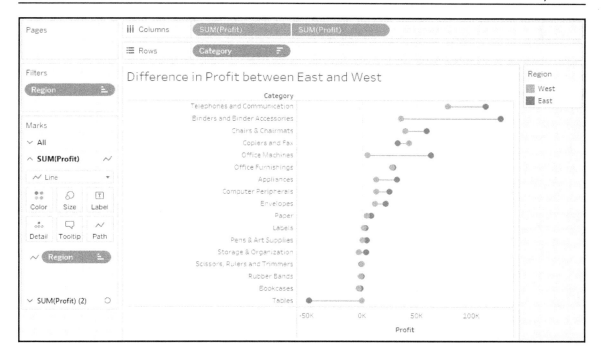

This chart was built using the following features and techniques:

- A *synchronized* dual axis of **SUM(Profit)** has been used, with one set to mark a type of **Circle** and the other set to **Line**.
- **Region** has been placed on the **Path** shelf for the line to tell Tableau to draw a line between the two regions.

> The **Path** shelf is available for **Line** and **Polygon** mark types. When you place a field on the path shelf, it gives Tableau the order to connect the points (following the sort order of the field placed on Path). Paths are often used with geographic visualizations to connect origins and destinations on routes, but can also be used with other visualization types.

- **Region** is placed on **Color** for the circle mark type.

# Unit chart/symbol chart

A **unit chart** can be used to show individual items, often using shapes or symbols to represent each individual. These charts can elicit a powerful emotional response, because the representations of the data are less abstract and more easily identified as representing something real. For example, here is a chart showing how many customers had late shipments for each region:

The view was created with the following techniques:

- The view is filtered where **Late Shipping** is true. **Late Shipping** is a calculated field that determines if it took more than 14 days to ship and order. The code is:

```
DATEDIFF('day', [Order Date], [Ship Date]) > 14
```

- **Region** has been sorted descending by the distinct count of **Customer ID**.
- **Customer ID** has been placed on **Detail** so that there is a mark for each distinct customer.
- The mark type has been changed to **Shape** and the shape has been changed to the included person shape in the **Gender** shape palette. To change shapes, click on the **Shape** shelf and select the desired shape(s).

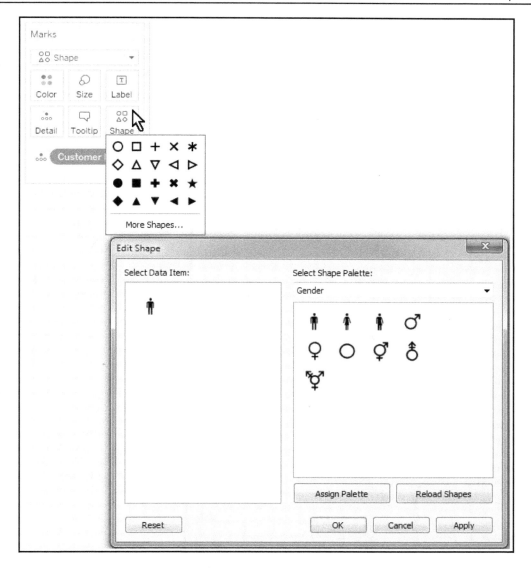

The preceding unit chart might elicit more of a response from regional managers than a standard bar chart when they are gently reminded that poor customer service impacts real people. Granted, the shapes are still abstract, but they more closely represent an actual person. You could also consider labeling the mark with the customer name or using other techniques to further engage your audience.

Remember that normally in Tableau, a mark is drawn for each distinct intersection of dimensional values. So it is rather difficult to draw, for example, 10 individual shapes for a single row of data that simply contains the value 10 for a field. This means that you will need to consider the shape of your data and include enough rows to draw the units you wish to represent.

Concrete shapes, in any type of visualization, can also dramatically reduce the amount of time it takes to comprehend the data. Contrast the amount of effort required to identify the departments in these two scatter plots:

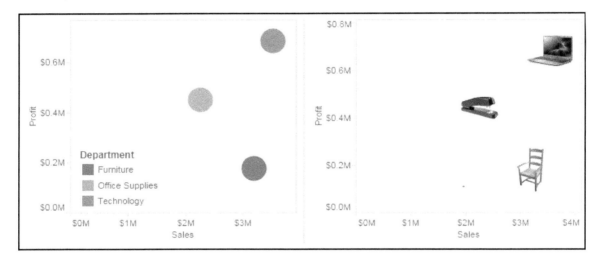

Once you know the meaning of a shape, you no longer have to reference a legend.

Placing a discrete field on the **Shape** shelf allows you to assign shapes to individual values of the field.

Shapes are images located in the `My Tableau Repository\Shapes` directory. You can include your own **custom shapes** in subfolders of that directory.

# Marimekko chart

A **Marimekko chart** (sometimes also called a **Mekko chart**) is similar a to stacked bar chart, but additionally uses varying widths of bars to communicate additional information about the data. Here, for example, is a Marimekko chart showing the breakdown of sales by region and department. The width of the bars communicates the total sales for the **Region** while the height of each segment gives you the percentage of sales for the **Department** within the **Region**:

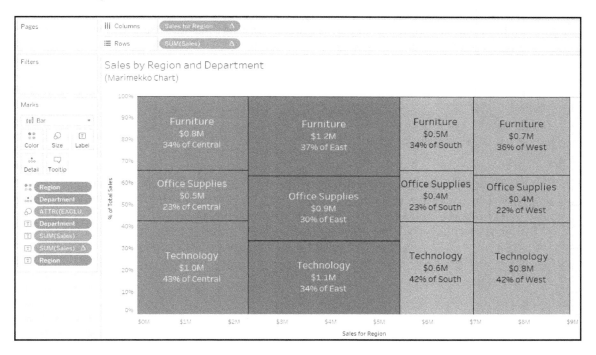

Creating Marimekko charts in Tableau leverages a feature introduced in version 10. Specifically, we leverage the ability to fix the width of bars according to axis units.

Clicking on the **Size** shelf when a continuous (green) field is on **Columns** (thus defining a horizontal axis) and the mark type is set to **Bar** reveals options for a fixed size. You can manually enter **Size** and **Alignment** or drop a field on the **Size** shelf to vary the widths of the bars.

Here are some of the details:

- The mark type has been specifically set to **Bar**.
- **Region** and **Department** have been placed on **Color** and **Detail** respectively. They are the only dimensions in the view, so they define the **view level of detail**.
- **Sales** has been placed on **Rows** and a **Percentage of Total** quick table calculation applied. The **Compute Using** (addressing) has been set to **Department** so that we get the percentage of sales for each department within the partition of the **Region**.
- The calculated field **Sales for Region** calculates the X-axis location for the right-side position of each bar. The code is as follows:

```
IF FIRST() = 0
    THEN MIN({EXCLUDE [Department] : SUM(Sales)})
ELSEIF LOOKUP(MIN([Region]), -1) <> MIN([Region])
    THEN PREVIOUS_VALUE(0) + MIN({EXCLUDE [Department] : SUM(Sales)})
ELSE
    PREVIOUS_VALUE(0)
END
```

While this code may seem daunting at first, it is following a logical progression. Specifically, if this is the first bar segment, we'll want to know the sum of Sales for the entire region (which is why we exclude **Department** with an inline level of detail calculation). When the calculation moves to a new **Region**, we'll need to add the previous **Region** total to the new **Region** total. Otherwise, the calculation is for another segment in the same **Region**, so the **Regional** total is the same as the previous segment.

- The field on **Size** is an ad hoc level of detail calculation with the code `{EXCLUDE [Department] : SUM(Sales)}`. As before, this excludes the department and allows us to get the sum of sales at a **Region** level. This means that each bar is sized according to total sales for the given **Region**.
- Clicking on the **Size** shelf gives the option to set the **Alignment** of the bars to **Right**. Since the preceding calculation gave the right position of the bar, we need to make certain the bars are drawn from that starting point.
- Various fields have been copied to the **Label** shelf so that each bar segment more clearly communicates the meaning to the viewer.

To add labels to each **Region** column, you might consider creating a second view and placing both on a dashboard. Alternately, you might use annotations.

 For a more comprehensive discussion of Marimekko charts, along with approaches that work with sparse data, see Jonathan Drummey's blog post: `https://www.tableau.com/about/blog/2016/8/how-build-marimekko-chart-tableau-58153`.

In addition to allowing you to create Merimekko charts, the ability to control the size of bars in axis units opens up all kinds of possibilities for creating additional visualizations such as cascade charts or stepped area charts. The techniques would be similar to those used here. Additionally, you can leverage the sizing feature with **continuous bins** (use the drop down menu to change a bin field in the view to continuous from discrete). This allows you to have histograms without large spaces between bars.

# Sheet swapping and dynamic dashboards

**Sheet swapping**, sometimes also called **sheet selection**, is a technique in which views are dynamically shown and hidden on a dashboard, often with the appearance of swapping one view for another. The dynamic hiding and showing of views on a dashboard has an even broader application. When combined with floating objects and layout containers, this technique allows you to create rich and dynamic dashboards.

The basic principles are simple:

- A view *collapses* on a dashboard when at least one field is on **Rows** or **Columns** and filters and/or hiding prevent any marks from being rendered
- Titles and captions do not collapse, but can be hidden so that the view collapses entirely

Let's consider a simple example with a view showing profit by department and category with a **Department** quick filter. The dashboard has been formatted (from the menu, navigate to **Format** | **Dashboard**) with a gray shading to help us see the effect:

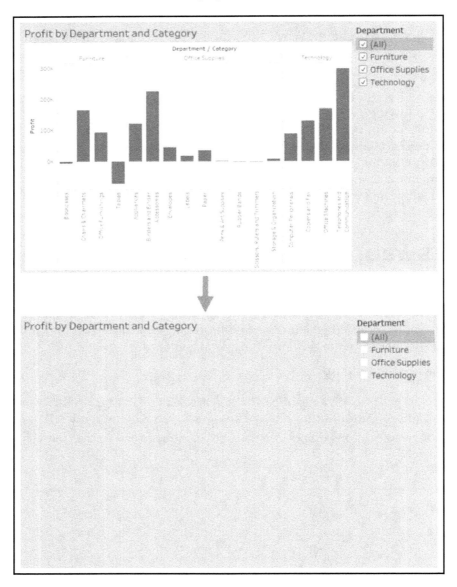

Observe how filtering out all departments results in the view collapsing. The title remains, but it could have been hidden.

In order to *swap* two different sheets, we simply take advantage of the collapsing behavior along with the properties of layout containers. We'll start by creating two different views filtered via a parameter and a calculated field. The parameter will allow us to determine which sheet is shown. Perform the following steps:

1. Create an integer parameter named `Show Sheet` with a **List** of **String** values set to `Bar Chart` and `Map`:

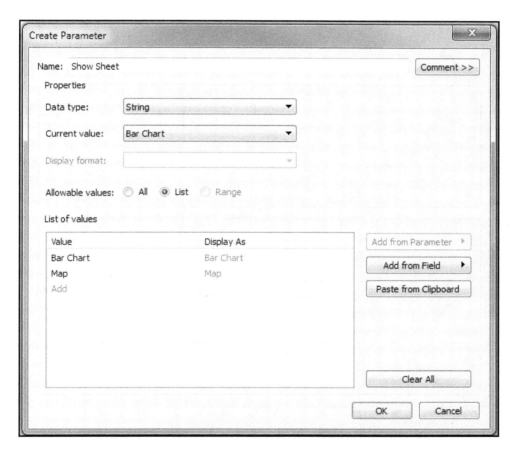

2. Since we want to filter based on the parameter selection and parameters cannot be directly added to the **Filters** shelf; instead we'll create a calculated field named `Show Sheet Filter` to return the selected value of the parameter. The code is simply `[Show Sheet]`, which is the parameter name and returns the current value of the parameter.

3. Create a new sheet named `Bar Chart` similar to the **Profitby Department** and **Category** view shown before.

4. Show the parameter control (right-click the parameter in the data window and select **Show Parameter Control**). Make sure the **Bar Chart** option is selected.

5. Add the **Show Sheet Filter** field to the **Filters** shelf and check **Bar Chart** to keep that value.

6. Create another sheet named `Map` that shows a filled map of states by **Profit**:

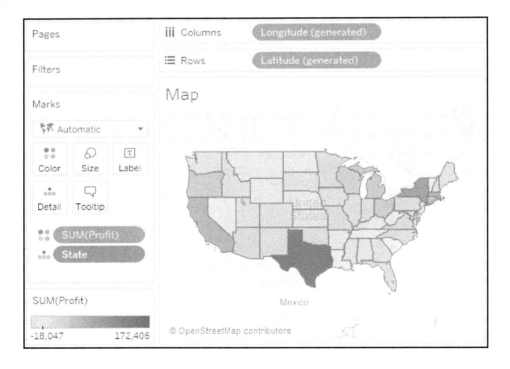

7. Show the parameter on this view and change the selection to **Map**. Remember that parameter selections are universal to the worksheet. If you were to switch back to the bar chart view, it should no longer be showing any data because of the filter.

8. Add the **Show Sheet Filter** field to the **Filters** shelf and check **Map** as the value to keep.

9. Create a new dashboard named `Sheet Swap`.

10. Add a horizontal layout container to the dashboard from the objects in the left window:

 A vertical layout container would work just as well in this case. The key is that a layout container will allow each view inside to expand to fill the container when the view is set to fit entire view, fit width (for horizontal containers), or fit height (for vertical containers). When one view collapses, the visible view will expand to fill the rest of the container.

11. Add each sheet to the layout container in the dashboard. The parameter control should be added automatically since it was visible in each view.

12. Using the drop down menu on the **Bar Chart** view, ensure the view is set to fill the container (navigate to **Fit | Entire View**). You won't have to set the fill for the map, as map visualizations automatically fill the container.

13. Hide the title for each view (right-click on the title and select **Hide Title**).

You now have a dashboard where changing the parameter results in one view or the other being shown. When **Map** is selected, the filter results in no data for the **Bar Chart**, so it collapses and Map fills the container:

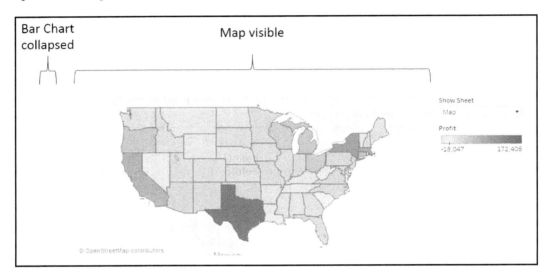

Alternately, when **Bar Chart** is selected, **Map** collapses due to the filter and the bar chart fills the container:

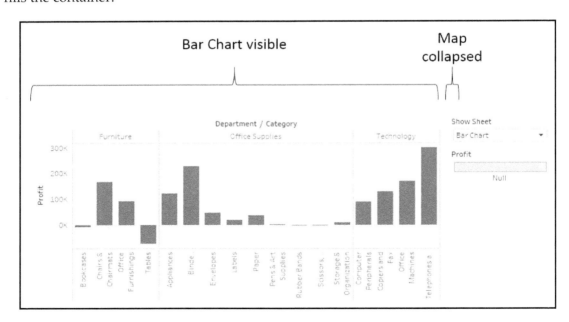

The key to collapsing a view is to have a filter or set of filters that ensures no rows of data. You do not have to use a parameter to control the filtering. You could use a regular filter or action filter to accomplish the same effect. This opens up all kinds of possibilities for dynamic behavior in dashboards.

# Dynamically showing and hiding other controls

Views will collapse based on filtering out all data. However, other controls such as quick filters, parameters, images, legends, and text boxes will not collapse and don't have an option to dynamically show or hide. Yet many times in a dynamic dashboard you might want to show or hide these objects. Sometimes certain parameters don't apply when other selections have been made. Look at the simple previous example. The color legend for Profit, which was automatically added to the dashboard by Tableau, applies to the map. But when the bar chart is shown, the legend is no longer applicable.

Fortunately, we can extend the technique we used previously to expand a view to push items we want to show out from under a floating object, and then collapse the view to allow the items that we want to hide to return to a position under the floating object.

Let's extend the previous example to show how to show and hide the **Color** legend:

1. Create a new sheet named **Show/Hide Legend**. This view is only used to show and hide the **Color** legend.
2. Create an ad hoc calculation by double-clicking on **Rows** and type the code MIN(1). We must have a field on **Rows** or **Columns** for the view to collapse, so we'll use this field to give us a single axis for **Rows** and a single axis for **Columns** without any other headers.
3. Duplicate the ad hoc calculation on **Columns**. You should now have a simple scatterplot with one mark.
4. As this is a helper sheet and not anything we want the user to see, we don't want it to show any marks or lines. Format the view using the menu **Format** | **Lines** to remove **Grid Lines** from **Rows** and **Columns** along with **Axis Rulers**. Additionally, hide the axes (right-click on each axis or field and uncheck **Show Headers**). Also, set the **Color** to full transparency to hide the mark.

5. We will want this view to show when the **Map** option is selected, so show the parameter control and ensure it is set to **Map**. Then add **Show Sheet Filter** to Filters and check **Map**.

6. On the **Sheet Swap Dashboard**, add the **Show/Hide Legend** sheet to the layout container between the **Show Sheet** parameter dropdown and the **Color** legend. Hide the title for the **Show/Hide Legend** sheet.

7. Ensure that **Map** is selected. The **Color** legend should be pushed all the way to the bottom.

8. Add a **Layout Container** as a floating object. Size and position it to completely cover the area where the **Color** legend used to be. It should cover the title of the **Show/Hide Legend** sheet but not the parameter dropdown.

 Objects and sheets can be added as floating objects by holding the *Shift* key while dragging, setting the **New Objects** option to **Floating**, or using the drop-down menu on the object. You may also change the default behavior for new objects from **Tiled** to **Floating** in the dashboard pane.

9. The **Layout Container** is transparent by e from the background.

At this point, you have a dynamic dashboard where the legend is shown when **Map** is shown, and it is applicable and hidden when the bar chart is visible. When **Map** is selected, the **Show/Hide Legend** sheet is shown and pushes the legend to the bottom of the layout container:

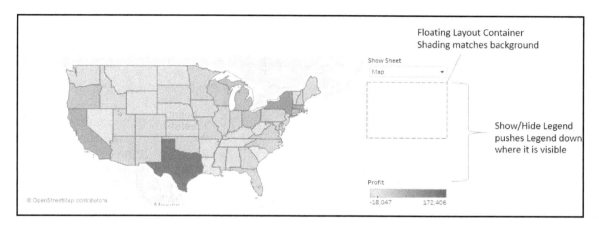

When **Bar Chart** is selected, the **Show/Hide Legend** sheet collapses and the legend, which is no longer applicable to the view, falls under the floating layout container:

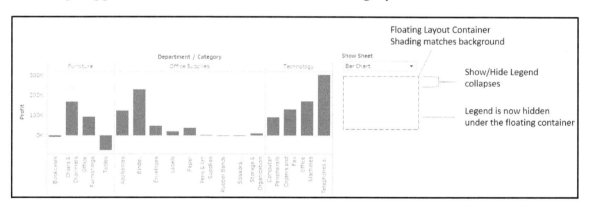

There is no limit to how many variations of this technique you can use on a dashboard. You can have as many layers as you'd like. You can even use combinations of these techniques to push views and objects on and off the dashboard. The possibilities for creating richly interactive user experience are endless.

# Advanced mapping techniques

We've touched on geographic visualization throughout the book. You've seen symbol maps and filled maps. Here we'll take a look at supplying your own geocoded data along with creating custom territories.

# Supplementing the standard in geographic data

We saw in `Chapter 1`, *Creating Your First Visualizations and Dashboard,* that Tableau generates **Latitude** and **Longitude** fields when the data source contains geographic fields that Tableau can match with its internal geographic database. Fields such as country, state, zip code, MSA, and congressional district are contained in Tableau's internal geography. As Tableau continues to add geographic capabilities, you'll want to consult the documentation to determine some specifics on what the internal database contains.

However, if you have latitude and longitude in your dataset or are able to supplement your data source with that data, you can create geographic visualizations with great precision. There are several options for supplying latitude and longitude for use in Tableau:

- Include latitude and longitude as fields in your data source. If possible, this option will provide the easiest approach to creating custom geographic visualizations, because you can simply place **Latitude** on **Rows**, **Longitude** on **Columns** to get a geographic plot.
- Create a calculated field for latitude and another for longitude using `if...then` logic or case statements to assign latitude and longitude values based on other values in your data. This would also be tedious and difficult to maintain with many locations.
- Import a custom geographic file. From the menu, navigate to **Map** | **Geocoding** | **Import Custom Geocoding...** The import dialog contains a link to documentation describing the option in further detail.
- Connect to the data containing your latitudes and longitudes as a secondary data source and use cross database joins or data blending to achieve geographic visualization. For example, here is a visualization that has been created by joining in a file containing exact latitudes and longitudes for each address:

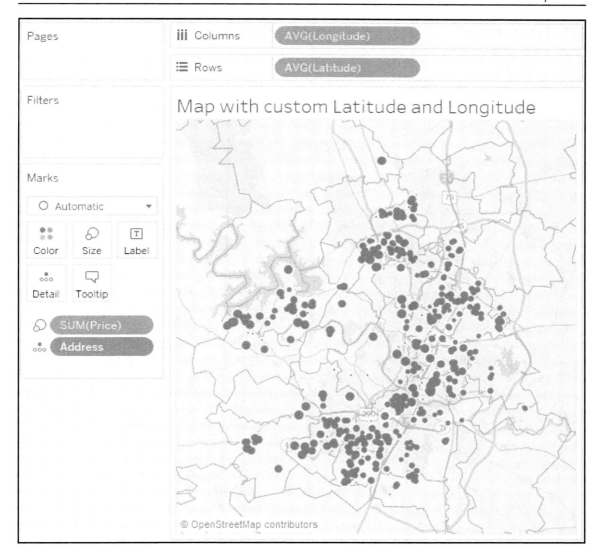

- Assign a field to a geographic role and assign unrecognized values to desired latitude and longitude locations. This option is most often used to correct unrecognized locations in standard geographic fields, such as city or zip code, but it can be used to create custom geographies as well–though this would be tedious and difficult to maintain with more than a few locations. You can assign unknown geographic locations as indicated in the following section.

# Manually assigning geographic locations

Assign unknown locations by clicking on the **unknown** indicator in the lower right of a geographic visualization, as shown here:

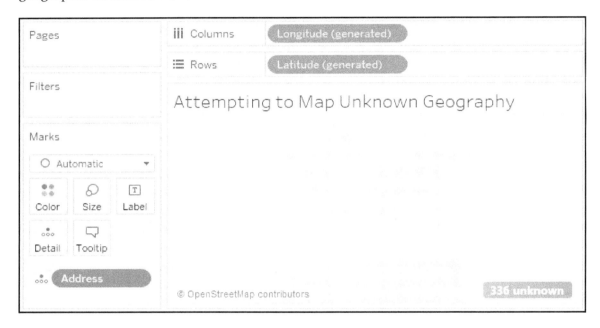

This will give you the following options:

- **Edit Locations**
- Filter out unknown locations
- Plot at the default location (latitude and longitude of 0, a location that is sometimes humorously referred to as **Null Island**, just off the west coast of Africa)

The indicator in the preceding screenshot shows **336 unknown** locations. Clicking the indicator and selecting the **Edit Locations** option allows you to correct unmatched locations by selecting a known location or entering your own latitude and longitude information, as shown here:

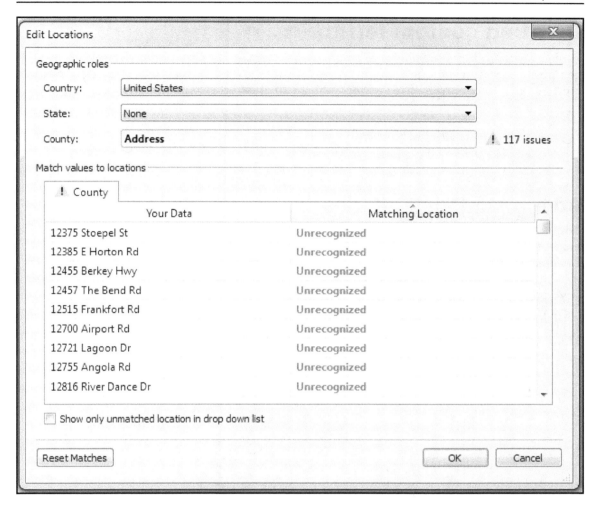

The first three options allow you to specify the geographic context by which Tableau determines the location of a field value. You may specify a **Country**, **State**, and/or **County**.

For example, Tableau will not recognize the city Mansfield until you specify the state (in the United States alone, there is a Mansfield, Texas; Mansfield, Ohio; Mansfield, Kansas; and about a dozen more!) In this example, you may specifically select a constant **State** or let Tableau know which field in the data set defines state.

You may also set individual locations by clicking the **Unrecognized** label in the table and matching to a known location or by entering a specific latitude and longitude.

# Creating custom territories

Tableau 10 introduces the ability to create custom territories. **Custom territories** are geographic areas or regions that you create (or that the data defines) as opposed to those built in (such as country or area code). Tableau 10 gives you two options for creating custom territories:

- Ad hoc custom territories
- Field – defined custom territories

## Ad hoc custom territories

You can create custom territories in an ad hoc way by selecting and grouping marks on a map. Simply select one or more marks, hover over one, and then use the **Group** icon. Alternately, right-click on one of the marks to find the option. You can create custom territories by grouping by any dimension if you have latitude and longitude in the data or any geographic dimension if you are using Tableau's generated latitude and longitude. Here we'll consider an example using **Zip Code**:

You'll notice that Tableau creates a new field, **Zip Code (group)** in this example. The new field has a paperclip and globe icon in the data pane, indicating it is a group and a geographic field. Tableau automatically includes the group field on color.

You may continue to select and group marks until you have all the custom territories you'd like. With **Zip Code** still part of the view level of detail, you will have a mark for each zip code (and any measure will be sliced by zip code). However, when you remove **Zip Code** from the view, leaving only the **Zip Code (group)** field, Tableau will draw the marks based on the new group:

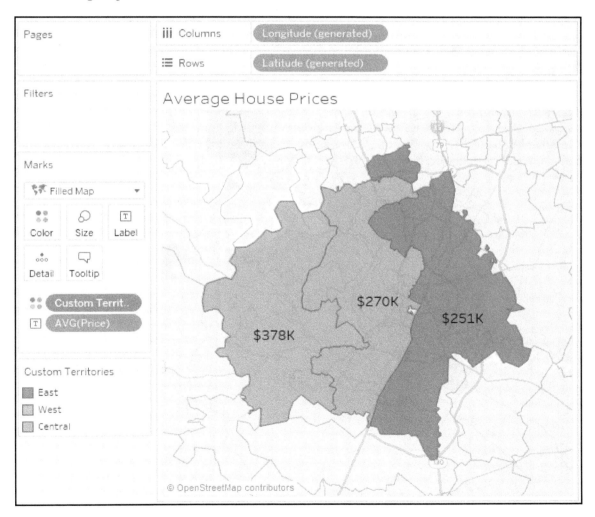

Here, the group field has been renamed to **Custom Territories** and the group names have been aliased as **East**, **West**, and **Central**.

 With a filled map, Tableau will connect all contiguous areas and still include disconnected areas as part of selections and highlighting. With a symbol map, Tableau will draw the mark in the geographic center of all grouped areas.

## Field – defined custom territories

Sometimes your data includes the definition of custom territories. For example, let's say your data had a field named **Region** that already grouped zip codes into various regions. That is, every zip code was contained in only one region. You might not want to take the time to select the marks and group them manually.

Instead, you can tell Tableau the relationship already exists in the data. In this example, you'd use the drop-down menu of the **Region** field in the data pane and navigate to **Geographic Role** | **Create From...** | **Zip Code**. **Region** is now recognized as a geographic field that defines custom territories as shown here:

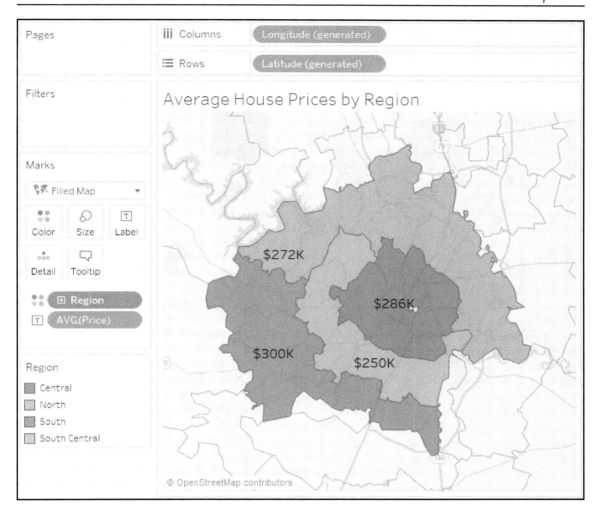

Pages

iii Columns | Longitude (generated)

≡ Rows | Latitude (generated)

Filters

## Average House Prices by Region

Marks

⬥⬥ Filled Map ▼

Color | Size | Label

Detail | Tooltip

⊞ Region

T AVG(Price)

Region

■ Central
■ North
■ South
■ South Central

$272K

$286K

$300K

$250K

© OpenStreetMap contributors

Use ad hoc custom territories to perform quick analysis, but consider field-defined custom territories for long-term solutions, because you can then redefine the territories in the data without manually editing any groups in the Tableau data source.

# Some final map tips

Here are some final tips to keep in mind when creating geographic visualizations. Various controls will appear when you hover over the map:

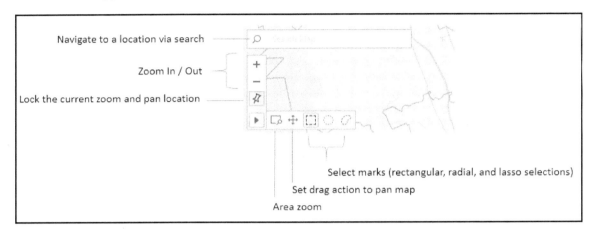

These controls allow you to search the map, zoom in and out, pin the map to the current location, and use various types of selections.

Additional options will appear when you go to **Map** | **Map Options** from the top menu:

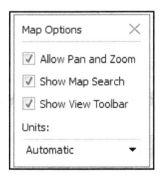

These options give you the ability to set what map actions are allowed for the end user. Additionally, you can set the units displayed for **radial selections**. Options are **Automatic** (based on system configuration), **Metric** (meters and kilometers), and **US** (feet and miles).

There are a few other tips to consider when working with geographic visualizations:

- Use the top menu to go to **Map | Map Layers** for numerous options for what layers of background to show as part of the map.
- Other options for zooming include using the mouse wheel, double-clicking, *Shift + Alt* + click, and *Shift + Alt + Ctrl* + click.
- You can click and hold for a few seconds to switch to pan mode.
- You can show or hide the zoom controls and/or map search by right clicking the map and selecting the appropriate option.
- Zoom controls can be shown on any visualization type that uses an axis.
- The pushpin on the zoom controls alternately returns the map to the best fit of visible data or locks the current zoom and location.
- You can create a dual axis map by duplicating *(Ctrl* + drag/drop) either the **Latitude** on **Columns** or **Longitude** on **Rows** and then using the field's dropdown menu to select **Dual Axis**. You can use this technique to combine multiple mark types on a single map:

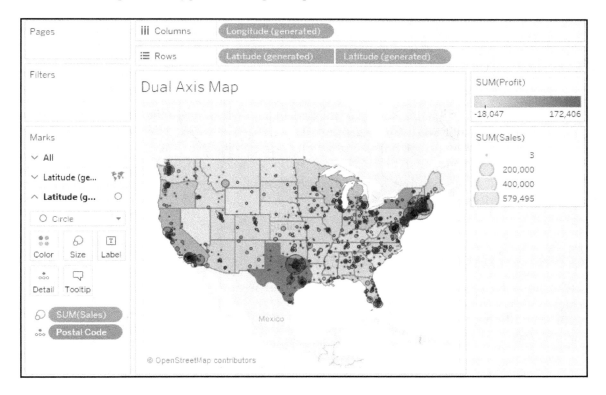

- When using filled maps, setting **Washout** to 100% in the **Map Layers** window can result in very clean-looking maps. However, only filled shapes will show, so any missing states (or counties, countries, and so on) will not be drawn:

- You can change the source of the background map image tiles using the menu and selecting **Map** | **Background Maps**. This allows you to choose between None, Offline (which is useful when you don't have an internet connection, but is limited in the detail that can be shown), or Tableau (the default).
- Additionally, from the same menu option, you can specify **Map Services...** to use a **WMS server** or **Mapbox**.

# Using background images

Background images allow you to plot data on top of any image. Consider the possibilities! You could plot ticket sales by seat on an image of a stadium, room use on the floor plan of an office building, the number of errors by piece of equipment on a network diagram, or meteor impacts on the surface of the moon.

In this example, we'll plot the number of patients per month in various rooms in a hospital. We'll use two images of floor plans for the ground floor and 2nd floor of the hospital. The data source is located in the Chapter 10 directory and is named Hospital.xlsx. It consists of two tabs: one for patient counts and another for room locations based on the x/y coordinates mapped to the images. We'll consider shortly how that works. You can view the completed example in the Chapter 10 Complete.twbx workbook or start from scratch using Chapter 10 Starter.twbx.

To specify a background image, use the top menu to navigate to **Map** à **Background Images** and then click the data source for which the image applies (in this example, Hospitals). On the **Add Background Images** screen you can add one or more images.

Here, we'll start with Hospital - Ground Floor.png, located in the Chapter 10 directory:

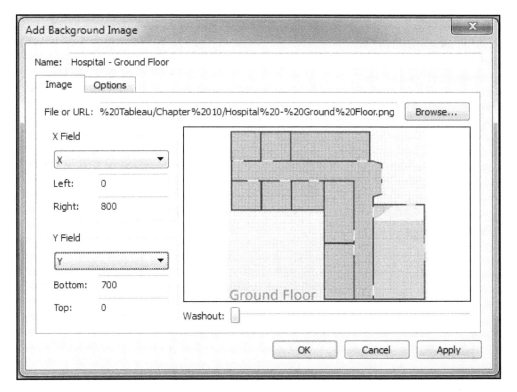

You'll notice that we mapped the fields **X** and **Y** (from the Locations tab) and specified the **Right** at **800** and **Bottom** at **700**. This is based on the size of the image in pixels.

You don't have to use pixels, but most of the time it makes it far easier to map the locations for the data. In this case, we have a tab of an Excel file with the locations already mapped to the X and Y coordinates on the image (in pixels). With cross-database joins in Tableau 10, you can create a simple text or Excel file containing mappings for your images and join them to an existing data source. You can map points manually (using a graphics application) or use one of many free online tools that allow you to quickly map coordinates on images.

We'll only want to show this blueprint for the ground floor, so switching to the **Options** tab, we'll ensure that the condition is set based on the data. We'll also make sure to check **Always Show Entire Image**:

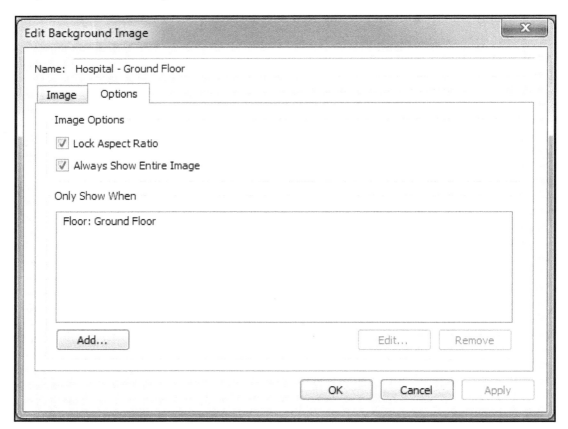

Next, repeating the previous steps, we'll add the second image (Hospital - 2nd Floor.png) to the data source, ensuring it only shows for the 2nd Floor.

Once we have the images defined and mapped, we're ready to build a visualization. The basic idea is to build a scatterplot using the **X** and **Y** fields for axes. But we'll have to ensure that X and Y are not summed because if they are added together for multiple records, we'll no longer have a correct mapping to pixel locations. There are a couple of options:

- Use X and Y as continuous dimensions
- Use MIN, MAX, or AVG instead of SUM; and ensure that **Location** is used to define the view level of detail.

Additionally, images are measured from 0 at the top to Y at the bottom, but scatter plots start with 0 at the bottom and values increase up. So, initially, you may see your background images appear upside down. To get around this, we'll edit the Y axis (right click and select **Edit Axis**) and check the option for **Reversed**.

We also need to ensure that the **Floor** field is used in the view. This is necessary to tell Tableau which image should be displayed. At this point, we should be able to get a visualization like this:

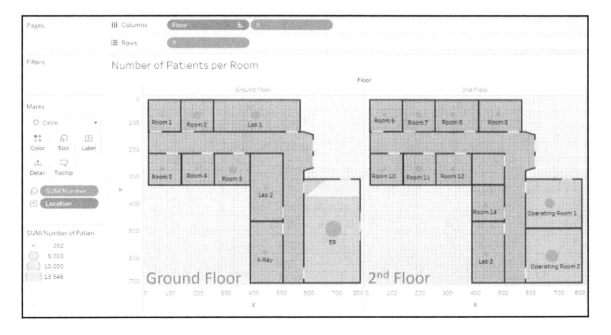

Here, we've plotted circles with size based on the number of patients in each room. We could cleanup and modify the visualization in various ways:

- Hide the X and Y axes (right-click on the axis and uncheck **Show Header**)
- Hide the header for **Floor** as the image already includes the label
- Add **Floor** to the **Filter** shelf so that the end user can choose to see one floor at a time

# Animation

**Animated visualizations** can bring data storytelling to life by revealing patterns that happen over time or emphasize dramatic events. Adding a field to the **Pages** shelf will show playback controls that allow you to *page* through each value of that field. You can do this manually, or click the play button to watch the visualization as values change automatically.

The `Chapter 10 Completed` workbook contains an example that animates the hospital floorplan shown above. You can create the same effect by adding the **Month** field to the **Pages** shelf (as a **Month date value**). Then watch as the circles change size month by month.

Experiment with the **Show History** options to see how you can view marks for previous pages.

 When you use multiple views on a dashboard, each having the same combination of fields on the **Pages** shelf, you can synchronize the playback controls (using the caret drop-down menu on the playback controls) to create a fully animated dashboard.

Animations can be shared with other users of Tableau Desktop or Tableau Reader. As of this writing, automatic playback controls are not available for Tableau Server, Tableau Online, or Tableau Public. However, end users are able to manually page through the values.

# Summary

We've covered a wide variety of techniques in this chapter! We looked at advanced visualizations, sheet swapping, dynamic dashboards, some advanced mapping techniques including supplementing geographic data, custom territories, using custom background images, and animating visualizations.

There is no way to cover every possible visualization type, technique, way of solving problems. Instead, we explored some of what can be accomplished using a few advanced techniques. The examples in this chapter build on the foundations laid in the preceding chapters. From here, you will be able to creatively modify and combine techniques in new and innovative ways to solve problems and achieve incredible results! Next, we'll turn our focus on how to share those results.

# Sharing Your Data Story **11**

Tableau enables you to share your work using a variety of methods. In this chapter, we'll take a look at the various ways to share visualizations and dashboards along with what to consider when deciding how you will share.

Specifically, we'll take a look at:

- Presenting, printing, and exporting
- Sharing with users of Tableau Desktop and Tableau Reader
- Sharing with users of Tableau Server, Tableau Online, and Tableau Public
- Additional distribution options with Tableau Server

# Presenting, printing, and exporting

When it comes to telling a data story, Tableau is primarily designed to build richly interactive visualizations and dashboards for consumption on a screen. Often you will expect users to interact with your dashboards and visualizations. However, there are good options for presenting, printing, and exporting in a variety of formats.

# Presenting

Tableau Desktop and Reader features a **Presentation Mode**, which is available from the **Window** menu, by pressing the *F7* key, or using the option on the toolbar. This mode removes all authoring controls and displays only the view and navigation tabs without any toolbars, panes, or authoring objects. Press the *F7* key or *Esc* key to exit **Presentation Mode**.

 When used with effective dashboards and stories, the **Presentation Mode** makes for an effective way to personally walk your audience through the data story. If you save a workbook by pressing *Ctrl+S* while in presentation mode, the workbook will be opened in presentation mode by default.

# Printing

Tableau enables printing for individual visualizations, dashboards, and stories. From the **File** menu, you can select **Print** to print the currently active sheet in the workbook to the printer, or the **Print to PDF** option to export as a PDF. Either option allows you to export the active sheet, selected sheets, or the entire workbook as a PDF. To select multiple sheets, hold the *Ctrl* key and click on individual tabs.

When printing, you also have the option to **Show Selections**. When this option is checked, marks that have been interactively selected or highlighted on a view or dashboard will be printed as selected. Otherwise, marks will print as though no selections have been made. The map in the following dashboard has marks for the western half of the United States selected:

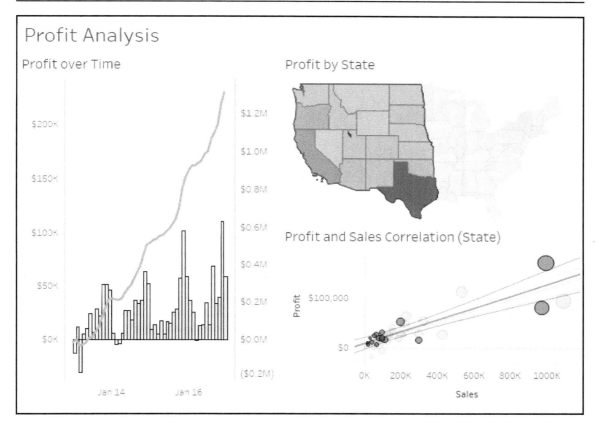

Here are some considerations, tips, and suggestions for printing:

- If a dashboard is being designed for print, select a predefined paper size as the fixed size for the dashboard or use a custom size that matches the same aspect ratio.
- Use the **Page Setup** screen (available from the **File** menu) to define specific print options, such as what elements (legends, title, or caption) will be included, the layout (including margins and centering), and how the view or dashboard should be scaled to match the paper size. The **Page Setup** options are specific to each view.

Duplicating or copying a sheet will include any changes to the page setup settings.

If you are designing multiple sheets or dashboards for print, consider creating one as a template, set up all the desired print settings, and then duplicate it for each new sheet.

- Fields used on the **Pages** shelf will define page breaks in printing (for individual sheets, but not dashboards or stories). The number of *pages* defined by the **Pages** shelf is not necessarily equal to the number of printed pages. This is because a single *page* defined by the **Pages** shelf might require more than one printed page.
- Each story point in a **Story** will be printed on a new page.
- Printing the entire workbook can be an effective way to generate a single PDF document for distribution. Each visible sheet will be included in the PDF in the order of the tabs, left to right. You may hide sheets to prevent inclusion in the PDF or reorder sheets to adjust the order of the resulting document. Also consider creating dashboards with images and text for title pages, tables of contents, page numbers, and commentary.
- Avoid scrollbars in dashboards, as they will print as scrollbars and anything outside the visible window will not be printed.

- You can also select multiple sheets in the workbook (hold the *Ctrl* key while clicking on each tab) and then print only selected sheets.

Sheets may be hidden if they are views that are used in one or more dashboards or if they are dashboards used in one or more stories. To hide a view, right-click on the tab or thumbnail on the bottom strip or in the left pane of the dashboard or story workspace, and select **Hide Sheet**. To show a sheet, locate it in the left pane of the dashboard or story workspace, right-click on it, and uncheck **Hide Sheet**. You can also right-click on a dashboard or story tab and hide or show all sheets used. If you don't see a **Hide Sheet** option, it means this sheet is not used in any dashboard and can then only be deleted.

# Exporting

Tableau also makes it easy to export images of views, dashboards, and stories for use in documents, PowerPoint, and even books like this one! Images may be exported as .png, .emf, .jpg, or .bmp. You can also copy an image to the clipboard to paste into other applications. To export or copy an image, use the menu options for **Worksheet**, **Dashboard**, or **Story**.

We'll take a look at using Tableau Server, Tableau Online, and Tableau Public in detail shortly. For now, let's consider some of the exporting features available on these platforms. When interacting with a view on Tableau Server, Online or Public, you will see a toolbar, unless you don't have the required permissions or the toolbar has been specifically disabled by a Tableau Server administrator:

The **Download** dropdown on the toolbar allows you to download **Image**, **Data**, **Crosstab** (Excel), **PDF**, or **Tableau workbook**. Images are exported in .png format and render the dashboard in its current state. Exporting a PDF document will give the user many options, including layout, scaling, and whether to print the current dashboard, all sheets in the workbook, or all sheets in the current dashboard.

Exporting data or a crosstab will export for the *active* view in the dashboard. That is, if you click on a view in the dashboard, it becomes *active* and you can export the data or crosstab for that particular view.

# Sharing with users of Tableau Desktop and Tableau Reader

Often, you'll want to share your dashboards and data stories with other Tableau users. There are some considerations for sharing with other users of Tableau Desktop and some different considerations for sharing with users of Tableau Reader.

## Sharing with Tableau Desktop users

Sharing a workbook with other Tableau Desktop users is fairly straightforward, but there are a few things to consider.

One of the major considerations is whether you will be sharing a packaged workbook (.twbx) or an unpackaged workbook (.twb). Packaged workbooks are single files that contain the workbook (.twb), extracts (.tde), file-based data sources that have not been extracted (.xls, .xlsx, .txt, .cub, .mdb, and so on), custom images, and various other related files.

To share with users of **Tableau Desktop**, do this:

- You may share either a packaged (.twbx) or unpackaged (.twb) workbook by simply sharing the file with another user who has the same or newer version of Tableau Desktop.

Workbook files will be updated when saved in a newer version of Tableau Desktop. You cannot open a workbook saved with a newer version of Tableau in an older version. You will be prompted about updates when you first open the workbook and again when you attempt to save it.

- If you share an unpackaged (.twb) workbook, then anyone else using it must be able to access any data sources and any referenced images must be visible to the user in the *same* directory where the original files were referenced. For example, if the workbook uses a live connection to an Excel (.xlsx) file on a network path and includes images on a dashboard located in C:\Images, then all users must be able to access the Excel file on the network path and have a local C:\Images directory with image files of the same name.

Consider using a UNC (for example, \\servername\directory\file.xlsx) path for common files if you use this approach.

Similarly, if you share a packaged workbook (.twbx) that uses live connections, anyone using the workbook must be able to access the live connection data source and have appropriate permissions.

# Sharing with Tableau Reader users

**Tableau Reader** is a free product provided by Tableau Software that allows users to interact with visualizations, dashboards, and stories created in Tableau Desktop. Unlike Tableau Desktop, it does not allow authoring of visualizations or dashboards. However, all interactivity such as filtering, drill-down, actions, and highlighting is available to the end user.

Think of Tableau Reader as being similar to many PDF readers that allow you to read and navigate the document, but do not allow for authoring or saving of changes.

To share with users of Tableau Reader, consider the following:

- Reader will only open packaged (.twbx) workbooks
- The packaged workbook may not contain live connections to server or cloud-based data sources. Those connections must be extracted

Be certain to take into consideration security concerns when sharing packaged workbooks (.twbx). Since packaged workbooks most often contain data, you must be certain that the data is not sensitive. Even if the data is not shown on any view or dashboard, it is still accessible in the packaged extract (.tde) or file-based data source.

# Sharing with users of Tableau Server, Tableau Online, and Tableau Public

**Tableau Server**, **Tableau Online**, and **Tableau Public** are all variations of the same concept: hosting visualizations and dashboards on a server and allowing users to access them via a web browser.

The following table provides some of the similarities and differences between the products, but as details may change, please consult a Tableau representative prior to making any purchasing decisions:

| Product | Tableau Server | Tableau Online | Tableau Public |
|---------|----------------|----------------|----------------|
| Description | A server application installed on one or more server machines that hosts views, dashboards, and stories created with Tableau Desktop. | A cloud-based service maintained by Tableau Software that hosts views, dashboards, and stories created with Tableau Desktop. | A cloud-based service maintained by Tableau software that hosts views, dashboards, and stories created with Tableau Desktop or the free Tableau Public client. |
| Licensing | Named user (set number of users) or core (unlimited users on a set number of cores). | Named user. | Free. |
| Administration | Fully maintained, managed, and administered by the individual or organization that purchased the license. | Managed and maintained by Tableau Software, with some options for project and user management by users. | Managed and maintained by Tableau Software. |
| Authoring and publishing | Users of Tableau Desktop may author and publish workbooks to Tableau Server. Web authoring gives Tableau Server users the capability to edit and create visualizations and dashboards in a web browser. | Users of Tableau Desktop may author and publish workbooks to Tableau Online. Web authoring allows Tableau Online users to edit and create visualizations and dashboards in a web browser. | Users of Tableau Desktop or the free Tableau Public client can publish workbooks to Tableau Public. |

| | Licensed Tableau Server users, even those without Tableau Desktop, may interact with hosted views. Views may also be embedded in intranet sites, SharePoint, and custom portals. | Licensed Tableau Online users, even those without Tableau Desktop, may interact with hosted views. Views may also be embedded in intranet sites, SharePoint, and custom portals. | Everything is public-facing. Anyone may interact with hosted views. Views may be embedded in public websites and blogs. |
|---|---|---|---|
| Interaction | | | |
| Limitations | None. | Most data sources must be extracted before workbooks can be published. Most non-cloud-based data sources must have extracts refreshed using Tableau Desktop on a local machine or via the Tableau Online Sync Client. | All data must be extracted and each data source is limited to 10 million rows. |
| Security | The Tableau Server administrator may create sites, projects, and users and adjust permissions for each. Access to the underlying data and downloading of the workbook or data can be restricted. | The Tableau Server administrator may create projects and users and adjust permissions for each. Access to the underlying data and downloading of the workbook or data can be restricted. | By default, anyone may download and view data, but access to these options may be restricted by the author. |
| Good uses | Internal dashboards and analytics, and/or use across departments/ divisions/clients via multi-tenant sites. | Internal dashboards and analytics. Sharing and collaboration with remote users. | Sharing visualizations and dashboards using embedded views on public-facing websites or blogs. |

# Publishing to Tableau Public

You may open and save workbooks to Tableau Public using either Tableau Desktop or the free Tableau Public client application. Please keep the following points in mind:

- In order to use Tableau Public, you will need to register an account
- With Tableau Desktop, you may save and open workbooks to and from Tableau Public by using the **Server** menu and selecting options under **Tableau Public**
- With the free Tableau Public client, you may only save workbooks to and from the Web. Anyone in the world can view what you publish

- Selecting the option to **Manage Workbooks** will open a browser so that you can log in to your Tableau Public account and manage all your workbooks online
- Workbooks saved to Tableau Public may contain any number of data source connections, but they must all be extracted and must not contain more than 10 million rows of extracted data each

# Publishing to Tableau Server and Tableau Online

Publishing to Tableau Server and Tableau Online is a similar experience. To publish to Tableau Server or Tableau Online, from the menu, navigate to **Server | Publish Workbook**. If you are not signed in to a server, you will be prompted to sign in:

You must have a user account with publish permissions for one or more projects. Enter the URL or IP address of the Tableau server or the Tableau Online URL, your username, and password. Once signed in, you will be prompted to select a site, if you have access to more than one. Finally, you will see the publish screen:

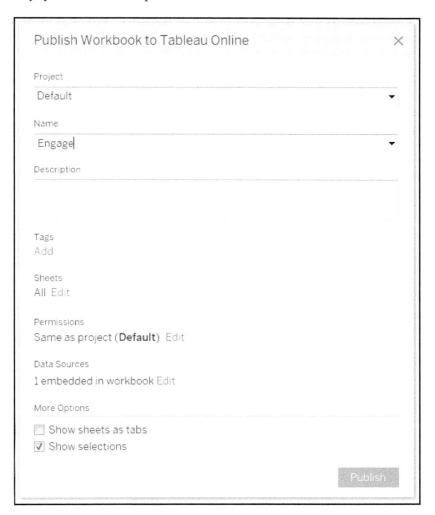

Here you will be able to select the **Project** to which you wish to publish and **Name** your workbook. If a workbook has already been published with the same name as the selected project, you will be prompted to overwrite it. You may give the workbook a **Description** and use **Add Tags** to make searching for and finding your workbook easier.

You may also specify which **Sheets** to include in the published workbook. Any sheets you check will be included; any you uncheck will not.

You may **Edit** user and group **Permissions** to define who has permissions to view, interact with and alter your workbook. By default, the project settings are used.

You also have the option to **Show Sheets as Tabs**. When checked, users on Tableau Server will be able to navigate between sheets using tabs similar to those shown at the bottom of Tableau Desktop. This option must be checked if you plan to have actions that navigate between views. **Show Selections** indicates that you wish any active selections of marks to be retained in the published views.

Editing the **Data Sources** gives you options for authentication and scheduling:

- For each data connection used in the workbook, you may determine how database connections are authenticated. The options will depend on the data source as well the configuration of Tableau Server. Various options include embedding a password, impersonating a user, or prompting a Tableau Server user for credentials.
- You may specify a schedule for Tableau Server to run refreshes of any data extracts.

Any live connections or extracted connections that will be refreshed on the server must define connections that work from the server. This means that all applicable database drivers must be installed on the server; all network, Internet connections, and ports required for accessing database servers and cloud-based data must be open. Additionally, any external files referenced by a workbook (for example, image files and non-extracted file-based data sources) that were not included when the workbook was published must be referenced using a location that is accessible by Tableau Server (for example, a network path with security settings allowing the Tableau Server process read access).

# Interacting with Tableau Server

After a workbook is published to Tableau Server, other users will be able to view and interact with the visualizations and dashboards using a web browser. Once logged in to Tableau Server, they will be able to browse content for which they have appropriate permissions. These users will be able to use any features built into the dashboards such as quick filters, parameters, actions, or drill-downs. Everything is rendered as HTML 5, so the only requirement for the user to view and interact with views and dashboards is a modern web browser.

 The **Tableau Mobile** app, available for iOS and Android devices, can enhance the experience for mobile users as can effective use of Tableau 10's device designer. While providing a great user experience, the app is not required to access Tableau Server from a mobile device.

For the most part, interacting with a workbook on Server or Online is very similar to interacting with a workbook in Tableau Desktop or Reader. Quick filters, parameters, actions, and tooltips all look and behave similarly.

You will find some additional features:

- The top menu gives you various options related to managing and navigating Tableau Server.
- Below that, you'll find a breadcrumb trail informing you which workbook and view you are currently viewing.
- Beneath that, you'll find a toolbar that includes several features. It is shown in the following screenshot:

- **Undo** and **Redo** give you the ability to step back and forward through interactions.
- **Revert** gives you the ability to undo all changes and revert to the original dashboard.
- **Refresh** reloads the dashboard with a refresh of the data. However, this does not refresh any extracts of the data.
- **Pause** allows you to pause refreshing of the dashboard based on actions, filter selections, or parameter value changes until you have made all the changes you wish.

- Additional options are included to the right:

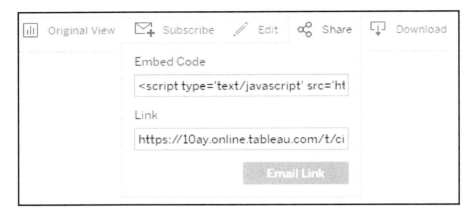

- **Original View** allows you to save the current state of the dashboard based on selections, filters, and parameter values so that you can quickly return to it at a later point. You can also find your saved views here.
- **Subscribe** allows you to schedule periodic e-mails of a screenshot of the dashboard. Tableau 10 also allows administrators to subscribe other users.
- **Edit** allows you to edit the dashboard. The interface is very similar to Tableau Desktop. Tableau 10 allows for editing individual views as well as dashboards. The Tableau Administrator can enable or disable web editing per user or group and also control permissions for saving of edited views.
- **Share** gives you options for sharing the workbook. These options include a URL you can distribute to other licensed users as well as code for embedding the dashboard in a web page.
- The **Download** button allows you to download the data, images of the dashboard, PDF, or the workbook as described previously.

# Additional distribution options using Tableau Server

Tableau Server allows for several other options for sharing your views, dashboards, and data. Along with allowing users to sign in to Tableau Server, you might consider the following options:

- Dashboards, views, and story points can be embedded in websites, portals, and SharePoint. Single sign on options exists to allow your website authentication to integrate seamlessly with Tableau Server.
- Tableau Server allows users to subscribe to views and dashboards and schedule email delivery. The email will contain an up-to-date image of the view and link to the dashboard on Tableau Server. Server admins may also manage user subscriptions.
- The **TABCMD** utility is provided with Tableau Server and may be installed on other machines. The utility provides the ability to automate many functions of Tableau Server including export features, publishing, and user and security management. This opens up quite a few possibilities for automating delivery.
- The **REST API** allows for programmatic interaction with Tableau Server.

# Summary

Tableau is an amazing platform for building useful and meaningful visualizations and dashboards based on your data. We've considered how to connect to the data, write calculated fields, and design entire stories based on your data. In this chapter, we considered how to share the results with others.

You now have a solid foundation. At its core, Tableau is intuitive, transparent, and easy to use. As you dive deeper, the simplicity becomes increasingly beautiful. As you discover new ways to understand your data, solve complex problems, ask new questions, and find new answers in your data, your new Tableau skills will help you uncover and share new insights hidden in your data.

# Catching Up with Tableau 2018 **12**

In this chapter, we'll cover the new features in Tableau's 2018 releases (Tableau 2018.1, 2018.2, and 2018.3).

 With the 2018.1 version, Tableau has changed the version numeration. All versions now start with the year, then the release number during that year. For example, Tableau 2018.3 is the third major release of 2018.

This chapter will be divided into two parts, as follows:

- Tableau Desktop
- Tableau Server

For each part, each major feature has its proper section. Next to the name of the feature, between brackets, the version that introduced the new feature is specified. For example, the section spatial Join (2018.2) covers the feature spatial Join, added in version 2018.2.

 This book focuses on data visualization with Tableau Desktop and Tableau Server/Online. The new product that allows you to clean and prepare your data, Tableau Prep, is not covered, as it fulfills a different need. Learn more about Tableau Prep at https://www.tableau.com/products/prep.

Let's start with Tableau Desktop; get ready to discover many great new features!

# Tableau Desktop

This first section, covering Tableau Desktop, is divided into three parts, as follows:

- **Data source improvements**: All of the new ways to connect your data and increase performance
- **Visualization improvements**: All of the things that you can do on a Worksheet, to create better visualizations
- **Dashboard improvements**: All of the options and new features to help you create better Dashboards

To understand and reproduce the examples provided in this chapter, you need to know how to connect to data, build a Data Source, and create Worksheets and Dashboards.

# Data Source improvements

In this section of the book, we'll focus on two major improvements: the normalized extract and the spatial join.

## Normalized extract (2018.3)

Previously, when creating an extract, Tableau always generated a single table. This was sometimes problematic, especially when a Join duplicated the number of lines. Now, when you Join multiple tables, you can choose the schema, creating either a **Single Table** or **Multiple Tables**:

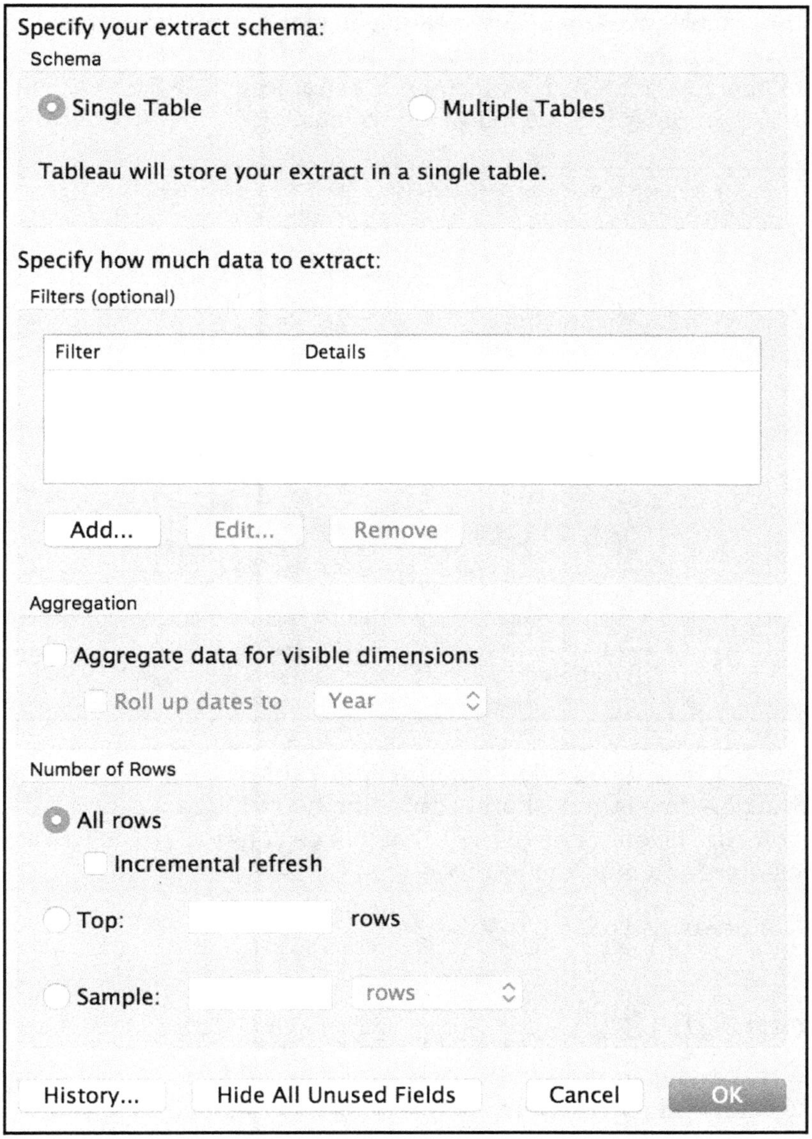

Specify your extract schema:

Schema

● Single Table                    ○ Multiple Tables

Tableau will store your extract in a single table.

Specify how much data to extract:

Filters (optional)

| Filter | Details |
| --- | --- |
|  |  |

    Add...        Edit...        Remove

Aggregation

☐ Aggregate data for visible dimensions

    ☐ Roll up dates to    Year    ⌄

Number of Rows

● All rows

    ☐ Incremental refresh

○ Top:  [          ]  **rows**

○ Sample:  [          ]  rows  ⌄

History...        Hide All Unused Fields        Cancel        **OK**

For example, you can download the Excel file `Multiple Table Storage Test` from the *Chapter 1* section of my website, `book.ladataviz.com` (or, browse to `https://ladataviz.com/wp-content/uploads/2018/09/Multiple-Table-Storage-Test.xlsx`). This file contains the an `Orders` sheet, with approximately 10,000 rows and another sheet, `User Access`, with 6,000 rows.

Individually, those tables are small, and creating an extract only takes a few seconds. When you Join the two tables, the data is duplicated. The result of the Join produces more than 11 million rows. When you created an extract, prior to Tableau 2018.3, the 11 million rows had to be retrieved, as you can see in the following screenshot:

Thanks to Tableau 2018.3, if you select the **Multiple Tables** schema when creating an extract, the extraction time is very short because the two tables are generated separately, prior to being joined. The only drawback is that you can't use all of the Extract options (**Filters**, **Aggregation**, and **Number of rows**).

The next new feature is also related to Joins.

# Spatial join (2018.2)

A new type of Join, called an **Intersect**, is now available, and it was created especially for spatial files. You can find it in the **Join** configuration, highlighted as follows:

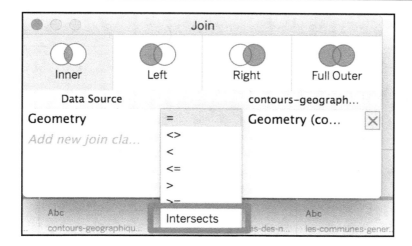

Intersects are useful when the only common field between the two tables is the spatial one. Tableau joins the data when there is a spatial intersection between a polygon and a point.

For example, let's look at how to join the two following shapefiles. The first one contains the polygons of the French regions:

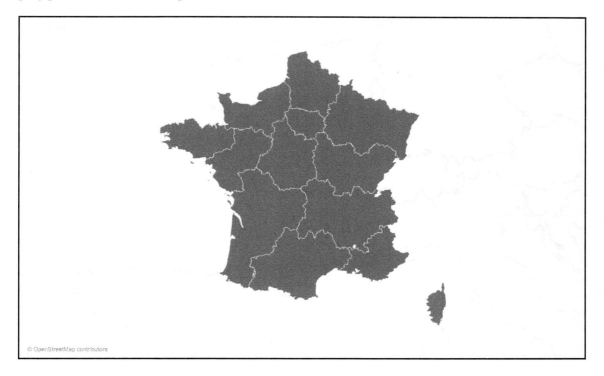

The second one contains a list of ports around the world:

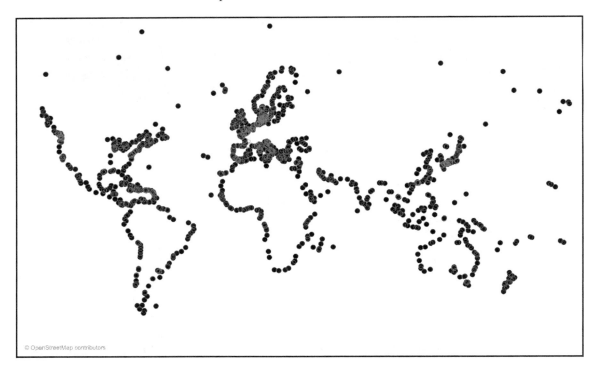

To recreate the example, you can download the ZIP file `Spatial Join` from the *Chapter 1* section of my website, `book.ladataviz.com` (or, browse to `https://ladataviz.com/wp-content/uploads/2018/09/Spatial-Join.zip`).

Let's create a spatial Join between the two spatial files, as follows:

1. Open Tableau and connect to the first spatial file, `contours-geographiques-des-nouvelles-regions-metropole.shp`.

2. Add a second spatial connection in the same Data Source, and choose the `ne_10m_ports.shp` file.

3. Choose an **Inner** interest Join between the two tables, shown as follows:

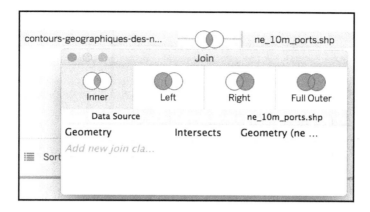

4. You can test your Data Source; the remaining French regions are the ones with ports, and the remaining ports are only French ones. If you create a Dual Axis map, you can show both the regions and the ports on the same map, as follows:

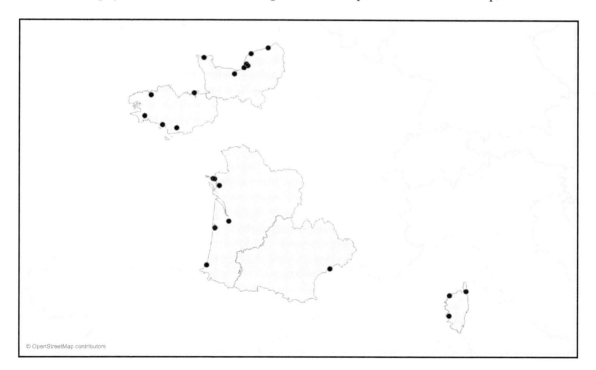

This is surely a great advancement for using spatial files in Tableau. Let's finish this section by looking at other Data Source improvements.

## Other Data Source improvements

Some other Data Source improvements are as follows:

- From Tableau 2018.1, Tableau can recognize spatial columns in SQL Server and use them for mapping. You can also use Custom SQL to write an advanced analysis using your spatial fields.
- Cross-database Joins and MDX queries have improved in performance since Tableau 2018.2.

Now, let's take a look at visualization improvements.

# Visualization improvements

Many new features are available when speaking about visualizations. With the new versions of Tableau, you can use a new type of Marks, create Dual Axis mapping, step lines, jump lines, save and reuse your clusters, and much more. Let's start with the new Density Mark.

## Density Mark (2018.3)

Density is the newest Marks type, introduced in Tableau 2018.3 and represented with the following icon: ◯ Density

This new mark fills a gap: to show the Density of Marks. The superposition of multiple Marks determines the color intensity. It's a straightforward Marks type; you can use it in various cases, as long as you have many Marks overlapping.

In the following example, you can see that the concentration of customers by **Sales** and
**Quantity**:

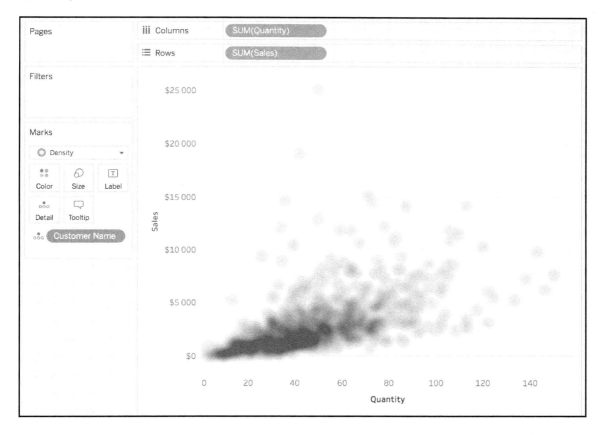

The most important property for the Density Mark is the color. Thanks to the intensity of the color, you can see the **Density** of the Marks. To deal with this particularity, there is a new option when you click on the **Color** property: **Intensity**. Changing the intensity of the color tells different stories. In the following screenshot, the **Intensity** is set to 90%:

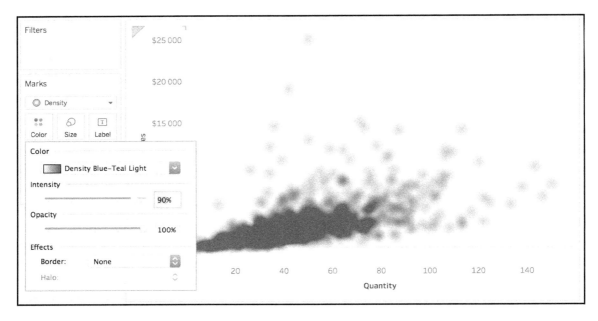

In the following screenshot, the **Intensity** is set to 40%:

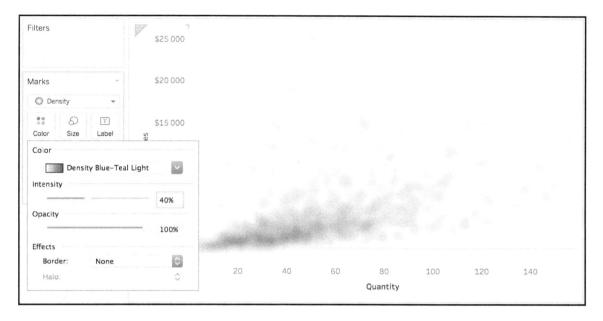

Tableau has also added new color palettes, specially designed for the Density Mark. You'll find palettes for bright and dark backgrounds. Currently, the only drawback is the impossibility to open the **Edit Color** menu and select a color on your screen or enter a color code. You can, however, use your custom palette, specified in the Preference.tps file of your Tableau Repository.

## Step and jump lines (2018.1)

Since version 2018.1, when you use the Line Marks type, a click on the **Path** button has opened a menu where you can select the **Line Type**: **Linear**, **Step**, or **Jump**. The following screenshot shows an example of a step line:

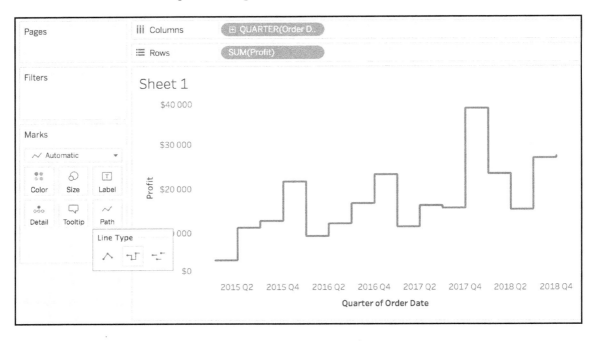

Although it's not the most spectacular new feature, it's nevertheless a great addition, simplifying a complicated procedure to build the same visualization.

## Worksheet transparency (2018.3)

A long-awaited feature is the Worksheet transparency. It is a great addition, allowing you to build better visualizations; but it's also an open door to terrible practices and designs.

 **Data** is the most crucial element in data visualization—not the design. The design is important, as it's a vector of success for your Dashboards, but it's not the primary concern. Please, always focus on the clarity of the data, and keep in mind the Data-Ink Ratio introduced by Edward Tufte: https://infovis-wiki.net/wiki/Data-Ink_Ratio.

To make the background of a Worksheet transparent, follow these steps:

1. Click on **Format...** in the Worksheet options, as highlighted in the following screenshot:

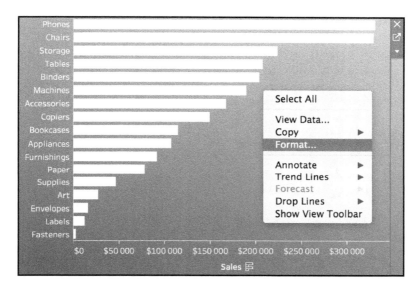

2. Click on the third icon, **Shading**, to modify the shading format.
3. Select **None** in the **Default** Worksheet shading, highlighted as follows:

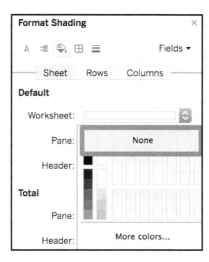

Use this new feature with caution! The next new feature is the ability to create Dual Axis, with different types of coordinates.

# Dual Axis mapping (2018.1)

Before Tableau 2018.1, you could already build a Dual Axis map. To do so, duplicate the longitude in columns, or latitude in rows, and select **Dual Axis** in the pill option. Thanks to the **Dual Axis** option, it is possible to have two different Mark types and a different level of detail in each Marks layer. In the following screenshot, you can see a Dual Axis map, with a filled map for the state with the **Sales** in color in the first layer, and circles for each city, colored in black, in the second Marks layer:

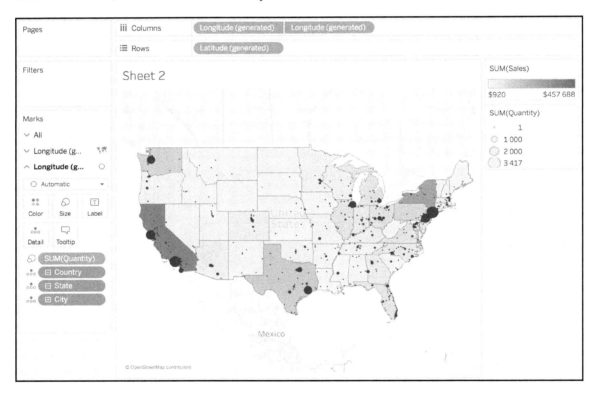

Unfortunately, in previous versions of Tableau, it was impossible to create a Dual Axis map by combining Tableau-generated coordinates and custom coordinates in your data. Since Tableau 2018.1, it's been possible. Let's look at how to do it.

To reproduce the example, download the `Orders without City` file from my website, `book.ladataviz.com`, or browse to `https://ladataviz.com/wp-content/uploads/2018/09/Orders-without-City.xlsx`.

In the `Orders without City` file, the cities have been removed and replaced by their latitude and longitude, in two different columns: `Latitude City` and `Longitude City`. The goal is to rebuild the preceding example with this new file. Do as follows:

1. Open Tableau and connect to the `Orders without City` file.
2. Right-click on the **Latitude City** field and select **Convert to Dimension**. Repeat the same for **Longitude City**.
3. Double-click on **State** to create a map, and put **Sales** in color.
4. Add **Latitude (generated)** next to the existing **Latitude (generated)** pill.
5. Right-click on the second **Latitude (generated)** pill and click on **Dual Axis**.
6. On the second Marks layer, change the **Type** to **Circle**, add **Latitude City** and **Longitude City** in **Detail**, change the **Quantity** from **Color** to **Size**, and, finally, change the color of the **Marks** to black. The final result is as follows:

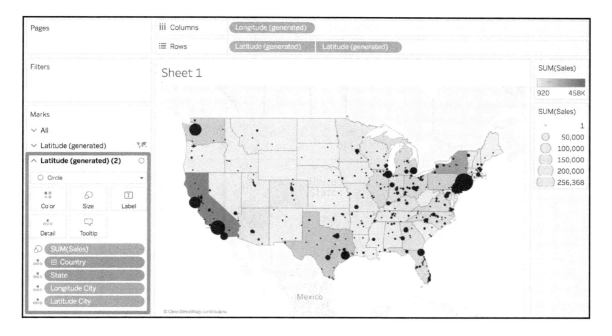

As you can see, since Tableau 2018.1, you can combine generated coordinates with custom ones.

The next enhancement was one of the longest-standing requests from the community: the nested sort.

# Nested sort (2018.2)

Sorting a measure across two dimensions was inexplicably difficult prior to Tableau 2018.2. If you tried to sort the categories by Sales for each dimension, you would see the following:

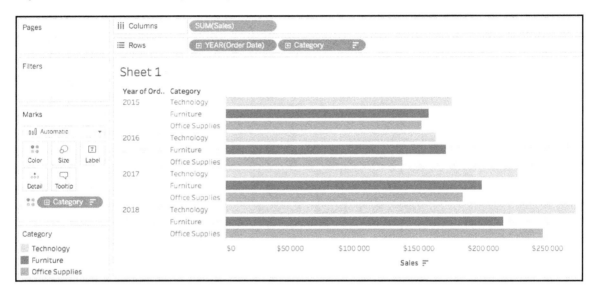

As you can see, the categories were sorted without taking the years into account (making it difficult to rank the categories in *2016* or *2018*, for example). It was possible to get the desired sort with a hidden combined field or some table calculations, but everyone agrees that it was unnecessarily complicated.

From Tableau 2018.2, if you click on the **Sort** button on the axis, Tableau creates a nested sort, displaying the best **Category** per year as follows:

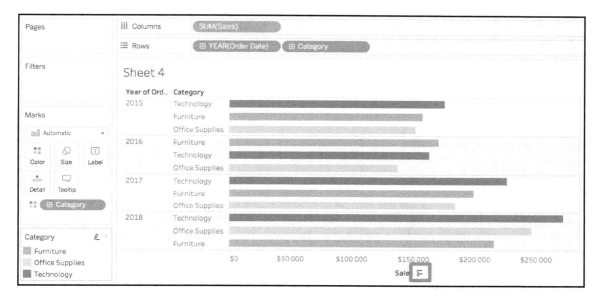

If you still want to use the previous method of sorting, you can use the sorting icon in the toolbar.

This small enhancement makes the product a lot simpler to use. The next feature is quite similar, with a simple addition having a tremendous positive impact.

# Hierarchy filtering (2018.1)

If you display the **Quick Filter** of a field that is part of a hierarchy, a new option is now available: **All Values in Hierarchy**. This new option is applied by default.

With this option, the **Quick Filter** only shows the possible values, considering the filtered parent value of the hierarchy. It produces the same result as the **Only relevant values** option, but automatically, and with better performance.

Let's finish by looking at a list of other small enhancements that will make your life easier (when using Tableau, of course).

# Other improvements

The following is a list of other small visualization improvements:

- Tableau 10.5 introduced the **Viz In Tooltip** feature. Unfortunately, in previous versions, it was impossible to hide a worksheet that was only used in a tooltip. You can now hide those Worksheets in every Tableau 2018 version.
- From Tableau 2018.1, saved clusters are no longer just groups, but are a special field with this icon: You can reuse saved clusters, and, with a right-click, you can refit the clusters to take the new data into account.
- You can revert your workbook to Tableau 10.2 by using the option **Export as Version** in the top **File** menu. From Tableau 2018.2, you also get clear information about the compatibility and lost functions.
- When you hover over a grayed option in the **Analytics** pane, Tableau now gives you information about why you can't use that option.
- Tableau now displays the link to the *Driver Installation* page in the **Connection** menu, for a specific connection.
- You can display negative values on a logarithmic axis, from Tableau 2018.2.
- Dates can be represented in ISO 8601 format, from Tableau 2018.2.
- Geocoding has been improved in the 2018.2 version, with Japanese municipalities, wards, seven-digit postal codes, and 2018 Pennsylvania Congressional Districts.
- Cross-database Joins and multi-dimensional expression queries for cubes have improved performance since Tableau 2018.2.
- In Tableau 2018.3, you can connect to the ESRI Geodatabase, KML, and the TopoJSON file.

Now, we'll look at the new features available for Dashboards.

# Dashboard improvements

This year, two new Dashboard items, two new actions, the Grid, and the automatic Mobile layout were released by Tableau.

Let's start with the extensions, which are likely the most important new feature in this book.

## Extensions (2018.2)

If you have been a Tableau user for a long time, I'm sure that you have dreamed about one of the following features: dynamic parameters, an automatic date updater, export to CSV buttons, an automatic radar chart or Sankey diagram, and more. Thanks to the extensions, all of these features are now available! And the best part is: this is just the beginning.

Extensions provide the ability to interact with other applications or services, directly inside Tableau, without leaving your Dashboard. You can also use them to expand Tableau's limits. The extensions are supported on Tableau Desktop and Tableau Server.

You can add new extensions from the **Dashboard** pane, on the left-hand side, as follows:

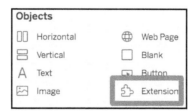

When you add an **Extension** object, Tableau opens a new window, where you have to select a .TREX file. You can either download existing .TREX files in the **Extension Gallery**, or create your own.

The **Extension Gallery** is available at `https://extensiongallery.tableau.com`. From here, you can find and download many extensions, developed by Tableau and their partners. One example is the **Data-Driven Parameters** extension page, with the **Download** button highlighted, as follows:

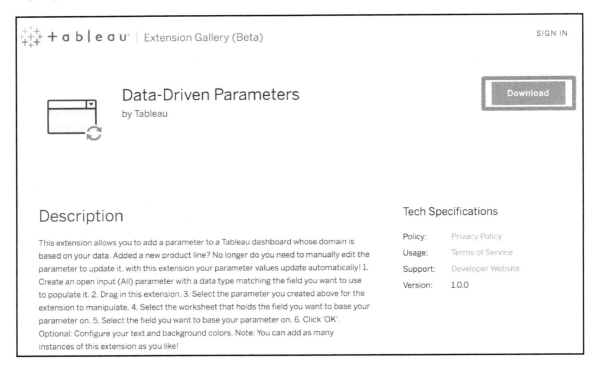

When you add an extension, Tableau opens a warning, asking you to allow and trust the extension. Then, you'll likely have to configure the extension. As every extension is different, each configuration window is different. The following is an example of the **Data-Driven Parameter Configuration** window, where you have to select a parameter, a worksheet, and a field:

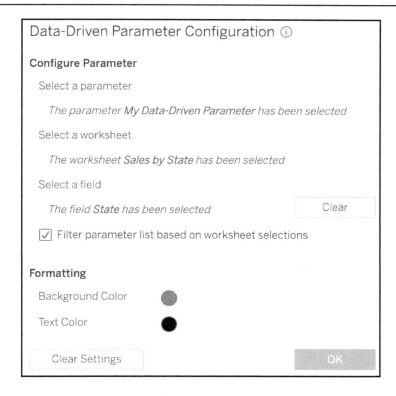

Using the Extensions API, you can also develop new extensions in Node.js to create new interactions with your applications. Unfortunately, you will not learn how to code in Node.js in this book. However, if you want to learn how to build your own extensions, you'll find tutorials, samples, and clear explanations in the Tableau Extensions GitHub page, at `https://tableau.github.io/extensions-api`.

As you can see, the possibilities are infinite. Tableau will frequently update the Extension Gallery, offering new ways to work with Tableau.

The next feature is also a new Dashboard object!

# Dashboard navigation button (2018.3)

Have you ever created a navigation button in Tableau, to change from one Dashboard to another? It was one of those unnecessarily complicated processes: you had to add a Worksheet with a custom shape on a Dashboard and add an action to another Dashboard: complicated, long, and now, obsolete.

Since Tableau 2018.3, the **Button** object is available on the Dashboard pane, as highlighted in the following screenshot:

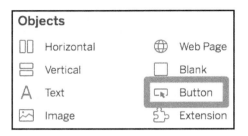

You can add a Button to your Dashboard as follows:

1. Drag and drop the **Button** object to wherever you please.
2. When you add a Button, Tableau will display it, and you can then configure it with a right-click, as follows:

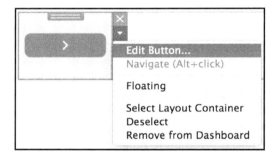

3. On the configuration window, you will have to specify a target sheet (a Worksheet, Dashboard, or Story), and you can change the image and add a tooltip. The following is an example of a button that redirects to the **Product Dashboard**, with a personalized image and a tooltip:

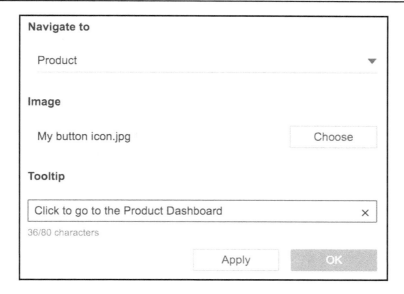

4. Finally, without having to use shapes and actions, you can add navigation buttons to your Dashboard, as highlighted in the following screenshot:

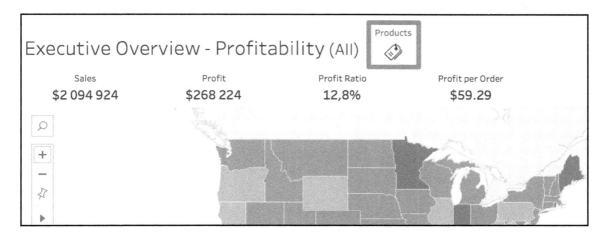

In 2018, Tableau added two new Dashboard objects, and also two new actions. Let's start with the first one, which is really close to the **Button** object.

# Navigation action (2018.3)

In Tableau 2018.3, when you add an **Action**, you will find the **Go to Sheet...** action, highlighted as follows:

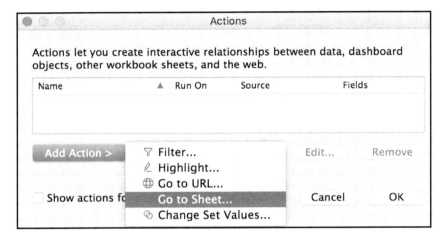

This action is straightforward: from one or multiple source Worksheets, you can navigate to a **Target Sheet** (Worksheet, Dashboard, or Story). The following screenshot shows the configuration window, when you add a **Go to Sheet...** action:

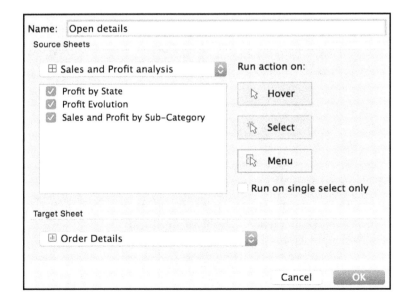

In this configuration window, you can specify the following:

- The **Name** of the action
- The **Source Sheets**
- The trigger (**Hover**, **Select**, or **Menu**)
- The **Target Sheet** (Worksheet, Dashboard, or Story)

This action is quite similar to the **Button** object, as both allow you to navigate between your sheets. The difference, however, is crucial: one is a configurable Dashboard object, while the other is an action based on a sheet and a trigger.

The second new action allows you to create new ways to interact with your Worksheets.

# The Change Set Values action (2018.3)

The **Change Set Values** action allows you to visually select the values to put in a set. From one or multiple source Worksheets, you can update the values of a set in your Data Source to impact other visualization in your Workbook.

When you create a **Change Set Values** action, a configuration window will open, where you can specify the following:

- The **Name** of the action
- The **Source Sheets**
- The trigger (**Hover**, **Select**, or **Menu**)
- The **set**—you have to specify the Data Source and the set

As for the action filter, you can dictate the behavior when clearing the action. There are three different behaviors, as follows:

- **Keep set value**: When you clear the selection, the current values of the set stay as selected.
- **Add all values to set**: When you clear the selection, all of the values will be in the set.
- **Remove all values from set**: When you clear the selection, all of the values will be out of the set.

Let's go through a guided tutorial, using **Sample-Superstore**, to see how to configure and use this new action:

1. Create a first Worksheet, `Sales by State` a map of **State** with **Sales** in color, as shown in the following screenshot:

2. Create a set, `State Set`, based on **State** (right-click on the **State** field and go to **Create**, then **Set**). On the **Edit Set** window, select **Use all**, as follows:

3. Create a second Worksheet, `Sales by Sub-Category`, with **Sales** in **Columns**, **Sub-Category** in **Rows**, and the new **State Set** in **Color**. The following screenshot shows what your Worksheet should look like:

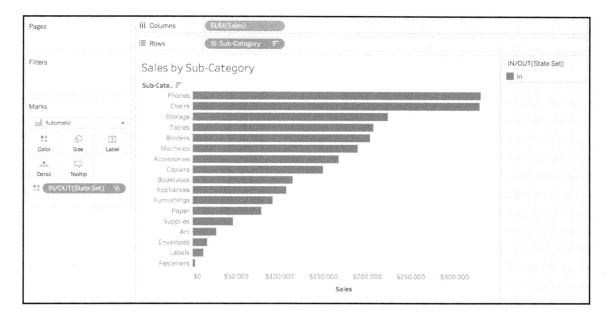

4. Create a Dashboard. First, add **Sales by State**, then add **Sales by Sub-Category** to the right. Add an action and choose **Change Set Values**. We want to update **State Set** when we click on a state on the map. When we clear the selection, all of the values will be **In** the set. The following screenshot illustrates the required configuration:

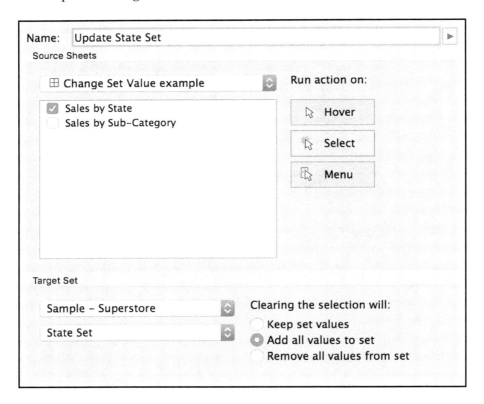

5. Let's test our action! When you select one or multiple states on the map, you should see the portion of sales coming from the selected state(s) on the right. In the following screenshot, you can see the portion of Sales coming from the state of California:

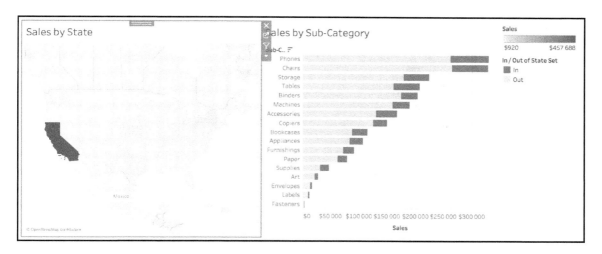

The ability to visually select the values of a set will surely provide great opportunities.

The next feature will be a great time saver if you have to create Mobile layouts.

# Automatic Mobile layouts (2018.2)

From Tableau 2018.2, when you add a Phone or Tablet layout, Tableau automatically rearranges the Dashboard layout, making it ready to use. In the previous versions, you had to reorder it yourself.

Consider the automatic Phone layout created by Tableau before 2018.2, as shown in the following screenshot:

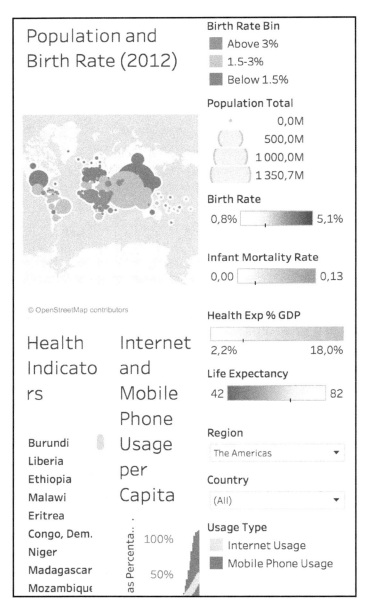

The following is the same layout, automatically built by Tableau in 2018.2:

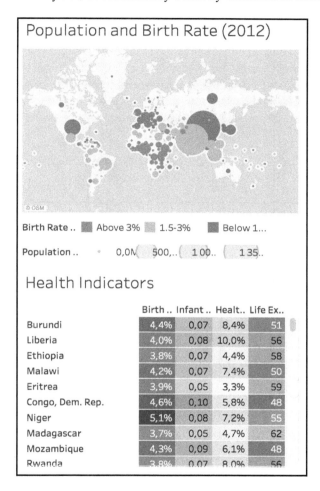

If you decide to change something inside of your custom layout, you can use the **Rearrange layout** option. It will automatically reorder the items and change the sizes. The option is available when you click on the three dots (...) next to a layout, highlighted as follows:

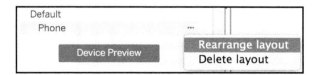

This feature doesn't allow you to create new things, but it'll save you a lot of time. The next feature is similar.

# Grids (2018.2)

Whether you are working with floating or container layouts, the goal is the same: to have a nice-looking Dashboard. With Grids, Tableau makes it easier for you to achieve this. You can show or hide the Grid from the Dashboard menu, or by pressing the *G* key on your keyboard.

From the Dashboard menu, you can also open the **Grid** option and choose its size in pixels. The following screenshot shows an example of a ten-pixel grid:

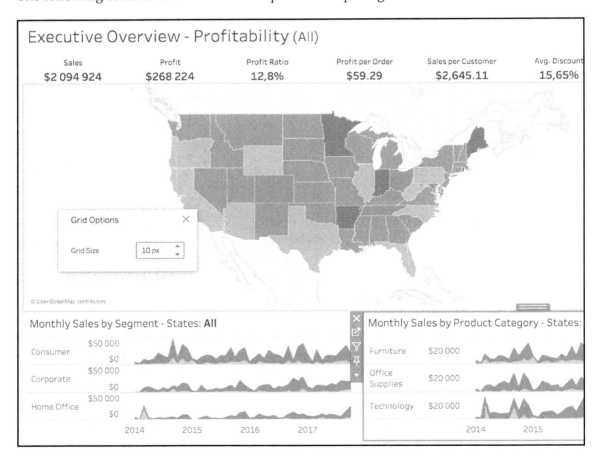

The Grid comes with another great enhancement: you can move the floating items, pixel by pixel, with the keyboard arrows. Achieving great designs has never been simpler!

This ends the section about Tableau Desktop. As always, Tableau has improved both Tableau Desktop and Tableau Server. Now, let's look at all of the new features available in Tableau Server and Tableau Online.

# Tableau Server/Online

This second section, about Tableau Server, is also divided into three parts, as follows:

- **Interacting**: The new features available when you open a published Workbook
- **Web authoring**: The new features available when you create a new Workbook online
- **Administration**: The changes and enhancements involved in administrating a Tableau Server

To reproduce the examples presented in this chapter, you will have to know how to connect to Tableau Server, open published Workbooks, and create new Workbooks online.

# Interacting

The major change comes in Tableau 2018.3 with the new browsing experience: mixed content. However, there are other nice new features when interacting with a view like the preview for Mobile layout and the ability to tag people in the comments.

## Mixed content (2018.3)

From version 2018.3, Tableau Server has two ways to display the content. The new default way is called **mixed content**, and it shows different types of content in the same place.

Before Tableau Server 2018.3, the different types of content were separated into different tabs, and you had to select a specific tab to see its content. In the following screenshot, you can see an example of a project called **Sales**:

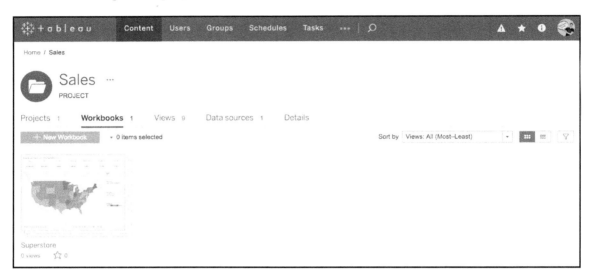

As you can see in the preceding screenshot, each tab contains a different type of content. In the following screenshot, you can see the same sales project with the sub-project (**Sales Projection**), one Workbook, and one Data Source, all displayed in the same place:

This new browsing method is simpler, and it keeps all of the same functionalities. If you prefer to keep the traditional browsing experience, you can deactivate the option in the **Settings** of Tableau Server, as follows:

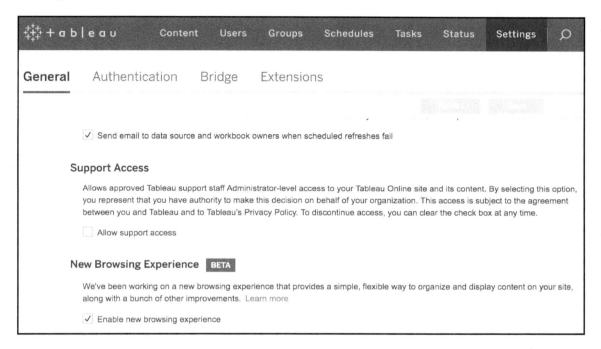

In Tableau Desktop 2018.2, the Automatic Mobile layout feature allows you to build great Phone and Tablet layouts more efficiently. With the next feature, you'll be able to test them online in seconds.

# Mobile preview (2018.3)

From Tableau 2018.3, you can preview the different layouts in Tableau Server. Above the toolbar, when you open a **View**, a new button, **Preview Device Layouts**, is now available, as follows:

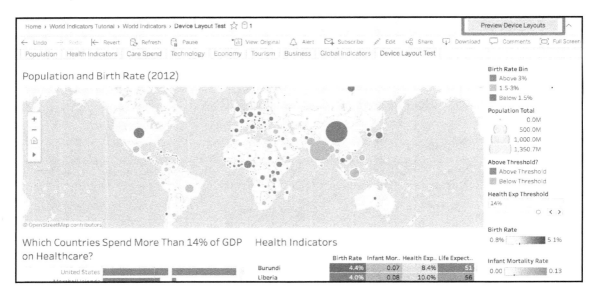

When you click on the button, Tableau opens the preview mode, where you can select **Laptop**, **Tablet**, or **Phone**, to see how your Dashboard renders. For example, if you preview the preceding Dashboard, you can see the Phone layout, as follows:

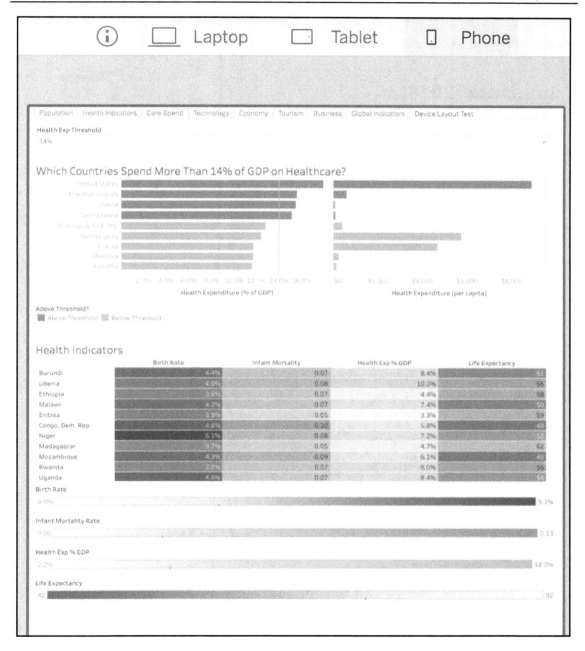

Phone layout view

This new feature is a great addition to test your different layouts, without having to use the devices or special tools.

## Comments (2018.2)

From Tableau Server 2018.3, you can mention Tableau Server/Online users by using the @ symbol in the comments. They will be notified by email, making it easier to follow the discussions and answer questions.

Let's move on to the web authoring improvements.

# Web authoring

Web authoring is getting better and better with each release of Tableau Server. Tableau Server 2018.1 added a significant new feature: the ability to connect to data directly from the web.

## Connecting to data (2018.1)

In Tableau 2018.1, Tableau changed its Tableau License model, with three new roles: creator, explorer, and viewer. A particularity of the creator role is the ability to create a new Data Source, directly on the web.

When you create a new Workbook in Tableau Server, Tableau opens the web authoring mode and asks you to connect to data. From this page, you can connect to files and servers directly from the web! There are four types of data connections available, as follows:

- **File**: Drag and drop an Excel file or CSV on the web page; you can choose the sheets and build a new Data Source, just like in Tableau Desktop.
- **Connectors**: A list of server-hosted databases available directly from Tableau Server.
- **On this site**: Use an existing, published Data Source.
- **Dashboard Starters**: Start with pre-built templates of cloud-based systems.

 Users that don't have a creator license can always use published Data Sources to create new analyses, but they can't connect to new data from files or servers.

---

You can also add a new Data Source to an existing workbook in the web authoring, just like in Tableau Desktop.

## Other web authoring improvements

As you know, the web authoring mode of Tableau Server does not yet include all of the functionalities of Tableau Desktop. However, each new version adds a list of new capabilities, getting closer and closer to Tableau Desktop. The following are some of the important missing functionalities, which are now available online:

- Adding, removing, and editing annotations
- Updating axes and resizing headers
- Using **Show Me** from a Dashboard
- Finding fields in your Data Source by using the search button
- Adding images to a Dashboard
- Connecting to Google BigQuery and opening files from Dropbox and OneDrive
- Creating Joins, cross-database Joins, Unions, and Pivots

 You can find all of the differences between Tableau Desktop and Tableau Server/Online at `https://public.tableau.com/views/TableauDesktopvTableauWebEditing/DesktopvsWebEdit,` created by Andrew Pick.

From Tableau Server 2018.1, the toolbar used to interact with a view is WCAG 2.0 AA compliant. Thanks to this improvement, the experience of using Tableau Online has been better for people that use screen readers, keyboards in braille, or keyboards only.

The time when saving a workbook online was also optimized in Tableau Server 2018.3. Of course, many of the new features of the latest Tableau Desktop version, such as extensions, buttons, and the Density Mark, are also included in the web authoring mode.

In the last section, we'll focus on the improvements for Tableau Server administrators.

# Administration

The major change for administrators is the new Tableau Service Manager, but you'll find many other enhancements.

# Tableau Service Manager (2018.2)

The first version of **Tableau Service Manager** (**TSM**) was introduced in Tableau Server 10.5, on Linux, with the TSM **command-line interface** (**CLI**). Now, with Tableau Server 2018.2, the TSM is available for both Windows and Linux, and contains three major components, as follows:

- A TSM CLI that replaces the previous `tabadmin` commands.

> If you migrate from Tabadmin to the TSM CLI, the corresponding commands are available at `https://onlinehelp.tableau.com/current/server/en-us/tabadmin_to_tsm_cli.htm`.

- A Tableau Service Manager API (currently in alpha) that allows you to perform administrative tasks through an API.

> You can find the documentation of the API at `https://onlinehelp.tableau.com/v0.0/api/tsm_api/en-us/index.htm#get-started`.

- A web UI interface that allows Tableau Server administrators to configure and manage the server directly from the web, without having to connect to the machine to open the configuration.

The most interesting feature is undoubtedly the web interface. You can access the administrative Tableau Server web page by using a URL, as if you were logging in to Tableau Server. From the web page, you can directly stop and start Tableau Server. The administration web page contains three tabs, as follows:

- **Status**: Check the current state of your Tableau Server.
- **Maintenance**: Generate, download, and analyze the log files, as well as other maintenance tasks.
- **Configuration**: Modify the topology of the server (the number of processes and nodes), the security, the user identity access, the notifications, and the licensing.

In short, all of the actions that require the administrators to connect to the machine where the server is installed to perform administrative tasks can now be done from the web, or by using the API. This improvement will surely make life easier for all administrators and DevOps teams!

To finish, let's review some other administrative improvements.

## Other administrative improvements

The following is a list of other improvements for admins:

- Tableau Bridge handles load-balanced live connections across multiple pooled clients.
- Two new backgrounder API functions are available: the GetJobList API (pulls the list of all jobs) and the CancelJob API (reclaims the resources of running and pending jobs).
- Tableau Online users are notified by email when they are added to a Tableau Online site.
- New admin Data Sources are available online, to create administrative views.
- You can activate **System for Cross-Domain Identity Provider** (**SCMI**) to manage the Tableau Server users with an external identity provider, such as Okta or OneLogin.

# Summary

With version 10.5, Tableau introduced a new data engine, Hyper, and included a long-awaited feature, the Viz in Tooltip. The 2018 releases have nothing to be ashamed of, in comparison! Every release brings a lot of new features and improvements.

In Tableau Desktop, with the multiple table schema and the spatial Join, you can create better Data Sources with improved performances. Visualizing the data has also improved considerably, with the new Density Marks type, step and jump lines, Worksheet transparency, and many more improvements for Dual Axis map, hierarchy filters, and nested sorts.

The most notable new features concern Dashboards. The ability to download and add extensions developed by Tableau and their partners from the Extension Gallery provides tons of new uses for Tableau. A few of the Tableau user dreams have already come true, thanks to the extensions. Also, you can develop your extensions to create the interactions that meet your needs. That's just one new feature! The navigation button and action, the update set value action, the automatic Mobile layout, and the grid, are some of the other features that will have huge impacts on building a Dashboard.

Tableau Server was not left out! A new browsing experience, a Mobile layout preview, and improved comments are now available when you interact with Tableau Server. Administrators also have some great new ways to perform their work, with the TSM allowing them to manage the server from a web page. However, the biggest change has come with the 2018.1 version and the ability to connect to data directly from a browser.

# 13
# Deal with Security

In this last advanced chapter, we'll speak about security, an essential aspect of working with data. To add protection, you need to have Tableau Server. In this chapter, we'll focus on three ways of dealing with security:

- Tableau Server security
- User filters
- Row-level filters

To manage the security on Tableau Server, you need to have sufficient privilege on it. To add the user filter and build the row-level security filter, you need at least one access to Tableau Server. Let's start with the most straightforward way of securing your data on Tableau Server.

## Tableau Server security

To protect your Tableau Server contents, you can click on the three dots **...** on any element (**Project**, **Workbooks**, **Views**, or **Data Sources**) to show the options and select **Permissions**. When you click on **Permissions**, Tableau opens a new window where you can specify many security options.

Here's the **Permissions** menu:

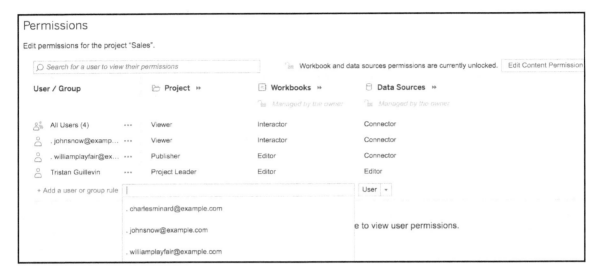

On this menu, you'll always see the **All Users** permissions. You can click on the dots to edit them. You can also click on **Add a user or group rule** to specify new permissions for specific Users or Group. When you edit the permissions, you can see, for each element, a list of pre-configured roles.

If you click on the arrows next to an element (Project, Workbooks, or Data Sources), you get more detail and the possibility to edit each permission individually. Each Permission can be allowed (green), denied (red), or unspecified (grey). To edit an individual Permission, click on its box.

Here's an example of a Permissions edition with a detailed view for Workbooks:

Know that all options are not available for all elements. Here's the complete list of Permissions, grouped by elements where they appear:

- **Global permissions**:
    - **View** 👁 : Specifies whether a user can see the element
    - **Save** 🖫 : Overwrites the existing element on the server
- **Project permissions**:
    - **Project leader** 👤: Someone with a project leader Permission has all Permissions on that project
- **Workbook and Data Sources Permissions**:
    - **Download** 🗄/🗄 : Downloads the Data Source or the Workbook
    - **Delete** 🗑 : Removes the element from the server
    - **Set Permissions** ✅ : Gives us the ability to change and define the Permissions
- **Workbook Permissions**:
    - **Download image** 🖼 : Downloads an image of the visualization
    - **Download summary data** ⬇ : Downloads a summary of the data in a visualization
    - **View comments** 💬 : Sees the comments posted under a visualization
    - **Add comments** 💬+ : Adds comments under a visualization
    - **Filter** ▽ : Uses the Filters available and the **Keep Only** and **Exclude** features
    - **Download full data** ⬇ : Downloads the complete data used in a visualization, with all the rows and columns
    - **Share customized** 📊 : Gives us the ability to create and share a customized view
    - **Web edit** ✎ : Opens the Tableau Server edition window where a user can modify the visualization or create new ones
    - **Move** 🗂 : Changes the Project of a Workbook

- **Data Sources Permissions**:
    - **Connect** 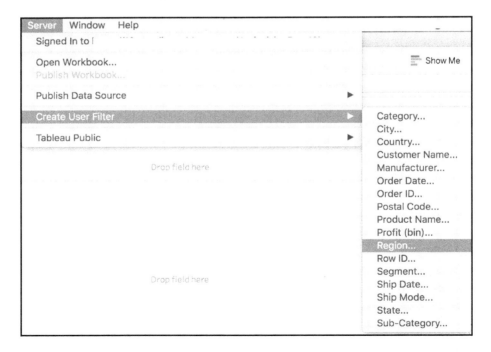 : Gives us the ability to connect to the Data Sources to create further analysis on Tableau Server or Tableau Desktop

With those Permissions, you can control who has access to what on Tableau Server. You can, for example, allow only a few users to access your Workbook. But what if you want to control what those users can see? Let's say that, based on the Sample-Superstore Data Source, you want to control the Region that the users can see. To do that, you need to set a User Filter.

# User Filters

User Filters are among Sets on Tableau Desktop and are based on a Dimension. Depending on who is the current logged-in user on Tableau Server, you can what data the user sees:

1. To add a User Filter, click on **Server** in the top menu, go to **Create a User Filter**, and choose the Field to secure. The following screenshot illustrates the creation of a User Filter on **Region...**:

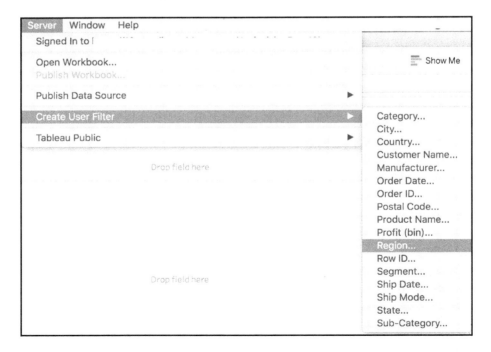

2. Tableau opens a new window where you can select, on the left, a User or a Group and select the values of the field that the User or Group can see.

3. Once you've created the User Filter, you'll see a new set in your Data Source.

4. To use a User Filter, add the corresponding set to the Filter shelf or, better, as a Data Source filter (with **Use all** option).

The reason it's better to add a User Filter on the Data Source filters rather than the Filter shelf is to increase the security. If you put a User Filter in the Filter shelf, and if a User can download or edit the Workbook, they can remove the User Filter from the Filters shelf, and they'll have access to all the data. Also, if someone starts a new analysis based on this Data Source, they'll also have access to all the data. Always put the User Filter on the Data Source Filters to make sure that no one can access data they're not supposed to see.

Now, to illustrate the usage of a User Filter, let's see an example with the Sample-Superstore Data Source. For this example, I created five Groups on Tableau Server: *Central, South, West, East,* and *Top Management*.

It's not a problem if you can't create the same groups as me to replicate this example. Just use existing Groups or Users on your Tableau Server, you can't break anything.

Let's start:

1. Create a new **User Filter** on **Region** and name it `Region Filter`.

2. In the User Filter configuration window, for each Group, select the members of the field that they are allowed to see. For example, for the **West** group, select the **West** value. For the **Top Management** group, select all members, and for **All Users**, select none.

Here's an example of the configuration for the **West** group:

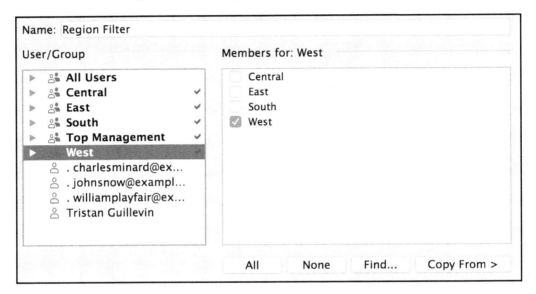

3. Build a simple visualization: double click on **State**, then add **Sales** on **Color**.
4. Put the **Region Filter Set** in the Filter shelf to test it. If you're not inside one of the Groups where we define access, you should not see anything.

5. At the very bottom of the Tableau window, you can see the current logged-in
   User in Tableau Server, as framed in the following screenshot:

6. Beside the name of the logged-in User, you can click on the arrow to select another User or Group.
7. With this option, choose the **West** group and the User Filter will automatically filter the Region to keep only the **West** value, as you can see here:

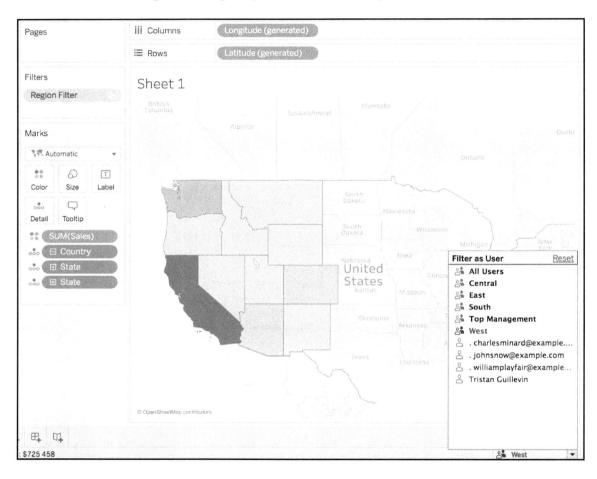

8. You can test the same with **Top Management**—all the regions will be displayed:

9. When you're confident that the User Filter works fine, you can remove it from the Filters shelf.
10. Right-click on the Data Source and select **Edit Data Source Filters**.
11. Click on the **Add** button, and select the **Region** Filter.
12. Select the **Use all** option, and click on **OK**. The User Filter is applied on all the data source, thereby enhancing the security of your data.

This is the first way of securing your data. As you may have guessed, if you have hundreds of Users to give access to and hundreds of different values in a Field, the User Filter will be extremely long to create and impossible to maintain. In those cases, we create a Row-level filter.

# Row-level filters

To create a Row-lever filter, your Data Source must contain a field with the name of the User. It is a great solution when access is already defined in your data. This option uses a Tableau function: USERNAME(). This function returns the username of the current logged-in User.

Again, the best way to understand it is with an example. You can reproduce the tutorial with the Users and Groups in your Tableau Server and the Sample-Superstore Data Source. For this tutorial, I've created three Users in Tableau Server and the following Excel File, which I named User Access:

| Region | User |
|--------|------|
| Central | johnsnow@example.com |
| West | johnsnow@example.com |
| East | johnsnow@example.com |
| South | johnsnow@example.com |
| West | williamplayfair@example.com |
| Central | charlesminard@example.com |

In the **Excel File**, we specified that:

- *John Snow* has access to all the Regions (*do not confuse John Snow, a famous epidemiologist who discovered, in 1854, that Cholera deaths were clustered around the water pumps in London thanks to data visualization, with Jon Snow, who knows nothing*)
- *William Playfair* only has access to *West*
- *Charles Minard* only has access to *Central*

Here's the step-by-step guide of how to create a Row-level filter between the data and Tableau Server:

1. Open Tableau and connect to the **Sample-Superstore** Excel File.
2. Add a new Excel connection to the **User Access** file.
3. Create a cross-database join between **Orders** and **User Access** on the common **Region** field:

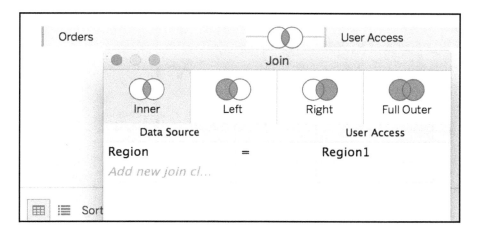

 This join duplicates the data by the number of Users, but as you never show multiple users at the same time, it's not a problem.

4. On a Worksheet, create a new Calculated Field, name it User has access, and write the USERNAME()=[User] calculation. This calculation returns True if the current logged-in User is the same as the **User** field in the Data Source.

5.  Create a new Data Source filter, add the **User has access** Calculated Field, and keep only the **True** value. The Data Source filter should look as follows:

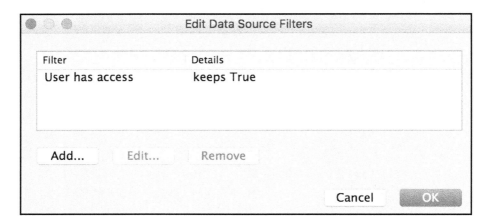

6.  You can test the Filter by selecting different Users on Tableau Server with the bottom menu. Here are two examples with the user *John Snow*, who has access to all regions, and *Charles Minard*, who only has access to the *Central* region:

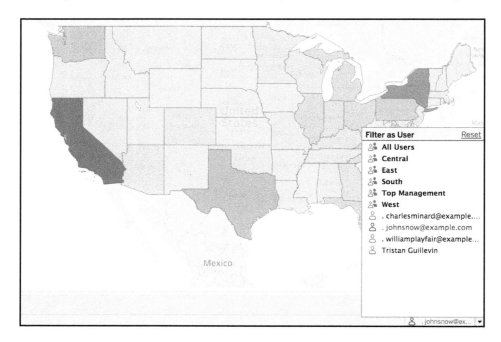

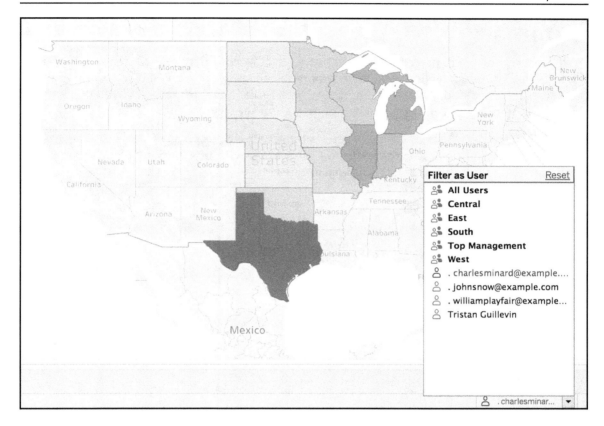

With this solution, you let the data control the security. It's a great way to handle complex situations because you can create Row-level filters based on multiple fields.

Before Tableau 2018.3, the only drawback was the data duplication: when using an extract, all the duplicated lines must be generated, which makes the Extract gigantic. Since Tableau 2018.3, you can use the multiple table schema when creating an Extract with joins. It drastically decreases the Extract size when using a Row-Level filter.

# Summary

In this last technical chapter, you learned how to secure your data and content on Tableau Server. The Permissions allow you to control who can see your work and what power they have over it (download, save, edit, and more). On Tableau Desktop, with User Filters and Row-Level filters, you can control what the users can see in your data.

This book is almost finished. We've covered all the technical aspects of Tableau. The last chapter is an invitation to join the Tableau Community with tips on how to get better and better each day with different Community Projects.

# How to Keep Growing Your **14** Skills

That's it! You are now all set to use Tableau in a professional environment. Starting with connecting to your data, building your data source, then your first visualizations and Dashboards to publish all your work in a secure and online environment. But there is still a lot to discover and many ways to become better at using Tableau.

In this short chapter, we'll speak about:

- The Tableau Community
- Tableau Public
- Community projects
- Ambassadors, Zen Masters, and Iron Viz

Let's start with the reason Tableau is the best tool for data visualization: the Community.

## The Tableau Community

Tableau is an excellent tool for many reasons. But there are a lot of great tools for data visualization. If you ask me why Tableau is better than the others, my answer would be, *the Community*.

When I started using Tableau, the Tableau Community Forums helped me a lot. No questions are left unanswered, and you'll find a lot of people eager to help you. Don't hesitate to ask any questions here: `https://community.tableau.com/community/forums`.

The Community is all about sharing. There are many events where the Tableau Community gather to share. The **Tableau User Group** (**TUG**) is a regional event (check whether there's one near your area!) where senior users meet new users and discuss new features, tips, use cases, and more. It's also a great place to share pizzas and beers!

Don't be sad if there is no TUG near you; there are many online events, such as the Fringe Festival, organized by the Tableau Community: http://www.thefringefestival.rocks/.

Of course, there are also two major official events: the Tableau Conference in the US and the European Tableau Conference in Europe. It is the biggest Tableau event and the best place to meet people, discover all the new features to be released and cheer on your favorite competitor at the Iron Viz event.

You'll find all the events, groups, forums, links, and webinars here: https://www.tableau.com/community.

The other great way to learn is on Tableau Public.

# Tableau Public

Tableau Public is software, similar to Tableau Desktop, that you can download and use for free with some limitations: you need to publish your work online in a public environment, and you don't have access to all the connectors available in Tableau Desktop.

Tableau Public is, in fact, much more than that.

Tableau Public is like a social network, but while people are sharing pictures of their cats and kids on Facebook, you can only find the best visualizations available in Tableau Public. As we are data lovers, here are some figures: 250,000 Tableau Public users have published more than 1,000,000 Workbooks, generating more than 1,000,000,000 views.

On the Tableau Public website, you can find a **Viz Of The Day** section on the homepage (every day, a new Workbook is promoted by Tableau: https://public.tableau.com/en-us/s/), and many Featured visualizations in different categories (Greatest Hits, Sports, Social Goof, and so on). You can find a list of the current Featured Authors, a blog, and many resources to keep learning. You can also search for any author or interest. But wait, the best is yet to come.

At the bottom of every visualization published in Tableau Public, there are some buttons to open the visualization in fullscreen, share, and the best: download. When you click on the download button, you can get an image, the data, a crosstab, a PDF, and – *are you ready?* – the Workbook itself! Even the most beautiful Workbooks can usually be downloaded (it's the author's choice). It is one of the greatest ways to learn. I discover a lot by downloading the Workbooks and figuring out how the authors built them.

Creating a Tableau Public account is very simple. Once you have an account, you can start to follow authors you like and publish Workbooks. If you post a visualization, you can make it featured, delete it, or hide it with the icons you see here:

Finally, for all your published visualizations, you can edit the description and specify whether you'll allow the Workbook and its data to be downloaded. It may be against the philosophy of Tableau Public to refuse it to be downloaded, but some companies use Tableau Public as a communication tool, and they can't share all their data.

Here's what you can edit on your published Workbooks:

The main reason why people don't share Workbooks in Tableau Public is that they don't know what data to share. The next section resolves that problem.

# Community projects

This section is all about growing your Tableau skills. There are many projects created by the Community for the Community. Participating in those projects doesn't engage you in anything, you can only learn and become better. For the majority of those projects, people interact through Twitter, so I advise you to create an account to follow those projects.

Here are some Community projects:

- **Viz For Social Good – #VizForSocialGood** by *Chloe Tseng*: This project gives you the opportunity to work for non-profit organizations such as UNICEF and the United Nations. There is a new project almost every month, with a deadline to respect. You can register as a volunteer to be informed of new projects. At the end of every project, the non-profit organization chooses one visualization to feature on its communication channels. As Chloe says:

*We help mission-driven organizations to promote social good and understand their own data through beautiful and informative data visualization.*

**Viz For Social Good** was awarded a Silver for Community at the 2017 Information is Beautiful Awards. All the information that is required to join is mentioned here: `https://www.vizforsocialgood.com`.

- **Make Over Monday – *#MakeOverMonday*—**by *Eva Murray* and *Andy Kriebel*: Probably the most-followed project and the best way to practice your creativity in Tableau. Every Sunday they share a new dataset to visualize in Tableau. On Wednesday, there is a webinar where Eva and Andy review some visualizations (*#MMVizReview*) and, during the weekend, they publish a blog post with all the lessons learned and the favorite makeovers. The best definition is on their website:

*Makeover Monday is your weekly learning and development appointment with yourself and hundreds of passionate data people. For free!*

You'll find all the information, data sets, and links here: `https://www.makeovermonday.co.uk/`.

- **Workout Wednesday – *#WorkOutWednesday*—**currently run by Rody Zachovich, Ann Jackson, Luke Stanke, Curtis Harris, and guests: The most challenging Community project. Every Wednesday, they share a new visualization and the Dataset required to reproduce it. The goal is to rebuild the same visualization. Of course, it's more difficult than you think. If **Make Over Monday** helps you practice the creativity, **Workout Wednesday** is all about technical challenges. As you can read on their website:

*Workout Wednesday is a set of weekly challenges [...] designed to test your knowledge of Tableau and help you kick on in your development.*

Find all the challenges at `http://www.workout-wednesday.com/weekly-overview/`.

There are other projects such as **Data For a Cause** *#DataForACause* (`www.olgatsubiks.com/data-for-a-cause`) by Olga Tsubiks, and **Sports Viz Sunday** *#SportsVizSunday* (`https://data.world/sportsvizsunday`) by Simon Beaumont and Spencer Baucke, that I invite you to follow.

As you can see, there are many ways to learn and become better at using Tableau. Maybe, after some time, you'll compete as an Iron Viz contestant, or you'll be recognized as one of the Ambassadors or Zen Masters. Don't know what I'm talking about? The next – and last – section explains everything.

# Ambassadors, Zen Masters, and Iron Viz

When you start in the Tableau Community, it may be hard to know whom to follow. Tableau has decided to help you by recognizing the investment and spirit of some people in the Community.

## Ambassadors

The first set of amazing people are the **Ambassadors**. They are split into four groups:

- **Forums Ambassadors**: They are there to your questions in the Forum
- **Social Media Ambassadors**: They are the social network gurus, follow them to get all the news
- **User Group Leader Ambassadors**: They help the Community meet in real life by organizing the Tableau User Groups
- **Tableau Public Ambassadors**: Check their Tableau Public profiles and be ready to be blown away

Find all the current **Ambassadors** here: `https://www.tableau.com/tableau-ambassadors`.

## Zen Masters

The second set of amazing people is the **Zen Masters**. They are the faces of Tableau Community. They passionately dedicate a huge amount of time to help everyone excel in Tableau. They not only create great visualizations, but they also share their knowledge as much as they can. Everyone in the Tableau Community has learned at least one thing from a **Zen Master**.

Discover who the **Zen Masters** are and what they are doing at `https://www.tableau.com/zen-masters`.

# Iron Viz

As you enhance your skills, you may want to try to compete against other people in the Community. For that, you have the Iron Viz. The competition is divided into two parts: three qualification contests, the Feeders, and one Final. For the Feeders, only the theme is imposed, and the contestants have approximately one month to find the data and create the best possible visualization. There is one winner per Feeder.

The three winners of the Feeders battle during the Iron Viz Final at the annual Tableau Conference. There is no way to prepare for the Final: build a Workbook from the start, in 20 minutes, live, in front of thousands of screaming people. A jury, composed of four peoples, and the public, vote on Twitter to determine the annual Iron Viz champion. Since 2017, they have also started a European Iron Viz competition.

I advise you to participate. Not for the purpose of winning, but to push yourself further than you've ever gone in Tableau. You cannot lose; either you win, or you learn.

# Summary

This chapter, even though it's not technical, is really important. This chapter is the key to continuing your journey with Tableau. Even if you don't plan on sharing a lot or getting involved (which is understandable), keep in mind that the Community Forum is the first place to go if you have any questions regarding Tableau. Even though I tried my best to explain all the concepts in this book, no books or training sessions can cover every use case you will encounter in real life. Also, if you're searching for resources, blogs, inspiration, or webinars, you'll find it on Tableau Public or through the Community Projects.

# Other Books You May Enjoy

If you enjoyed this book, you may be interested in these other books by Packt:

**Advanced Analytics with R and Tableau**
Jen Stirrup

ISBN: 9781786460110

- Integrate Tableau's analytics with the industry-standard, statistical prowess of R.
- Make R function calls in Tableau, and visualize R functions with Tableau using RServe.
- Use the CRISP-DM methodology to create a roadmap for analytics investigations.
- Implement various supervised and unsupervised learning algorithms in R to return values to Tableau.
- Make quick, cogent, and data-driven decisions for your business using advanced analytical techniques such as forecasting, predictions, association rules, clustering, classification, and other advanced Tableau/R calculated field functions.

**Mastering Tableau**
David Baldwin

ISBN: 9781784397692

- Create a worksheet that can display the current balance for any given period in time
- Recreate a star schema from in a data warehouse in Tableau
- Combine level of detail calculations with table calculations, sets, and parameters
- Create custom polygons to build filled maps for area codes in the USA
- Visualize data using a set of analytical and advanced charting techniques
- Know when to use Tableau instead of PowerPoint
- Build a dashboard and export it to PowerPoint

# Leave a review - let other readers know what you think

Please share your thoughts on this book with others by leaving a review on the site that you bought it from. If you purchased the book from Amazon, please leave us an honest review on this book's Amazon page. This is vital so that other potential readers can see and use your unbiased opinion to make purchasing decisions, we can understand what our customers think about our products, and our authors can see your feedback on the title that they have worked with Packt to create. It will only take a few minutes of your time but is valuable to other potential customers, our authors, and Packt. Thank you!

# Index

www.ingramcontent.com/pod-product-compliance
Lightning Source LLC
LaVergne TN
LVHW081509050326
832903LV00025B/1421